Race, Class, and Education

LA FOLLETTE PUBLIC POLICY SERIES

The Robert M. La Follette
Institute of Public Affairs

Robert H. Haveman, Director

Race, Class, and Education

The Politics of Second-Generation Discrimination

Kenneth J. Meier,
Joseph Stewart, Jr., and
Robert E. England

The University of Wisconsin Press

The University of Wisconsin Press
114 North Murray Street
Madison, Wisconsin 53715

3 Henrietta Street
London WC2E 8LU, England

Library of Congress Cataloging-in-Publication Data
Meier, Kenneth.
    Race, class, and education: the politics of second-generation discrimina-
tion/Kenneth Meier, Joseph Stewart, Jr., and Robert E. England.
    208 pp.   cm.—(La Follette public policy series)
    Includes bibliographical references.
    1. Discrimination in education—United States. 2. Afro-American
children—Education. 3. Educational equalization—United States. 4. School
boards—United States—Membership, Afro-American. 5. Education and
state—United States. I. Stewart, Joseph, 1951- II. England, Robert E.
III. Title. IV. Series.
LC212.2 M45   1989
370'. 89' 96073—dc20   89-40262
ISBN 0-299-12210-7   CIP

To Theodore P. Robinson,
colleague and friend

Contents

Tables and Figures

Figures

Acknowledgments

This book has research antecedents dating to 1977. Joe Stewart's dissertation represents the first systematic effort by a political scientist to examine second-generation discrimination on a broad scale. Published work resulting from this first effort encouraged Ken Meier and Bob England to begin their studies of black representation in 1980. That research appeared in the *American Political Science Review,* the *Journal of Politics,* and *American Politics Quarterly.* In 1987 the three of us joined forces to produce the final research project. The research in this book builds on our prior research. Individuals who have followed this stream of research will see how the theories we examine here have developed gradually over time. This research does not contradict anything that we have previously done, but it goes well beyond what was previously published.

In doing a project of this magnitude over such an extended period of time, we have obviously become indebted to many individuals. At various times we have been aided and assisted by numerous individuals who gave us good advice, critical comments, or insightful ideas. Michael Goldstein, Charles Bullock, Theodore P. Robinson, Susan Welch, James F. Sheffield, Lee Sigelman, Peter Eisinger, Gary Copeland, Grace Hall Saltzstein, Michael Preston, Frank J. Thompson, F. Chris Garcia, Michael Olivas, Cynthia Brown, and Chandler Davidson offered helpful comments on various parts of this extended research project. We are particularly indebted to those individuals who cheerfully responded to more than one manuscript. Our intellectual debts to individuals whose ideas and research allowed us to improve our work are simply too numerous to mention. They will have to be satisfied with citations in our bibliography. Franklin Wilson generously provided us with some of the data we used in the analysis. Ted Robinson deserves our special thanks for interesting us in school boards, and George Pasdirtz and Luis Fraga assisted in creating our data set. The University of Wisconsin Press and our editor Gordon Lester-

Massman deserve our thanks for their willingness to publish a controversial manuscript. Robin Whitaker deserves special thanks for her exceptional copy editing.

The surprising aspect of this research project is how little funding was obtained. Although serious efforts were made to obtain federal funding for this research, we were unsuccessful. The dean of the College of Arts and Sciences at Oklahoma State University provided summer support for Bob England and some modest funds to purchase data tapes. The Robert M. La Follette Institute for Public Affairs provided the funds to send out our 1985–86 school district survey. The graduate school at the University of Wisconsin–Madison provided a summer support grant for Ken Meier that included funds needed to access the university's computer system.

We would truly like to blame someone for any mistakes we might have made in writing this book. Individually we will blame each other, collectively we will assume responsibility for any errors of commission or omission.

Race, Class,
and Education

Introduction

B. J. was a 10-year-old black student who had always done his school work diligently with average results (Children's Defense Fund, 1974: 25–26). At the end of third grade, B. J.'s parents were told that he had done well enough to pass. The following September, without notice to his parents, B. J. was placed in a class for children who were either mentally retarded or had learning disabilities. B. J. was disappointed because he no longer went to class with his friends and because the class was boring. After two months in the class just wasting time, B. J. thought that the school was trying to make him act like the retarded children. This belief was reinforced by his friends in regular classes, who now avoided him. B. J. then quit going to school.

An evaluation of B. J.'s counseling file confirmed that he had an IQ of 85 and a low aptitude. A puzzling aspect of the folder was the assessments of his teachers, which indicated he was a normal, average student. A great deal of searching revealed that B. J. had been assigned an IQ score but had never actually been given an IQ test. How this bureaucratic error had occurred was not discovered, although B. J.'s third grade teacher had told his fourth grade teacher that B. J. was a "problem child" and needed to be watched. After B. J. was administered an IQ test, he was returned to a regular class.

T. R. was a black middle school student who had always done reasonably well in school. His middle school counselor went over a series of aptitude tests with him and urged him to enroll in the high school's vocational program for carpenters. T. R. did exceptionally well in the carpentry program receiving A's and B's. His morning class schedule for his senior year consisted of first period drafting, second period wood shop, third period construction planning, and fourth period gym. In the afternoons he took remedial English and basic math.

A local college began an aggressive affirmative action program and offered T. R. a scholarship after reviewing his grades. College came as a rude shock to T. R. Teachers made assignments; the reading load was massive; tests were unlike any he had ever seen. Because his high school background did not prepare him for college, he nearly flunked out. Through long hours and remedial tutoring, T. R. removed himself from academic probation and eventually graduated with a 2.0 grade point average.

Despite his low undergraduate grades, T. R. convinced an admissions director to admit him on probation to a master of public administration program at a major university. Having finally acquired good study habits as a result of undergraduate trial and error, T. R. received his MPA degree two years later with a 3.5 GPA. He then took the Law School Aptitude Test and was admitted to study law at Northwestern University.

B. J. and T. R. are only two examples of how the use of academic grouping and tracking can limit the educational opportunities available to black students. Although both B. J. and T. R. experienced happy endings, thousands of students do not. Racial biases in special education, ability grouping, curriculum tracking, and discipline have replaced segregation as the single greatest obstacle to equal educational opportunities. Desegregation—the mechanical mixing of races in equal percentages—is not enough; desegregated schools often have little interracial contact and unequal educational opportunities because black students are grouped or tracked into classes different from those for the majority of white students. What is needed is integration—the interaction of students in a multiracial learning environment both in and outside the classroom. Integrated education provides students with equal status and equal opportunities to excel.

This research examines equal educational opportunities in 174 United States school districts with at least 15,000 students and 1 percent black enrollment. Several themes permeate the study and should be clarified at the outset. First, we view education as the single most important civil rights issue affecting blacks in the United States. Equal access to educational opportunities is the key to good jobs, quality housing, and political influence. Second, our analysis focuses on the political forces that affect education. Other influences on education policies such as the family, the economy, or parent groups are not stressed. Third, discrimination in education is complex; it is based on both race and class. Fourth, our intent is not only to study equal education opportunities but also to change them; a series of reforms is proposed and defended.

Findings of This Study

Schools use academic grouping to sort students into homogeneous subsets. Within the regular curriculum, ability grouping is used to sort students according to academic potential. At the top of this spectrum are the honors and gifted classes; at the bottom are remedial classes. Those students unable to benefit from the normal curriculum are further sorted into special education classes, with special education students then sorted into classes for the educable mentally retarded, the trainable mentally retarded, specific learning disabilities, and so on. At the secondary level curriculum tracking supplements ability grouping so that students are clustered by career aspirations ranging from college preparation to vocational education. Different academic groups receive vastly different educations, with the greatest resources and the highest-quality education provided for the highest academic groups.

Schools also use disciplinary actions to sort students. Corporal punishment, suspensions, and even expulsions seek to encourage students to conform to school rules and regulations. Those who fail to do so are sorted out via expulsions. Schools also sort students when they leave school. Some students receive degrees, others fail, and some drop out.

The sorting practices of schools are associated with racial disproportions (see chapter 4). A black student is nearly three times more likely to be placed in a class for the educable mentally retarded than is a white student. A black student is 30 percent more likely to be assigned to a trainable mentally retarded class than a white student. At the other end of the sorting spectrum, a white student is 3.2 times more likely to be assigned to a gifted class than is a black student.

In terms of discipline, a black student is more than twice as likely as a white student to be corporally punished or suspended. A black student is 3.5 times more likely than a white student to be expelled. Educational outcomes form a similar but less severe pattern. A black student is 18 percent more likely to drop out of school and 27 percent less likely to graduate from high school.

What do these patterns of racial difference mean? Our analysis indicates that they form a consistent pattern of action that should be termed second-generation educational discrimination. Three findings produce this conclusion (see chapter 5). First, schools that disproportionately sort black students into lower academic groups also disproportionately subject these students to the school's disciplinary practices. In these schools white students gain better access to gifted classes, are less likely to drop out of school, and are more likely to graduate. This pattern is consistent with a denial of equal educational opportunities for black students. Second, an extensive analysis of disciplinary practices reveals that their greater use does not have a deterrent effect on behavior problems. If discipline does not deter, it must have other goals. Discrimination is one possibility. Third, school districts that disproportionately group and discipline black students are able to limit the withdrawal of white students from their schools. The overall pattern demonstrates that black students are denied access to the same educational opportunities that white students have.

Why did policies of second-generation discrimination develop? Initial efforts to gain access to educational opportunities for black students focused on eliminating segregated schools and gaining access to the white school system (see chapter 2). Policy-making institutions over time defined equal educational opportunities as desegregated education. Such a policy definition ignored the continued resistance to integration and permitted the development of other methods of limiting access. By disproportionately sorting black students into lower academic groups and white students into higher academic groups and by disproportionately using disciplinary action against black students, school systems were able to limit interracial contact. In the process, most black students attending desegregated schools received lower-quality educational opportunities than their white school mates.

Not all school districts are equally successful in implementing policies of second-generation discrimination (see chapter 4). Variation in discrimination is linked directly to the political process. In school districts with a politically powerful black community, with a large population of lower-class white students, and with a large percentage of black teachers, black students experience less second-generation discrimination. Of these factors, black teachers are without a doubt the key. Black teachers are the single most effective force in limiting the amount of second-generation discrimination against black students.

Increasing the number of black teachers is difficult, but one factor that has shown a strong correlation is the employment of black school administrators (see chapter 3). Increases in the number of black school administrators are directly tied to increases in the number of black school board members. Black representation on the school board, in turn, is a function of black political resources and the use of district rather than at-large elections. Political action, in short, is an effective route to combat second-generation discrimination and provide equal access to educational opportunities.

Policy Recommendations

The results of this study suggest that several changes in public policy are needed to provide equal educational opportunities for black students (see chapter 6). First, at-large school district elections should be abolished to provide greater opportunities for minority representation. Second, efforts must be made to increase significantly the number of black teachers. Increasing the number of black teachers is counter to current trends. We suggest that special scholarship and loan programs be devised, that black administrators be hired from a wider pool of candidates, and that teacher certification and testing requirements be made more flexible.

Third, the federal Office for Civil Rights needs to be transformed from a data-collection agency to an aggressive civil rights action agency. In addition, OCR needs to collect better and different data to permit more accurate monitoring of second-generation discrimination. Fourth, the federal Equal Employment Opportunity Commission should be empowered to release aggregate data on racial employment by individual school districts.

Fifth, academic grouping must be reevaluated. The optimal solution is to eliminate academic grouping and replace it with a variety of proven educational techniques that permit equal status learning. The second best solution is to limit severely the use of academic grouping. To place a student in special education, for example, the school district should have to prove that the student has been exposed to quality teaching in regular classes and has been unable to learn. Placements should be for a limited term with specific goals and a schedule for when the student can return to regular classes.

Sixth, corporal punishment should be banned. No evidence exists that corporal punishment is more effective than other disciplinary measures. The deterrent impact of all forms of discipline, in fact, is questionable. Seventh, schools need to review and restructure disciplinary processes; this review should focus on what offenses require discipline and how discipline can be administered in a manner that enhances the potential for improved academic achievement.

Limitations of This Study

This study has three limitations that readers should note. Our sample is limited to large urban school districts enrolling 15,000 or more students. We have not analyzed smaller districts. Given the large number of students who reside in these districts, particularly the high percentage of black population, and given what we feel is a highly representative sample, we are confident that our findings can be generalized to the educational experiences of most black students.

This study is also limited in that it addresses the problems of access to quality education only for black students. Nothing in this work necessarily applies to Hispanic, American Indian, Asian, or lower-class white students. The educational process varies for each of these groups, and we are reasonably confident that access to quality education for blacks is different from access for Hispanics and others. We are currently engaged in research to assess the equal education opportunities for Hispanic students.

Finally, this study is limited by the availability of data. The Office for Civil Rights, our prime data source, does not gather data on all forms of academic grouping that take place, nor does it gather data on all forms of discipline. In situations where our analysis was limited by available data, we note this.

Structure of the Book

Chapter 1 introduces the theoretical framework used in this book. It presents and justifies a political view of school systems and links school district policies to the political process. Chapter 2 examines the historical evolution of equal education policies. The school desegregation effort is summarized, and an argument is presented that second-generation discrimination was inevitable because policy-makers incorrectly defined the problem as one of segregation rather than equal access to educational opportunities.

Chapter 3 examines the political process of black representation. Black political resources, social class, region, and election systems are used to explain black representation on urban school boards. Similar models are used to examine black representation among school administrators and on teaching faculties.

Chapter 4 focuses on the individual elements of second-generation discrimination. Racial disparities in academic grouping, discipline, and educational outcomes are presented. These racial disparities are then explained in terms of the political theory introduced in chapter 1.

Chapter 5 probes the interrelationships of second-generation discrimination indicators. First, each indicator is related to other indicators to show how the various elements of second-generation discrimination form a pattern. Next, whether or not greater use of discipline can be justified as a deterrent of unacceptable behavior is addressed. Finally, the chapter links policies of second-generation discrimination to school district efforts to limit declining white-student enrollments. Chapter 6 provides a summary of the findings and presents our policy recommendations in detail.

Black Representation and Educational Policy

Race and education is a perennially salient policy issue that predates the Supreme Court's ruling in *Plessy* v. *Ferguson* (1896) that states could maintain racially separate facilities if they were equal. Legal challenges to the principle of segregated schools culminated in the Court's rejection of "separate but equal" schools in *Brown* v. *Board of Education* (1954), the focus then shifted to the implementation of school desegregation by local school boards. Extended implementation battles were fought and eventually resolved, so that by the mid-1970's most southern school districts had desegregated (Rodgers and Bullock, 1976a; Bullock and Lamb, 1984). Northern districts were equally resistant to school desegregation, and progress in these de facto segregated systems was slow.

Lost in the desegregation battle was the initial goal of this effort—to obtain equal educational opportunities for black students. School districts can use a variety of techniques to limit black students' access to equal educational opportunities. This research focuses on one set of such techniques, those termed second-generation educational discrimination. Essentially second-generation discrimination is the use of academic grouping and disciplinary processes in order to separate black students from white students. The resulting education that black students receive is inferior to that received by white students.

This chapter generates a theory of educational policy-making that will be applied to school district policies of academic grouping, discipline, and equal educational opportunity. First, we stress the fundamental importance of education as the cornerstone of antidiscrimination policy. Second, our political focus predicts that the ability of blacks to gain access to policy-making positions is important in determining local educational policies. Third, a theory of black representation is presented to account for black access to positions as school board members, school administrators, and teachers. Fourth, black representation is linked to equal education policies through a theory of policy-making

9

that includes black political resources, social class, region, and school district size.

Why Study Education?

We believe that education is the single most important policy area in terms of racial discrimination. Discrimination in education directly affects the ability of blacks to earn a living. The human capital school of economics holds that the primary determinant of a person's rate of pay is that person's investment in education (either formal or on-the-job; see Schultz, 1961; Becker, 1975). Greg Duncan (1984: 109), a critic of the human capital approach, reports in his longitudinal study of poverty that "differences in the level of education can account for a substantial share of the long-run earnings differences between individuals." Education explains 20 percent of the variation in individual income; with controls for work experience, test scores, achievement motivation, father's education, and efficacy, it explains 15 percent of the variation in income (Duncan, 1984: 110). Although 15 percent might not seem like much, it is five times the explanation attributable to any other factor.

Some scholars (e.g., Feagin and Feagin [1986]) discount the importance of education, because early research findings show that an additional year of education for blacks does not increase income as much as it does for whites.[1] More recent research, however, finds that "the labor market . . . gives similar pay increments to those with higher levels of education regardless of race" (Duncan, 1984: 138; see also Featherman and Hauser, 1976; Smith and Welch, 1986: 33–34). According to Corcoran and Duncan's 1979 study, different levels of education by themselves explain 40 percent of the wage difference between blacks and whites. The increased impact of education on black earnings results from substantial improvements in the quality of black education (Smith and Welch, 1986: 39). To illustrate the strength of black education as a predictor of black income, we have used the percentage of blacks with high school diplomas to predict the black median income for our sample of school districts (see table 1.1).[2] The result is a strong relationship, with education accounting for 53 percent of the variation in income.

Education is also important because it helps individuals gain access to certain types of jobs. Hall and Saltzstein (1977: 868) have found a correlation of .68 between levels of black education and black employment in urban government jobs. Hutchins and Sigelman (1981: 84) have discovered that black educa-

1. We are somewhat surprised that later research does not result in black education being less valuable in income gains than white education (see Farley and Allen, 1987: 204). Since our basic argument is that blacks do not get the same quality education as whites do, we would expect that each year of education for blacks would not have the same impact it does for whites.

2. Data for table 1.1 are from 1986. This is true as well for all other tables in the book, unless otherwise noted.

Table 1.1. Impact of Black Education on Black Median Income

Dependent Variable = Black median income

Independent Variable	Regression Coefficient	t-score
High school graduates (%)	$223.78	13.62*

F = 185.60
r^2 = .53
Intercept = $3,467.07
N = 170

*p < .05

tion correlates at .76 with access to state and local government jobs and at .60 with black-white salary equity. Meier and Nigro (1976: 463) have found that the United States higher civil service is exactly representative of the population that holds master's degrees, no matter what variables are compared.

Educational attainment is also the key to both upward mobility (Cohen and Tyree, 1986) and the ability to pass socioeconomic status on to children (Blau and Duncan, 1976). Cohen and Tyree's (1986: 811) study credits education as the most important variable in allowing intergenerational escapes from poverty; they conclude, "Education . . . matters more for the children of the poor." Education teaches students about the impact of social institutions and provides them with the resources to influence those institutions (Sleeter and Grant, 1985: 54; Freire, 1970; Everhart, 1983; Barbagli and Dei, 1977). The results of our study (see chapter 4) also reveal that higher levels of education increase the ability of blacks to gain quality education for their children.

By stressing the crucial role of education in discrimination, we do not mean to underplay other areas of discrimination. Logically, however, if blacks are denied equal access to education, then discrimination in the job market is much easier, because blacks will lack the educational qualifications for many jobs. In such cases, an employer need not discriminate overtly; institutional use of job qualifications is sufficient to eliminate most blacks from consideration. Equalizing access to quality education means that discrimination in employment and other areas must be overt, and overt methods of discrimination are easier to document and combat.

Politics and Education

Education research often denies the role of politics in educational policy. As Meyer Weinberg (1983: 333) characterizes research on equal access to education, "Much of the research proceeds as though it were outside any political framework." The dominant ideology of both educators and educational research is that politics have no impact on educational policies.

In this book we define politics as the process of determining "who gets what" (Lasswell, 1936), and who gets what is a function of "who governs" (Dahl, 1961). For us the issue of who governs focuses on representing the interests of the black community at key decision points in the educational policy process. This implies that education is primarily a political process rather than the neutral application of professional criteria to individuals (Anderson et al., 1984; Tucker and Zeigler, 1980). The three key decision points in local educational policies are determining overall policy, translating overall policy into administrative rules and procedures, and implementing rules and procedures by applying them to individuals.

Different sets of individuals dominate these three stages of the policy process. School boards, at least in theory, set the overall school district policy, including policies on equal access to education. School district administrators play a role, perhaps a major role, in setting such overall policies; but the decision point they clearly dominate is the translation of general policies into specific administrative rules and procedures. Teachers, in turn, take the lead in applying administrative rules and procedures to individual students.

At each stage of the process, decision-makers have some discretion. School board members, although they face constraints such as the overall size of the budget, federal laws, and state mandates, still have substantial autonomy to affect district policies. We view school board members as autonomous decision-makers constrained somewhat but not totally by economic, social, and political forces (Nordlinger, 1981). When policy choices are made by school board members, we assume that they act similarly to other decision-makers, that they attempt to maximize their own personal policy preferences.

Legislative policy-makers, including local school boards, cannot make policies so specific that no discretion is left to administrators (Rourke, 1984). The policy-implementation literature contains numerous examples of legislatively established policies being altered by program administrators (Pressman and Wildavsky, 1973; Bullock and Lamb, 1984; Mazmanian and Sabatier, 1983). School district administrators also have policy preferences, and where possible they will seek to exercise discretion so that policies reflect their own preferences (Janowitz, 1969: 29; see also Scott, 1980).

Finally, most policies as they descend the administrative hierarchy are changed and adapted to individual situations (Downs, 1967). Teachers are akin to what Lipsky (1980) calls street-level bureaucrats.[3] They exercise discre-

---

3. We will often refer to teachers in this book as bureaucrats. This term has no pejorative connotations for us. A bureaucrat is simply a member of a large formal organization (Weber, 1946; Downs, 1967).

tion in using discipline, encouraging or discouraging students, recommending placement in various academic groups, and countless other ways (see Silver, 1973). Although "objective" criteria have been established for many of these actions, the teacher still retains some discretion. Exercising that discretion, in turn, affects the policies set down by school district administrators.

All three groups of decision-makers, we argue, exercise discretion; and they use that discretion to influence policies to be consistent with their own preferences. This book does not directly measure policy preferences but rather uses race as a surrogate measure of policy preferences. Essentially we assume that black school board members, administrators, and teachers favor policies that provide greater educational equity for black students and oppose policies that reduce the access to quality education for black students. As we argue in chapter 3, of all the demographic surrogates for individual values, race is the strongest and longest lasting. Our central concern is whether or not black access to positions of decision-making authority results in educational policies that benefit black students (Lineberry, 1978: 175).

A Political Theory of Representation

Although school board members, school administrators, and teachers are selected in different ways, we will use a similar political theory to explain black access to each set of positions. School board members are generally elected, except in those dependent school districts where they are appointed by other elected officials. School district administrators are usually hired by school boards, though at lower levels they may be hired by other administrators using merit criteria. Teachers are almost always hired by school administrators using elaborate merit-system criteria. Our theories of representation generally look at five forces that influence black representation—black political resources, district political structure, social class, region, and black access to other decision-making positions. Because the theory changes somewhat for school board members, administrators, and teachers, each is discussed separately. Figure 1.1 summarizes the influences hypothesized to affect blacks' access to all three decision-making positions.

Access to School Board Seats

Black Political Resources. To win elections, blacks must have political resources that can be converted into political successes (Karnig, 1979). Perhaps the most obvious political resource is simply black votes or the percentage of black population in the school district. If long-term white efforts to restrict black suffrage via white primaries, grandfather clauses, literacy tests, discriminatory registration procedures, and outright intimidation and violence are any

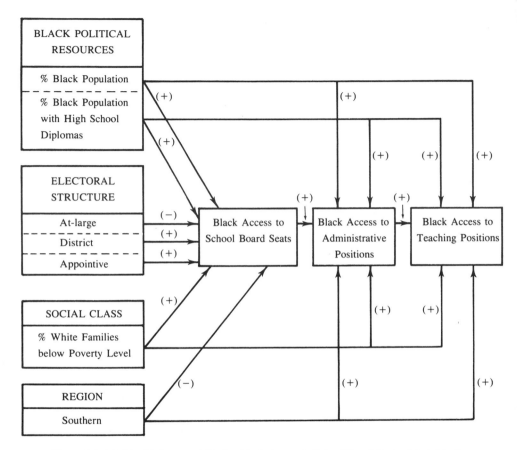

Figure 1.1. Model of Influences Affecting Black Access to School Board Seats, Administrative Positions, and Teaching Positions.

indication, black votes may be the most important political resource the black community has.[4]

Although votes are necessary for gaining positions of policy-making authority, they alone are not sufficient. Black election victories require black can-

4. We do not undervalue such black resources as group membership, the ability to generate protests, the use of litigation, and so on (Stewart and Sheffield, 1987; Gamson, 1975; Piven and Cloward, 1971; Browning, Marshall, and Tabb, 1984). Many of these were important in getting the right to vote and other basic civil rights. Restrictions on black voting have generally been

didates (Stewart and Sheffield, 1987). Studies of urban politics generally suggest that ethnic groups produce candidates for office once the ethnic group contains members who are middle class (Banfield and Wilson, 1963). Middle-class status for blacks might be measured in a variety of ways including income, business ownership, levels of education, and self-perception. In the representation stage of our theory, only one such indicator will be used—the percentage of blacks with high school diplomas.[5]

Electoral Structure. Translating black resources into black access to elected positions has been hampered by electoral structures that grew out of the urban reform movement (see chapter 3). Because educational policy was considered more compatible with neutral administrative procedures than is overall city policy, school districts were often "reformed" even in cities that were not (Banfield and Wilson, 1963). Nonpartisan elections, springtime elections, at-large elections, staggered terms for school board members, and professional school administrators were all adopted to limit the impact of certain types of politics on education (Tyack, 1974; Wakefield, 1971; Cistone, 1975).[6]

Of these urban reforms, the most detrimental to black representation is at-large elections (Davidson and Korbel, 1981; Engstrom and McDonald, 1981). At-large elections, in contrast with elections where candidates run in smaller districts or wards, require that candidates receive more votes to run a successful campaign. While a candidate might have sufficient electoral support to win in a district of 10,000 residents, he or she may not have sufficient support to be elected at-large from an electorate of 70,000 or more residents. At-large elections are particularly harmful to black candidates for school board positions when voting is polarized by race (a frequent condition) and blacks constitute a minority of the voting population.

School board selection plans differ from city council selection plans in that for school boards the normal choice between at-large and ward elections is

---

eliminated; and because we are focusing on election outcomes, the use of votes as the key resource is defensible.

5. High school education may indicate higher levels of turnout for school board elections rather than the willingness of more individuals to be candidates in these elections. College education percentages were tried in these models but did not predict nearly as well as high school education. Income, the other logical measure of middle-class status, will be used in the policy models to indicate both social class and the "power thesis" of interracial group relations.

6. These reforms do not limit the impact of politics on educational policy, they simply limit the political actors that are allowed to influence educational policy. The same decisions must still be made. Simply because a professional administrator or a "nonpartisan" school board makes a decision does not mean that decision has no political implications. Most decisions still determine who gets what from the educational system. By limiting participation in making such decisions, the outcome of the decisions is also affected.

expanded.[7] In a dependent school system, the school board is appointed by another group of elected officials such as the mayor, the city council, or the county commission. The politics of appointed boards differ from those of elected boards (Robinson, England, and Meier, 1985: 981). Selection for the school board in appointive systems becomes a function of access to other elected officials. In many cases, a "fair share" of seats is allocated to minorities from among the individuals who supported the winning electoral coalition. Our measure of school district structure, therefore, will include a measure of at-large, ward, and appointive systems (a dummy variable, coded as 1 or 0).

Social Class: Po' White Trash. The power thesis of intergroup relations argues that conflict is the result of social differences between two groups (Giles and Evans, 1985, 1986; Feagin, 1980). This thesis asserts that if a minority is similar to the majority, the majority will be less threatened by minority demands and less likely to oppose minority access to governing institutions. Giles and Evans (1986) contend that discrimination is less likely against middle-class blacks than against lower-class blacks, because middle-class blacks share many of the values of middle-class whites. They imply that discrimination has as much to do with social class as with race.[8]

Because we already have one indicator of black social class—black education—additional indicators of black-white differences at first glance might not seem necessary. Testing out the implications of the power thesis, however, reveals otherwise. If a fundamental cause of discrimination is social class, then such discrimination is as likely to affect poor whites as it is to affect poor blacks. Majority political institutions will deny access to poor whites as well as to blacks. In a community with a large number of poor whites, the political resources of the middle-class white community will be mobilized against the lower-class white community. In such a situation, blacks, particularly middle-class blacks, may be more acceptable to the middle-class white community and may even be seen as allies. This social-class aspect of representational politics will be measured by the percentage of the white community that resides in poverty.[9] This variable should be positively related to black school board representation.

7. We have treated those school districts with mixed election systems, where some members are elected by ward and others are elected at-large, as ward systems. Previous work on school board elections (Robinson, England, and Meier, 1985) has found that mixed electoral systems operate more like ward systems than at-large systems, so little is lost by combining these two categories.

8. Both Parent and Stekler (1985) and Welch and Foster (1987) find that social class is associated with attitudinal differences among blacks, but these differences are nowhere near as great as those between racial groups.

9. One needs to distinguish the power thesis from what we call the redneck thesis. The redneck thesis argues that political tolerance is positively related to social class and thus there is a greater

Region. The final variable of concern is the southern region. Region as a variable is clearly a surrogate, because location itself can hardly determine anything. In this case, southern region serves as a surrogate for the unique racial history of the South, some residual of *de jure* discrimination, and perhaps even some current political attitudes. For purposes of this analysis all states that maintained a *de jure* segregated school system in 1954 are considered southern. Southern districts are coded as 1; all others are coded as 0. Southern region should be negatively related to black representation on school boards.

Access to Administrative Positions

Black educators have disproportionately paid the price of desegregation (see Rodgers and Bullock, 1972: 94–97; Carter, 1982: 178–181; Adair, 1984: chap. 1). Arnez (1978: 40), for example, reports that as a result of school desegregation, many black principals were released or demoted. Black teachers suffered similar fates; their contracts were not renewed, or they were reassigned to teach lower grades or special remedial classes.

Discrimination in this matter, however, was difficult to prove because the process was subtle. With school desegregation came a plethora of techniques to mix schools racially. One common technique was school closing-consolidation (see Hughes, Gordon, and Hillman, 1980; Morgan and England, 1982). Under the principles of separate but equal, black schools were rarely accorded equal resources or facilities (see chapter 2). If consolidation was pursued, logic suggested closing all-black schools rather than all-white schools, because many all-black schools had smaller enrollments and/or were physically less desirable.

Many black educators simply lost their jobs during the consolidation process—for example, between 1964 and 1970, 600 black principals lost positions in Texas, and 200 black school professionals lost positions in West Virginia (Adair, 1984: 15; see also Moore, 1977). Testimony before the United States Senate (Epstein, 1971: 4906–4907) reveals that desegregation resulted in the termination of 90 percent of the black principals in Kentucky and Arkansas, 77 percent in South Carolina and Tennessee, 50 percent in Georgia, 78 percent in Virginia, 30 percent in Maryland, 80 percent in Alabama, and 96 percent in North Carolina. Smith and Smith (1974: 35) estimate that desegregation displaced more than 31,000 black teachers in southern states and those bordering them.

---

propensity for whites to vote for blacks. Such an argument suggests a negative relationship between white poverty and black representation. The power thesis supports the opposite hypothesis of a positive relationship between white poverty and black representation. For a discussion of tolerance in general and in regard to race, see Jackman 1978, 1981.

Discriminatory personnel practices affect more people than just those who lose their jobs. Advocates of a "representative bureaucracy," where administrators represent individuals who share their demographic origins, have long argued that such bureaucracies are more responsive (Kingsley, 1944; Long, 1952; Salzstein, 1979; see chapter 3). Minority educators also provide role models for young students. They are sensitive to the cultural norms and mores of minority children. Even today, argues Adair (1984: 14), with the special emphasis on equal employment opportunities and affirmative action programs, black principals, ministers, and teachers represent key leadership figures in the black community.

Research also suggests that the presence of a multiracial, multiethnic staff facilitates the integration process by dispelling myths of racial inferiority and incompetence. Day-to-day cross-racial contact among minority and majority teachers, administrators, and students helps eradicate such misconceptions. In addition, given the highly volatile nature of many school desegregation efforts, minority teachers and administrators can ease the adjustment of minority students, their parents, and majority teachers to the new heterogenous school population (see U.S. Commission on Civil Rights, 1976: 122–124).

Black access to administrative positions in schools uses the same model of representation used for school board members with some slight modifications. The variables sometimes indicate slightly different forces, but the direction of the impact remains the same.

School Board Members. One variable that must be added to the political theory of representation when applied to the administrative level is school board members. Districts with a large percentage of black school board members are more likely to employ a larger percentage of black school administrators. The school board can affect hiring decisions in at least two ways. First, the school board hires the superintendent, so the board members can choose a black person for the position or a white person who strongly supports minority hiring (see Thompson, 1978, on personnel hiring values). Second, the school board can enact formal policies or informally exert pressure on higher-level school administrators to hire more blacks at lower administrative levels.

Black Resources. Black resources could have two different meanings in terms of filling administrative positions. Black population and black education still could represent the potential political power of the minority community. Examining three Alabama counties, for example, Peterson (1976) has found that increases in black voting (mobilized population) have led to the employment of more black school administrators. For administrative positions, black population and education could also indicate favorable labor pool characteristics; that is, school districts with numerous blacks and a large percentage of educated blacks would have more individuals who are qualified to be school administrators (see Sigelman and Karnig, 1977; see Sigelman and Karnig, 1976, for a similar argument on public sector employment in general).[10]

Electoral Structure. How the school board is selected should have no direct impact on the hiring of black school administrators. If structure has any impact, it is by limiting the number of blacks on the school board. Because black representation on the school board can be measured directly and because structure cannot be logically defended as affecting the number of black administrators, it will be deleted from the black administrators model.

Social Class. The power thesis again holds that the majority community prefers black administrators with middle-class backgrounds to white administrators with lower-class backgrounds. The percentage of the white population residing in poverty, in addition, represents a white labor pool that is less conducive to producing school administrators. Such a labor pool should generate proportionately more opportunities for blacks.

Region. The southern region is again a surrogate for past politics, policies, and current attitudes. Region might have one additional impact that makes a difference in the opposite direction. Because the South maintained a dual school system, black teachers were in demand to teach and administer black schools (B. P. Cole, 1986: 326). A small group of black colleges including Fisk, Howard, and Morehouse met this demand. Predominantly black colleges produced 85 percent of all black college graduates before 1936 (Johnson, 1938: 10) and 75 percent as late as 1970 (Fisher, 1970: 19). This greater previous demand for black administrators and the southern location of black colleges might have some residual effect on today's distribution if the black administrators were able to avoid the demotions and terminations that accompanied the closing of all-black schools (Arnez, 1978).

Access to Teaching Positions

Black Administrators. With one slight modification the representation model for administrators will be used in the analysis of black teachers. Teachers are hired by administrators. As a result, school districts with a large number of black administrators should also hire a larger percentage of black teachers. Studies of public employment show that managers frequently hire individuals with characteristics similar to their own (Saltzstein, 1983; Thompson, 1978; Dye and Renick, 1981). The inclusion of black administrators is coupled with the deletion of black school board members from the teachers' model. School board members in large urban districts should not play a role in hiring

10. Black high school graduates are probably not qualified to become administrators for a school district, but the percentage of black high school graduates is highly collinear with the percentage of black college graduates. Rather than shift the variable designation, we have used the same indicator to maintain consistency.

teachers.[11] If black school board members have any impact on black teachers, it should indirectly manifest itself through black administrators.

Black Resources. Again black population and black education can have two separate effects on the proportion of black teachers. On the one hand, they represent potential black resources for pressuring a school district to hire more blacks (Freeman, 1977). On the other hand, they indicate a larger labor pool from which to recruit.

Social Class. White poverty, by reducing the potential white labor pool for teaching jobs and making black teachers from middle-class backgrounds more attractive, should increase the proportion of black teachers.

Region. Again region might have two different impacts. The southern region as a surrogate for past policies, politics, and current attitudes should result in lower percentages of black teachers. Alternatively, the residual impact of the dual school system plus the location of many black teachers' colleges in the South might well increase the proportion of black teachers in southern school districts.

Impact on Public Policy

The bottom line for black representation is whether or not it affects public policy. To assess the impact of black representation on public policy, public policy measures having the following three characteristics are needed: First, they must be variables that individual policy-makers can influence. Second, the policies must be tied closely to race, so that black representatives can clearly discern the benefits of such policies for the people they represent. Third, the policy must be capable of being measured over a wide variety of districts so that findings can be generalized.

Most research focusing on the impact of black representatives has failed on one or more of these criteria. Early studies have examined the impact of black mayors elected during the late 1960s and early 1970s on urban policies. Keech's (1968) case studies of Durham and Tuskeegee, for example, have found numerous specific instances where a black mayor made a public policy difference, particularly in Tuskeegee. A variety of other case studies have shown similar results (Campbell and Feagin, 1975; Levine, 1974; Nelson, 1972; Nelson and Meranto, 1976; Poinsett, 1970; Stone, 1971). Although these case studies provide a rich detail of policy impacts, they are highly specific to individual cities and policies, so generalizations concerning black representation are difficult to make. In addition, the case-study methodology does not permit the use of control variables to ensure that such findings are not spurious.

---

11. We can imagine that in small districts some school board members would actually get involved in hiring decisions. Our districts, with a minimum of 15,000 students, are very large and likely to have professionalized procedures for hiring teachers.

The one study that overcomes some of these limits is the excellent analysis of 10 northern California cities by Browning, Marshall, and Tabb (1984). Although 10 cases from the same geographic area limit generalizations, the Browning, Marshall, and Tabb effort revealed that precisely done analysis on a few cases can lead to valid findings.

A second set of studies has examined the expenditures of cities with black mayors and black members on the city council. At first such findings were disappointing. Keller (1978: 50) has reported from his study of three black and three white mayors that "black mayors do not, as a rule, spend less than white mayors on community wide items . . . and . . . it is not clear that they spend more on welfare type programs." The most systematic study of expenditures is Karnig and Welch's (1980: 152) multivariate analysis of major United States cities. They conclude that "black mayoral representation does result in some changes in the level of municipal expenditures. Black council representation makes little consistent difference."

Expenditure measures have produced modest findings, probably because expenditures lack two qualities of good policy indicators. First, elected officials often find it difficult to affect urban expenditures. The city's tax base, state laws on revenues, federal grant-in-aid requirements, and numerous other factors constrain the spending actions of mayors and members of the city council. Second, the linkage of expenditures to race is not always clear. Many hypothesize that black representatives should favor greater expenditures on welfare programs and less on community development, but welfare expenditures are rigidly constrained by state and federal laws and a well-designed community development program could in fact benefit black constituents.

An alternative to expenditure data that has been enthusiastically adopted by some social scientists is employment data (Dye and Renick, 1981; Eisinger, 1982a, b). A positive relationship has been found between black elected officials and municipal employment of blacks (see chapter 3). Black employment in the bureaucracy, although important, is still one step removed from actual policy. Treating employment as a policy output translates black representation into a patronage context and results in an extremely narrow view of black representation and public policy.

Equal Educational Opportunity

The policy area that this research addresses is black student access to equal educational opportunity. By equal educational opportunity we mean what others have termed integrated education: students are treated equally regardless of race, and learning takes place in a multiracial situation (Weinberg, 1983: 172). In our view desegregation and integration are not necessarily synonymous processes. Desegregation is a mechanical process; it requires mixing students of different races. Integration is social process, a possible outcome of desegregation. It as a process that "embodies the concepts of parity and equity along with equal opportunities and access to the legitimate means for exploiting the resources of a society" (Adair, 1984: 2; see also Hughes, Gordon, Hillman, 1980; McConahay, 1981).

Desegregation does not always lead to integrated schools, because the "quality of desegregation varies as much as quantity" (Hochschild, 1984: 33). In other words, a school system may deny equal access to education even after a desegregation plan has been fully implemented. Through the use of various overt (e.g., segregated classrooms, segregated buses) and more subtle institutional (e.g., academic grouping, selective use of disciplinary measures) discriminatory practices, schools may become resegregated and deny students equal educational opportunities (see Rodgers and Bullock, 1972; Children's Defense Fund, 1974; Levin and Moise, 1975; Yudof, 1975; Smith and Dziuban, 1977; Ogbu, 1978; Arnez, 1978; Fernandez and Guskin, 1981; Hawley et al., 1983: chap. 5; Eyler, Cook, and Ward, 1983; Adair, 1984; Hochschild, 1984; Brantlinger and Guskin, 1985; Shepard, 1987; Dunn, 1968; Gartner and Lipsky, 1987). Practices that impede the integration of schools and deny black students equal access to education have been collectively referred to as postdesegregation discrimination, or more commonly second-generation school discrimination (see Children's Defense Fund, 1977; Bullock and Stewart, 1978, 1979; Carter, 1982; Hochschild, 1984). Three types of policies are analyzed—academic grouping, discipline, and educational outcomes.

Academic Grouping[12]

Every day during the academic year millions of children make their way to local schools. After they arrive and the first-hour bell rings, schools become "sorters" (Kirp, 1973). Most schools, for example, group or track students based on their estimated intellectual abilities and/or interests (Oakes, 1985). Ability grouping is primarily an elementary school practice. Students are sorted by ability into instructional groups and assigned either to separate classrooms or to within-classroom groups: "Bluebirds, Robins, and Sparrows meet in their reading, spelling, and math groups" (Epstein, 1985: 24). Usually similar things are taught in the different groups, but the pace of instruction varies. By year's end, the swifter "Bluebirds" cover significantly more material than the slower "Sparrows."

12. *Academic grouping* is a generic term that encompasses all efforts to group students by ability, needs, or aspirations. Four main types of academic grouping will be discussed here—ability grouping, curriculum tracking, special education, and compensatory education. Each of these forms of academic grouping is defined in the text. When general grouping is discussed, the term *academic grouping* will be used. When a specific grouping technique is considered, the term for that form of academic grouping will be used.

Curriculum tracking generally is a secondary school practice and involves the assignment of students by ability and/or interest to different classes, or "tracks," of study that usually have different curricula (e.g., college-bound, general business, vocational). As Epstein (1985: 23–24) explains, in high schools students are assigned to curriculum tracks, "with some students going to honors courses and others to regular or remedial courses." In junior highs, youngsters go to "section 8-1, 8-2, 8-3, or 8-4 and on down the list of bright-to-dull classes."

Students who the school cannot sort into various ability groups or tracks *within the regular academic program* may be classified as "special" or "exceptional" and placed in separate special education classes.[13] In other words, special education is for "children considered unable to profit from regular instruction" (Heller, Holtzman, and Messick, 1982: 3; see also Dunn, 1968; Mercer, 1973; Hobbs, 1975). Most students with special needs are perceived to have some type of disability or handicap. The disability may be intellectual (mental retardation), physical (blindness, deafness), emotional (psychological disturbance), speech related (stuttering, voice disorders), or a specific learning disability (perceptual handicaps, dyslexia, developmental aphasia). The special education category that has evoked the greatest placement controversy is mental retardation, particularly educable mentally retarded classes (see Messick, 1984).

Schools also sort students through placement in compensatory education programs. Compensatory education is based on cultural deprivation theory (i.e., poor school performance is the result of a deprived home and/or neighborhood environment), therefore, related remedial programs are aimed at economically and educationally disadvantaged children (Flaxman, 1976; Ogbu, 1978: 81–100). As part of the War on Poverty, the principal source of federal dollars for remedial programs was Title I of the Elementary and Secondary Education Act (ESEA) of 1965.[14] Although school officials have historically possessed discretion in defining ESEA compensatory programs, most funds have been spent for instructional services (Eyler et al., 1981: 234).[15]

13. Special education students, especially those in mentally retarded classes, are often pulled out of regular classrooms and taught in isolation (Singer et al., 1986; Singer and Butler, 1987; Gartner and Lipsky, 1987).

14. In 1981 Title I of the ESEA was replaced by Chapter 1 of the Education Consolidation and Improvement Act Block Grant. Thirty-eight other previous ESEA categorical grants were folded into Chapter 2 of the block grant (General Accounting Office, 1984: 2).

15. We had hoped to address compensatory education as a manifestation of academic grouping, but were unable to secure data at the school district level. A telephone call to officials in the Compensatory Education Program, U.S. Department of Education, confirmed that our inability to find data was not simply an oversight on our part. Compensatory education data are collected by state officials from school districts and then submitted to the Department of Education. Data are thus available from the Department of Education aggregated at the state level and not at the school district level.

Academic grouping practices, including ability grouping, tracking, and special education, gained considerable prominence in the United States educational system in the 1920s, along with advances in the art and science of psychometrics (Morgenstern, 1966: 11).[16] The National Education Association (1968) estimates that 85 percent of secondary schools use ability grouping extensively; about 25 percent of elementary schools group class sections by ability (Rowan and Miracle, 1983: 135); and ability grouping within elementary school classes occurs in 74–84 percent of all schools (Austin and Morrison, 1963; Wilson and Schmits, 1978; Epstein, 1986: 26). Virtually all large school districts have special education classes. Despite massive use, academic grouping's history has been checkered. Since being introduced, academic grouping has been "tried, debated, discarded, revived, and debated again" (Findley and Bryan, 1975: 5).

Although academic grouping techniques are considered useful pedagogical tools for creating homogeneous instructional groups, for black students the reality is that ability grouping, tracking, special education, and compensatory sorting practices can be used to deny them equal educational opportunities. Through the arbitrary and capricious selection and subsequent placement of black children in special types of classes, they can be denied access to the best education the district has to offer (Zettel and Abeson, 1978; Hobbs, 1975). Gartner and Lipsky (1987: 387) contend that special education students receive inferior education as a result of "dumbing down" the curriculum. Education in lower-ability-group classes and vocational tracks is similarly less challenging (Oakes, 1985). In addition, each of the sorting practices can separate white students from black students, thus, resegregating a school system (see Eyler, Cook, and Ward, 1983; Epstein, 1985; Damico and Sparks, 1986). As a consequence, academic grouping practices in schools have been the focus of much research and controversy (see Polloway, 1984: 18). At least four explanations can be offered for the controversy.

First, the assignment of students to academic groups is based on tests, grades, and/or teacher reports. Performance on a test can make the difference between placement in a slow-learners group in the regular academic program or placement in a more stigmatizing educable mentally retarded class (Kirp, 1973: 755). Hobbs (1975: 29) contends that classification systems based on standardized tests have labeled a disproportionately large number of minority students as intellectually subnormal and a disproportionately small number as gifted. Fur-

16. Some evidence exists that ability grouping has always been used to separate white middle-class children from lower-class ethnic children (see Heller, Holtzman, and Messick, 1982: 28–29). For a discussion of ability grouping in Great Britain, see Davies 1975. Also Ogbu (1978) provides cross-cultural studies of minorities and educational opportunities in Britain, New Zealand, India, Japan, and Israel.

thermore he supports Mercer's (1972) contention that such classification tests are based on a statistical model that "institutionalizes the culture of the Anglo-American as the single monocultural frame of reference for 'normal' " (quoted in Hobbs, 1975: 29).

The timing of such placements is also questionable. Ogbu (1978: 135) asserts: "The use of IQ testing and related techniques to exclude black children from high-quality education intensified after the Supreme Court order of 1954 to desegregate schools. Blacks consistently score lower than whites of similar socioeconomic status in such tests because the tests are culturally biased . . ." (see also St. John, 1975; Mercer, 1973). Although objective data are lacking, interviews with staff members in 18 school districts have found increased use of tracking and ability grouping after court-ordered desegregation (Trent, 1981). Some evidence also links black assignments to special education classes with desegregation plans that required the busing of black children to previously white schools (Eyler, Cook, and Ward, 1983: 137).

Biased tests are rarely the only method of assigning students to academic groups (Findley and Bryan, 1975: 15 18). Teacher and/or administrator (e.g., counselors, school psychologists) judgments supplement these "objective" measurements (Simmons and Brady, 1981: 129; Oakes, 1985).[17] Because of racial, ethnic, or social-class stereotyping, disparities in low-group track placements for minorities or lower-income children may be even greater than if tests alone were used as the criterion (Persell, 1977; Metz, 1978; Rosenbaum, 1976; Lanier and Willmer, 1977).[18] Sometimes a teacher can make a "single decision [that] determines a student's program of classes for the entire day, semester, year, and perhaps even six years of secondary schooling" (Oakes, 1985: 3).

Academic grouping creates permanent educational routes for children. Approximately 85 percent of students in college-prep tracks go on to college, whereas only 15 percent of those in other tracks do so (Jencks et al., 1972). Upward academic mobility from one level to another either during the academic year or between years is rare (Groff, 1962; Hawkins, 1966; Mackler, 1969; Rist, 1970). Because special education programs are not usually considered remedial, as opposed to compensatory classes, the assumption is frequently made that once students are placed in special-needs classes they will always

17. A review of academic grouping programs that use educable mentally retarded (EMR) classes reveals that IQ tests are still the major reason for assigning students to EMR classes (Bickel, 1982: 197).

18. The impact of testing biases is subject to some dispute. If only IQ scores are used and 70 is the cutoff point for EMR classes, then the ratio of black to white students in EMR classes would be about eight to one (Heller, Holtzman, and Messick, 1982). The actual ratio is significantly less, indicating that teachers and others may be mitigating the discriminatory impact of IQ tests used for placement.

belong there (Heller, Holtzman, and Messick, 1982: 108). The Office of Education (now the Department of Education) concluded that fewer than 10 percent of children placed in special education classes are ever returned to regular classrooms (Gallagher, 1972: 529).[19]

Permanent classification involves two problems. Students are often misclassified for a number of different reasons, as we have just discusssed (Ysseldyke et al., 1983; Gartner and Lipsky, 1987). A self-study by the Washington, D.C., school system found that two-thirds of the special education students belonged in regular classes (Kirp, 1973: 719). A study of 378 Philadelphia EMR students concluded that 25 percent of the classifications were erroneous and another 43 percent were questionable (Garrison and Hammill, 1971: 18).[20] In addition, students grouped in homogeneous units progress at significantly different rates (Franseth, 1966: 17), so many students fail to "fit" their initial assignment after short periods of time.

Second, academic grouping practices are antithetical to the process of school *integration*. As Rosenbaum (1976: 6) argues, with ability grouping and tracking,

> 1. students are grouped with those who are similar to themselves and separated from those who are different.
>
> 2. grouping is based, at least in part, on a ranked criterion—ability or postschool plans (college is considered superior to jobs); thus groups are unequal in status.

Integration requires equal educational opportunities, equal group status, and cross-racial student contact (see Allport, 1954; Pettigrew, 1971; McConahay, 1981; Adair, 1984). Academic grouping clearly creates separate groups of unequal status.

Third, a consensus of academic research concludes that minority students are disproportionately overrepresented in lower-level academic groups (R. L. Jones, 1976; Ogbu, 1978; Hawley et al., 1983: chapter 7; Eyler, Cook, and Ward, 1983; Adair, 1984; Hochschild, 1984; Heller, Holtzman, and Messick, 1982; Chinn and Hughes, 1987). In addition, the use of ability grouping or tracking may have second-order consequences such as a negative effect on self-esteem (see Jones and Wilderson, 1976; Findley and Bryan, 1975; Metz, 1978: chap. 5; Eyler, Cook, and Ward, 1983; Oakes, 1985: chap. 7). It can

---

19. The use of IQ as a placement criterion may have no predictive ability. Shonkoff (1982: 145) notes that the large disparities between blacks and whites on IQ tests during school years decreases almost completely for individuals between the ages of 20 and 60. If the tests measure a temporary phenomenon, then they should not be the devices used to make permanent educational classifications.

20. Shepard (1987: 327) claims that about 90 percent of children served in special education are mildly handicapped and that these children are "indistinguishable from other low achievers."

also lead to an increase in student misconduct, delinquency, and dropouts (Children's Defense Fund, 1974; Findley and Bryan, 1975; Rosenbaum, 1976).

Fourth, the racial bias of academic grouping means that it can be justified only if such practices enhance the educational performance of students. Kulik and Kulik (1982) have examined 700 references on ability grouping, eventually focusing on 52 valid studies that could be used to assess the impact of ability grouping. Their findings are mixed. They find that ability grouping has no impact on average- and lower-ability groups but it has benefits for higher-ability groups.[21] This conclusion is based on slim findings, because only 10 of the 52 studies produced significant results and not all of these favored the ability grouped students. In addition, if high-ability groups benefit, the benefit is small. Kulik and Kulik (1982: 421) find that the positive impact is equivalent to improving performance from the 50th percentile to the 54th percentile, an especially modest improvement. Similarly Carlberg and Kavale's (1980: 304) meta-analysis of 50 special education studies has resulted in the finding that "special education class placement is an inferior alternative to regular class placement in [academically] benefiting children removed from the educational mainstream. . . . [There] is no justification for placement of low IQ children in special classes."

Findley and Bryan's (1975: 13) conclusion still appears to hold: ". . . ability grouping, as practiced, produces conflicting evidence of usefulness in promoting improved scholastic achievement in superior groups, and almost uniformly unfavorable evidence for promoting scholastic achievement in average-or-low achieving groups" (see also Goldberg, Passow, and Justman, 1966; Goldberg and Passow, 1966; Franseth, 1966; Heller, 1982). EMR classes in particular have not shown positive impacts on students (Corman and Gottlieb, 1978; Semmel, Gottlieb, and Robinson, 1979; Dunn, 1968; Gartner and Lipsky, 1987). Simmons and Brady (1981: 132) provide a similar critical appraisal of compensatory education programs: "Minority students are highly overrepresented in a situation that perpetuates their disadvantage. . . . [They] are resegregated, provided an inferior educational experience compared to that of their peers, stigmatized by staff and other students—in short, placed in learning environments that do little to close the gap in minority-majority achievement levels." Perhaps Oakes (1985:7) offers the most straightforward assessment of academic grouping: ". . . *no group of students has been found to benefit consistently from being in a homogeneous group.*"

Lower-academic groups are detrimental to student performance for three reasons. The differential-peers hypothesis suggests that, in low-academic groups, group dynamics lower student performance either through peer pressure

---

21. According to Oakes (1988: 43) the reason for greater improvement for high-ability groups is obvious. High-ability groups receive greater resources, more individual attention, a more challenging curriculum, and other instructional advantages.

or unfavorable learning environments (Alexander and Eckland, 1975; Alexander and McDill, 1976; Eder, 1981: 159; Felmlee and Eder, 1983). The instructor-effect hypothesis holds that lower teacher expectations produce lower student performance, because students respond to the cues that teachers give (Brophy and Good, 1970; Rist, 1973; Barr and Dreeben, 1977). The counselor-impact hypothesis suggests that non-college-prep students (and logically other students in lower-ability groups) receive far less attention and advice from counselors (Heyns, 1974; Cicourel and Kitsuse, 1963). Academic grouping not only reinforces initial differences between students but also actually widens those differences over time (Alexander and McDill, 1976; Chesler and Cave, 1981; Felmlee and Eder, 1983: 85). Accordingly many equal-education advocates have called for its elimination or suggest it should be used only under limited circumstances (see Smith and Dziuban, 1977; McConahay, 1981: 47; Epps, 1981: 103; Hawley, 1981: 299; Hawley et al., 1983: 119).

Disciplinary Practices

One goal of a school system as an organization is to maintain order and authority. The method for achieving this goal is discipline. Second-generation discrimination, however, can also be manifested in the process of maintaining school order. Most discipline is dispensed for relatively minor offenses such as truancy, cutting classes, tardiness, smoking, and cafeteria violations rather than for behavior that is violent or dangerous to persons or property (Arnez, 1978). Discipline for lesser offenses is more conducive to racial discrimination. Racially based disciplinary practices can lead to minority student "push out" (Children's Defense Fund, 1974) and, in the words of Yudof (1975: 374), represent "academic capital punishment."

A number of studies support the notion that disciplinary practices are "sometimes a mere pretense for punishing a child for other reasons" (Children's Defense Fund, 1974: 130). Being black, Hispanic, or poor is often adequate reason (see Children's Defense Fund, 1974, 1975; Southern Regional Council, 1973; U.S. Commission on Civil Rights, 1976; Arnez, 1978). Eyler and her associates (1983: 142), for example, report that black students are from two to five times more likely than white students to be suspended from school, they receive lengthier suspensions, and are more likely to be suspended repeatedly. Arnez (1978: 31) also suggests a strong linkage between disparities in disciplinary practices and minority-student dropout rates. She notes that in many newly desegregated schools "minority students were induced to drop out" and that often "the most aware and aggressive Black students . . . were removed."

Finally, research substantiates a racial bias in the discretionary power of school officials in dispensing justice. "Black students are punished for offenses allowed white students or given heavier penalties for similar offenses" (Eyler, Cook, and Ward, 1983: 144). On the individual level, Eyler, Cook and Ward (1983: 144) find that "powerful predictors of suspensions include low grade-point average, low IQ scores, low test scores as well as being male or black." Bennett and Harris (1982: 421) have found racial disparities in discipline associated with lack of administrative support for integration and with school environments generally hostile to black students. On the positive side, research also claims that school officials can mitigate the deleterious impact of discriminatory discipline practices on minority students by developing disciplinary rules that are perceived as fair and equitable by all students, by creating a school social environment of equal opportunity, and by employing teachers who are sensitive to different cultural norms and who display favorable expectations of their students (see Children's Defense Fund, 1974; U.S. Commission on Civil Rights, 1976; Felice and Richardson, 1977; Richardson and Gerlach, 1980; Eyer, Cook, and Ward, 1983).

Educational Outcomes

A school district that uses academic grouping and disciplinary procedures in a discriminatory way denies minority students access to the best quality education the district can provide. Three results of such a discriminatory process are possible. First, students can become disillusioned with school and drop out (or be pushed out in the case of suspensions or expulsions). Second, dropouts and students who continue to attend classes but lose interest might not graduate from high school. Third, even those students who overcome discriminatory academic grouping and disciplinary practices and do graduate from high school will not receive the same quality education as other students receive. The first two results—dropouts and high school graduation rates—can be measured and will be the final two policy variables in the study. The third result is probably even more important in this era of social promotion, but comparing the quality of high school diplomas is an extended research project in and of itself and is beyond the scope of this research.

Before progressing to our theory of black representation and public policy, one additional aspect of second-generation discrimination via academic grouping and discipline merits discussion. Academic grouping and discipline have become institutionalized as part of the normal process of education.

Institutional Second-Generation Discrimination

The subtle nature of second-generation discrimination requires one to recognize that schools are formal organizations. They have goals (e.g., the education of children, maintaining order and authority, serving as socialization and "leveling" agents, survival), structures (e.g., organization charts, classrooms, rules, curricula), and work processes (e.g., teaching to educate, disciplining to maintain order). Structures and work processes are instrumental in reaching goals, but schools are clearly open systems receptive to environmental influences. Schools can manipulate structures and work processes in response to environmental demands (Metz, 1978: 15). School officials must respond to pressures from students, parents, community groups, courts, school boards, federal and state bureaucracies, professional standards, labor unions, and so on. Such pressures may be either complementary or contradictory.

Environmental pressures played a significant role in school desegregation. Few schools desegregated voluntarily. Some were forced to desegregate by court orders, others were pressured to desegregate by civil rights groups, and still others desegregated to retain their state and federal funds. Second-generation discrimination can be viewed as a racist response to desegregation pressures. In some school districts, changes in curriculum were concomitant with desegregation efforts. Special education programs for the mentally retarded or ability grouping and tracking practices have been implemented for resegregative purposes (Levin and Moise, 1975; Bell, 1980; McConahay, 1981; Carter, 1982; Eyler, Cook, and Ward, 1983). Similarly, racially biased disciplinary practices have been used to eliminate minority students (Children's Defense Fund, 1974; Yudof, 1975; Arnez, 1978).

Blatant racism might be the reason for second-generation discrimination, but an equally likely explanation is institutional discrimination (see Feagin and Feagin, 1986). Institutional discrimination occurs when the norms, procedures, and rules of an organization discriminate against certain individuals. Three reasons suggest that academic grouping and discipline have become institutionalized discrimination. First, they are based on traditional, widely used, and legal work processes designed to achieve educational goals. Academic grouping and discipline have an educational history and a supporting literature that precedes efforts to desegregate schools. The maintenance of order requires disciplinary practices. Curriculum changes are often necessary to meet the new demands and perceived needs of heterogenous school populations.

Second, especially since the turbulant 1960s, federal and state laws have required local school officials to create programs for students with extra educational needs and/or have provided fiscal assistance for the development of such programs (e.g., Title I of the Elementary and Secondary Education Act of 1965, the Bilingual Education Act of 1968, the Education of All Handicapped Children Act of 1975). Special education classes (e.g., educable mentally retarded, learning disabled, emotionally disturbed), bilingual education (depending on the nature of the instruction), and compensatory programs for low-income and disadvantaged youth often require "pull out" of students from regular classes and result in de facto resegregation (see Eyler, Cook, and Ward,

1983: 132–140; Brady, 1980; Gartner and Lipsky, 1987). Federal and state grant programs often create an incentive to increase the size of special education and other pull-out classes (Magnetti, 1982).

Third, the practices have been consistent with accepted professional norms. Professional educational procedures require that students be evaluated and grouped according to ability. Discrimination has become imbedded in the regulations and informal rules of the institution and the roles of the organization's members (Feagin and Feagin, 1986: 12). This sanction of official rules and policy has allowed individual acts of discrimination to "occur without the presence of conscious bigotry" (Knowles and Prewitt, 1969: 5).[22] Thus institutional discrimination can occur even where individuals have "no intention of subordinating others because of color, or are totally unaware of doing so" (Downs, 1970: 7).

A Political Theory of Equal Access to Education

This book is concerned with the impact of black representation on a set of public policies that affect equal access to education. The focus is on political explanations of variations in equal access to education for black students. This focus does not mean other forces do not affect quality education; they do. Equal access to education is affected by the resources of the school district, the support from the families of school children, the curricula used, and countless other factors (Bridge, Judd, and Mock, 1979). Our intent is not to construct a theory of equal access to education that explains all the variation in access to education. Rather, our intent is to create a political theory of equal access to education to demonstrate that political forces affect equal educational opportunities. The political theory follows closely the logic of the previous models of black representation. Compare, for example, the black representation model in figure 1.1 with figure 1.2, which summarizes the influences affecting second-generation discrimination.

Black Teachers

Of the policy-making positions we have discussed, the most likely individuals to influence equal access to education are teachers (Heller, Holtzman, and Messick, 1982: 38). Although school board members can set policy limits on academic grouping and discipline, in most cases these policies were established long before the current board was elected. School board influence, as a result, will be only indirect. School administrators have a stronger hand in

22. Rosenbaum (1980: 85) discusses the institutional character of tracking. He concludes, ". . . gross coercion is not required to keep students in lower tracks; misinformation is sufficient to make students voluntarily choose to remain in tracks which will ultimately frustrate their plans [to attend college]."

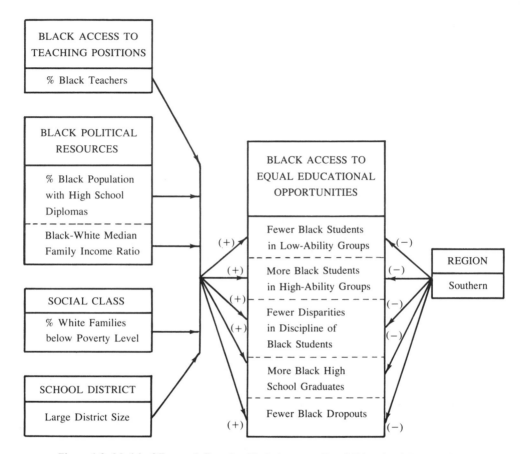

Figure 1.2. Model of Factors Influencing Black Access to Equal Educational Opportunities.

ability grouping, tracking, special education, and discipline; but their contact with students and their influence on access to education is fairly small when compared with that of teachers.

The education literature considers teachers the strongest single influence on the student's learning environment. Perhaps the most documented conclusion is that teachers can affect student performance (Brophy, 1983; Evertson, 1986); in the words of Hawley and Rosenholtz (1984: 4), ". . . teachers have a significant impact on . . . the nature of the student's experiences, whatever the formal policies and curricula of a school might be." Numerous studies have

demonstrated that teacher expectations are highly correlated with the performance of students (Brookover and Erickson, 1975; St. John, 1975; Good and
Cooper, 1983; Holliday, 1985: 76). Teachers provide more positive feedback
to high achievers and more negative feedback to low achievers, thus accen-
tuating the differences between these groups of students (Rosenthal and Jacobson, 1968; Heohn, 1954; Good, 1970).

Black students are no different from white students in that their performance
is also affected by teacher perceptions and interactions (Holliday, 1985: 72;
Rist, 1970; St. John, 1971; Brophy and Good, 1974; Leacock, 1969; Scritchfield and Picou, 1982). Rist (1970) and Persell (1977) argue that teachers have
lower expectations of black students and this adversely affects their performance (see also Dusek and Joseph, 1983; DeMeis and Turner, 1978; Marwit,
Marwit, and Walker, 1978; Rubovits and Maehr, 1973). Gay (1974) and
Mangold (1974) document that white students get more praise and positive
reinforcement than black students do. Grant (1984: 105) has found that the
praise black students did receive was more often qualified than the praise given
to white students.

Teacher expectations can easily influence decisions on ability grouping and
tracking. In a multivariate analysis of teachers' classifications of students,
Moore and Johnson (1983: 472) concluded, "Black students with low SES
[socioeconomic status] scores were more likely to be assigned to the unskilled
laborer category when grades were low, and less likely to be assigned to the
professional category when grades were high, than were students from other
ethnic groups with similar grade-SES combinations."

The massive literature on the different expectations and reinforcements of
students related to student race stands in stark contrast with the limited literature
on teacher race and its impact on students. Aaron and Powell (1982: 55) have
found that "white teachers had a rate of negative feedback to black pupils two
and one half times greater than that of black teachers to black students." Mathis
(1975: 71) has found that black third- and fourth-grade students were disciplined
less and fared better overall with black teachers. Logically other hypotheses
about the impact of black teachers on black students can be suggested. Because
a black teacher shares racial experiences with the black student and because
the black teacher has experienced the educational system as a black student,
a black teacher is more likely to be supportive of a black student who has trouble
in class. This implies that such a teacher would be less likely to discipline
a student inappropriately and less likely to conclude that a student belongs in
special education classes.

Black teachers can have a separate impact on black students simply by being in the classroom. A black teacher serves as a role model for black students;

black students are exposed to other black individuals who have been successful. The impact that black teachers can have as role models has been recognized even by the courts as important to the education experiences of black students (B. P. Cole, 1986: 332).

Our first political hypothesis about equal access to education for black students is that it should be positively correlated with the proportion of black teachers in the school district. If our expectations hold, we would expect that districts with larger proportions of black teachers would place fewer black students in special education and low-ability groups and more in high-ability groups. In addition, black students would not suffer disproportionate discipline and would be more likely to finish high school.[23]

Black Resources

Black resources should be associated with greater access to equal education for black students. Specifically higher levels of black resources should be associated with proportionately fewer black students in low academic groups and proportionately more in high academic groups. Black resources should be associated with less disproportionate discipline of black students and more black students finishing high school.

Black resources can affect equal educational opportunities in one of two ways. High levels of black resources will indicate that the black community has the potential as a group to pressure the school district for educational policies more favorable to the black community. High levels of black resources also indicate that individual black parents have the ability to resist a negative decision concerning their own child.

Two measures of black resources will be used. The first, black education, was also used in the representation models. The second resource variable will not be black population, because that was linked to black voters, and this study examines the implementation of policy decisions.[24] The second indicator of

23. We use the percentage of black teachers rather than some ratio of teachers to students because we are interested in the probability that a student will come in contact with a black teacher. A district with 25 percent black teachers means that a black student should have a 25 percent chance that the next teacher she or he meets will be black. A ratio has no substantive meaning. A school district with a 1.0 representation ratio of black teachers to black students tells us only that the percentage of black teachers in the district is equal to the percentage of its black students; it does not tell us anything about the probability that a black student will come in contact with a black teacher.

24. We experimented with the percentage of black population in the model. This variable was rarely significant and was highly collinear with black teachers. Because the variable black teachers was both more significantly correlated with the policy outputs and could be supported stronger from a theoretical standpoint, this variable was retained and black population was dropped.

black resources will be the ratio of black median family income to white median family income in the district. This measure taps black resources relative to white resources, relates to our social-class argument, and has frequently been used as an indicator of black resources (Karnig, 1979; Robinson, England, and Meier, 1985).

Social Class

The power thesis applied to black representation holds that the majority white community prefers black middle-class representatives to white lower-class representatives. Similarly, in terms of equal educational opportunities, the institutional biases of the educational system will also have some class preferences. Academic-grouping decisions are often based in part on standardized tests of reading and IQ. Such tests are positively associated with social class. In communities with a homogeneous middle-class white community, these tests will serve to segregate black students into lower academic groups. In a heterogeneous white community, however, the standardized tests will adversely affect lower-class white students as well. Blacks, at least middle-class blacks, should fare better in such a school system because the institutional discrimination will affect many more white students (see, for example, Alexander and McDill, 1976; Hauser, Sewell and Alwin, 1976; Rosenbaum, 1976). The limited size of lower-ability and special education classes means that fewer "discretionary" slots will be available for black students.

The indicator of social class will again be the percentage of white families living below the poverty level.[25] The black-white income ratio previously discussed as a black resources variable will also tap the social-class dimension of educational policy. A large white lower class will be associated with proportionately more blacks in higher-level ability groups and fewer in lower-level ability groups. Fewer black students should be disciplined, and more should graduate from high school.

Region

The southern region again serves as a surrogate variable for past policies and procedures and current attitudes. Given the historical use of *de jure* segregated schools in the South and the fact that second-generation discrimination was first identified in the South, the southern region should be associated with higher levels of second-generation school discrimination.[26]

25. Finn (1982: 346) has found a correlation of −.20 between the socioeconomic status of school districts and the degree of racial bias in EMR assignments. Finn used school lunch measures of social class and did not separate out the impact of white poverty from overall levels of poverty.

26. Southern districts are coded as 1, and all others are coded as 0.

District Size

District size has been negatively associated with the ability to desegregate school systems (England and Morgan, 1986: chapter 5). Primarily for logistical reasons, a school desegregation plan is harder to implement in a larger school district. To date only one brief assessment has been made of the relationships between district size and second-generation discrimination. Finn (1982: 344) has found a negative relationship between black EMR assignments and district size for large school districts ($\geq$ 30,000 students). Some explanation for this finding exists. Larger districts are more likely to be aware of civil rights laws and regulations and are more likely to have had contact with the Office for Civil Rights. In addition, large school districts are more likely to have a greater division of labor and thus be more professionalized. These factors suggest that larger school districts may be less likely to engage in second-generation school discrimination.

The Nature of the Survey

The universe for analysis is United States school districts with a minimum 1976 enrollment of 15,000 students, of which at least 1 percent were black. Large districts were selected because they are likely to represent the educational experiences of most black students in the United States. Districts without a sizable black population were eliminated from the universe, because one can hardly generalize about how educational policies affect blacks if a district does not have any blacks.

Four separate data sources were used in this analysis. Measures of ability grouping, special education, discipline, educational attainment, and student enrollment were originally gathered by the Office for Civil Rights (OCR, now in the Department of Education) in their "Elementary and Secondary School Civil Rights Survey." OCR conducted this survey every year from 1968 to 1974 and every two years thereafter. OCR does not survey every school district every year, but large school districts are likely to be included in the survey for most years. Two OCR data sources were used, one containing a panel of the surveys from 1968 to 1982 and a second with only the 1984 survey.[27]

27. Anyone working with OCR data can testify to the difficulties in using their data sets. The panel survey was constructed in such a way to make analysis across years impossible (that is, one cannot relate EMR classes in one year to EMR classes in another). The structure of the data set was such that vast blank spots (representing questions not asked in specific years) were included in the data matrix. This inefficient structuring made the data set time-consuming to read and difficult to analyze. For some analysis we reconstituted the data set so analysis over time was possible. The risk in this is that, with significant missing data, the number of cases dwindled rapidly. In addition, the number of coding or other types of error is not as low as one would associate with a clean data set. We made every effort to eliminate obvious coding errors by comparing OCR information with other information about the districts.

Information on black income, black education, white poverty, regions, and other similar demographic information was taken from the Bureau of the Census, *1980 Housing and Population Survey, File STF-3* (released in 1985). This file contains information aggregated by school district.

To gather information on black representation on school boards and among administrative and teaching positions, the authors sent a survey in the spring of 1986 to the superintendents of all districts with 15,000 or more students in 1976. A total of 306 surveys were sent. After a follow-up request, 205 surveys (or 67 percent) were returned. The requirement of 1 percent black student enrollment plus continued existence since 1968 reduced this sample to 174 usable responses. A listing of the school districts can be found in Appendix B.[28]

A statistical profile of the school districts in the sample is shown in table 1.2. The average district had around 50,000 students. Approximately three-fifths of the students were white, three-tenths black, and one-tenth Hispanic. Notable in this statistical profile of districts is the range of variation on a wide variety of measures. Such variation yields some confidence that these districts are representative of the educational experience in the United States.

One characteristic that these districts share is increasing minority enrollment. Table 1.3 shows that black enrollment in these districts has increased by 7 percentiles in the past 18 years. To determine if these districts are representative of all large school districts, we compared the dependent variables for

Table 1.2. Statistical Profile of School Districts in the Sample

Variable	Mean	Low	High
Student enrollment	50,065	10,500[a]	932,880
Whites (%)	59.2	2.0	97.0
Blacks (%)	26.5	2.0	92.0
Hispanics (%)	10.3	0.0	96.0
High school graduates			
Blacks (%)	58.6	28.9	94.6
Whites (%)	70.5	37.6	95.9
Median family income	$16,825	$9,285	$44,121
Black-white income ratio	0.70	0.50	1.07
White poverty (%)	9.6	2.2	30.8

N = 174

[a] Enrollments of less than 15,000 result because some districts lost enrollments after 1976.

28. Twenty-eight districts were omitted from the analysis because they had less than 1 percent black enrollment. Three were omitted because the districts were merged or consolidated. None was deleted as the result of missing data.

Table 1.3. Changes in Black Student Enrollment
in Districts in the Sample

	Black Students (%)	Standard Deviation
1968	19.4	17.3
1970	20.1	18.0
1972	21.3	18.8
1974	22.8	19.4
1976	23.2	19.8
1978	24.3	19.9
1980	24.8	20.5
1982	28.2	20.5
1984	26.3	20.6
1986	26.5	20.6

our districts with all districts in the United States. These figures, reproduced in table A.1 in Appendix A, reveal that our sample is extremely close to the universe on these policy indicators.

Finally, because we want to compare school desegregation with second-generation school discrimination, measures of school desegregation are needed. Professor Franklin Wilson of the University of Wisconsin provided us with Taeuber Dissimilarity Indexes measuring the level of segregation in each of our districts for every year from 1968 to 1976, except for 1975, when the Office for Civil Rights did not gather the base data.

Summary

This chapter has introduced the theory that we will use to examine the relationships between black representation and equal access to education. We perceive that education is a political process, and our theory has a distinctly political emphasis. We hypothesize that gaining access to positions on the school board is determined by black political resources, social class, region, and electoral structure. Representation on the school board is important for blacks, because school board representation is a major determinant of access to administrative positions. Our theory also argues that access to administrative positions is affected by black political resources, social class, and region. More black administrative representation, according to our theory, should translate into more black teachers. Additional factors that influence the hiring of black teachers include black political resources, social class, and region.

Black representation in policy-making positions is important, because teachers, administrators, and school board members make the decisions that affect equal access to education. Our theory suggests the most important decision-maker is the teacher. Other important factors are black political resources, social class, region, and school district size.

Our measure of equal access to education is based on the use of academic grouping and discipline to limit both educational attainment and the quality of education provided. The core of our theory argues that politics determines the degree of racial equity in these areas. Important to understanding these policies of equal access is the historical development of educational discrimination against black Americans. That subject is the focus of the following chapter.

2 From No Schools to Separate Schools to Desegregated Schools
Toward Equal Educational Opportunity

To people familiar with urban education, the argument that race and education are intertwined seems self-evident. Over the past four decades, the country has been vividly, and often violently, reminded of this fact. The *Brown* v. *Board of Education* (1954, 1955) school desegregation decisions engendered reactions seldom more moderate than the segregationist shibboleth, "As long as we can legislate, we can segregate" (Peltason, 1971: 93). Some districts went so far as to close their schools rather than desegregate voluntarily (Smith, 1965). In between such extremes were cases such as Little Rock, where a young black student returned home from her first day of desegregated schooling with her dress soaking wet from the human spittle rained on her by the gauntlet of angry antidesegregation protestors through whom she had to walk.

Racial problems in education have not been unique to southern states and those that border the south, and they did not arise only in the aftermath of *Plessy* v. *Ferguson* (1896). Policy-makers throughout United States history have tried to deny blacks access to education and to limit interracial contact in the process. This chapter briefly traces the saga of black education in the United States from the days when blacks were denied education by law through the era when blacks were educated in segregated schools to the more recent times of desegregated education. This story not only provides important historical background, but it also furnishes the context for understanding how second-generation discrimination has been able to arise and whether, perhaps, it should have been anticipated.

No Public Schooling

When a student of slavery in Mississippi concluded that "the education of slaves was almost entirely neglected" (Sydnor, 1966: 253), he was guilty only of understatement. After 1740 when South Carolina adopted the first compulsory illiteracy law, making it a crime to teach slaves to write (Birnie, 1927: 14), other states adopted similar, often more restrictive, laws. The Deep South states fell in line quickly, but this phenomenon was not limited to that region. Gerber's (1976: 4) account of the experiences of blacks in Ohio indicates that Ohio was "an exception to the almost universal denial of public education to blacks during the early nineteenth century." Other studies confirm this situation in other nonsouthern states such as Missouri (Traxler, 1914: 265) and Pennsylvania (Weinberg, 1977: 21). So pervasive were such laws and practices that in 1850 only 6.1 percent of the "free Negro children" nationwide attended school (Weinberg, 1977: 17; using data from Woodson, 1919). Only Maine had as many as one-fifth (20.7 percent) of its free black children enrolled in schools in that year. These figures apparently include those enrolled in secret schools and "Sabbath schools," alternatives devised by blacks interested in gaining an education. In short, before the Civil War an active effort, widespread and largely successful, prevented blacks from obtaining an education.

Segregated Public Schooling

Not until the Civil War and thereafter did schooling for blacks become somewhat more common.[1] Schools for blacks were sponsored by various philanthropic organizations, particularly the American Missionary Society and Freedmen's Aid Societies. These schools later gained public funding with the creation of the War Department's Freedmen's Bureau in 1865 (Johnson, 1938: 277–279), opening educational opportunities to unprecedented numbers of blacks in the South. Even with federal appropriations after 1865 removing some of the uncertainty about funding, the resources for these schools were scarce, and they were the targets of terrorism, so their impact was limited. Between 1860 and 1870 the enrollment rates for black children between ages 5 and 19 rose from 1.9 percent to 9.9 percent (Weinberg, 1977: 44). This increase represents both remarkable success and disappointment. In less than a decade the proportion of black children enrolled in school increased fivefold. Still the numbers were atrociously low.

Only after the Radical Republicans, fresh from their 1868 congressional election victories, dissolved the existing southern state governments, were universal, publicly financed educational systems established in the South. Thus, black enrollment in public schools did not increase greatly until after 1870. By 1880, just over one-third of black children between the ages of 5 and 19 were enrolled in schools, and enrollment remained close to that level into the first decade of the next century (Weinberg, 1977: 44). This newly provided education was

1. Although one might argue that public education was not commonly available to whites either, by modern standards, Weinberg's (1977: 44) calculations show that in 1860, when only 1.9 percent of black youths between the ages of 5 and 19 were enrolled in schools, 59.6 percent of white youths were enrolled.

invariably segregated in the South, just as the freedmen's and missionary schools had been (Weinberg, 1977: 51). Public education was commonly segregated in the North also. By 1860, for example, San Francisco had three elementary schools specifically built for blacks, but blacks were barred from attending the city's high schools (Peterson, 1985: 104). In 1863 Chicago attempted to segregate its schools by passing the Black School Law. The law required all black children to attend segregated schools, but black parents refused to comply, and the law was repealed two years later (Peterson, 1985: 111).

Several states mandated equal expenditures for black and white schools; but only briefly and only in the South, where blacks represented significant voting blocks, was any semblance of equal expenditures achieved. In the later half of the 1870s in Alabama and the Carolinas, expenditures on black schools were either comparable to white schools or slightly advantageous to blacks (H. A. Bullock, 1967: 86; Weinberg, 1977: 46). By the end of the decade, however, unequal expenditures for the education of blacks and whites became common pratice (Du Bois, 1901). Courtroom challenges to such discriminatory practices were apparently successful in Kentucky (*Claybrook* v. *City of Owensboro,* 1883) and North Carolina (*Puitt* v. *Commissioners,* 1886), but the implementation of these judicial declarations foreshadowed events to follow some 70 years later. State officials were ordered to allocate school monies in a racially nondiscriminatory manner, but local officials were left unmonitored when they spent the funds. South Carolina was certainly not the most extreme case when it changed from actually spending more on its black schools than on its white schools in 1880 to spending almost three times as much per pupil in white schools as it did in black schools in 1895 (Tindall, 1952: 216).

The ultimate legitimation of segregation occurred in 1896 when the U.S. Supreme Court, in *Plessy* v. *Ferguson,* upheld a Louisiana statute which mandated "separate but equal" accommodations in railway trains for blacks and whites; the Court found no violation of the Fourteenth Amendment's equal protection clause (Barth, 1974: 22–53). If public transportation facilities could be racially segregated, segregation of public education facilities was not a big step. In fact, Justice Brown, in *Plessy,* helped justify the Court's decision by noting that in Massachusetts, a state among those "where the political rights of the colored race have been longest and most earnestly enforced," the Massachusetts Supreme Judicial Court had upheld segregation of the Boston schools (*Roberts* v. *City of Boston,* 1849). Had he desired, he could also have noted that appellate courts in Arkansas, California, Kansas, Louisiana, Missouri, Nevada, Oklahoma, Oregon, South Carolina, and West Virginia, as well as lower federal courts, had cited *Roberts* while permitting segregated education (Levy, 1957: 109–117).

If any doubt existed about how far the Court was willing to let authorities go in ignoring the "but equal" part of the decision in educational systems, the Court clarified it in 1899 by allowing the Richmond County (Augusta), Georgia, school board to close its black high school but maintain its white one (*Cumming* v. *County Board of Education*). State control of education was held to be inviolable, and six decades of legally sanctioned segregated education were ushered in. Pretenses of equality were superfluous and generally avoided.

Segregated education was not imposed without black protest. One line of attack was based on principle. Frederick Douglass saw segregated schools as "a system that exalts one class and debases another" (Foner, 1955: 289). Delegates to the National Civil Rights Convention of 1873 declared, "It is an abridgement of the privileges of a citizen to say he shall not, because of his race and color, elect . . . the common school he shall attend . . . " (Aptheker, 1951: 639).

A second line of attack was more practical in nature. Bond (1934: 56) argued that blacks "were able to see that separate schools meant inferior schools. They wished to use mixed schools as a lever to obtain equality in efficiency," that is, as leverage for obtaining equal per capita expenditures for black and white students.

But these protests, regardless of their nature, were of little avail in the first half of the twentieth century. No matter what measure is used, blacks fared worse than whites in schooling (Lieberson, 1980: 142–143). The Great Depression exacerbated the funding differences for black and white schools, so that Bond, writing in 1934 (p. 171), concluded that "Negro children do now receive a smaller proportion of the public funds in the Southern States than they have at any time in past history." Davis' (1934: 52–99) study of early twentieth-century school systems in East Texas paints a picture of black education as incidental to white education. This description was apt in a wide variety of settings. Bond's (1934: 244) broader analysis of the same period produced what he referred to as the "old formula": "Negro schools are financed from the fragments which fall from the budget made up for white children. Where there are many Negro children, the available funds are given principally to the small white minority."

The position of blacks arguing for greater educational resources was not enhanced by their inability to present a unified front concerning the priorities for black education. Booker T. Washington, reflecting his philosophy on the primacy of black economic development, advocated practical "industrial education" and was perhaps the dominant voice of the day. But, a serious note of opposition was sounded by W. E. B. Du Bois, who demanded the education of youth according to ability, particularly in the liberal arts. This debate raged within the black leadership from shortly after the turn of the century through the 1934 ouster of Du Bois as editor of *The Crisis,* the official organ of the National Association for the Advancement of Colored People (NAACP). The debate continues today in political and social discourse (Cruse, 1987).

The War to Overturn Plessy

In such an environment the seeds for dismantling the segregated school systems took root. Many of these seeds were sown by the NAACP.[2] The NAACP developed a plan for using litigation as an instrument to strike at segregation in the mid-1920s and came to focus on education as the point of attack. According to Charles Houston, at the time the special counsel to the NAACP, attacking discrimination in education was seen as the key for the group's efforts, because it was "symbolic of all the more drastic discriminations." Discriminatory education precluded effective competition by blacks for jobs or effective self-defense of blacks' rights (Tushnet, 1987: 34).

Beginning in the early 1930s the NAACP implemented its campaign, focusing on the desegregation of public graduate and professional schools, the equalization of black and white public school teachers' salaries, and the equalization of physical facilities at segregated elementary and secondary schools (Tushnet, 1987: 34). Led by Thurgood Marshall after 1936, the campaign evolved as the organization won decisions, chipping away at the doctrine of separate but equal. On the first front, the NAACP won an appeal to the U.S. Supreme Court which held that a black applicant to the University of Missouri Law School had the same right to an opportunity for legal education as whites within that state (*Missouri ex rel Gaines* v. *Canada,* 1938). The Court specifically rejected Missouri's stated intention of opening a law school for blacks "whenever necessary or practical" and its plan to provide scholarships for black students to attend law school outside the state. In this case, the NAACP won its first decision by the U.S. Supreme Court, eroding the separate-but-equal principle articulated in *Plessy.*

On the second front, the NAACP won a salary equalization case at the Fourth U.S. Circuit Court of Appeals, and the U.S. Supreme Court refused to hear the losing side's appeal (*Alston* v. *School Board of Norfolk,* 1940). When the data showed clear differentials between what blacks and whites (and men and women) were paid after controlling for type of school assignment, the circuit court declared the situation to be clearly unconstitutional. Only in the target area of facilities equalization did the NAACP go without victory. Still the total effect of these and follow-up decisions made it virtually impossible for local school districts to have separate but unequal schools.

2. For a fuller account of the NAACP's efforts in this area, see Kluger 1975. For a more insightful account, upon which this presentation relies heavily, see Tushnet 1987.

The campaign's underlying premise seems to have been based on a combination of faith in the rule of law and simple cost-benefit analysis. If blacks could obtain authoritative legal pronouncements and sufficiently raise the costs of maintaining segregated schools, school officials would dismantle dual school systems because the law said to and to do so would be a more efficient expenditure of taxpayers' dollars. These expectations were, of course, disappointed (Tushnet, 1987: 49–104).

Only after almost a decade and a half of arduous work was the NAACP ready, in 1950, to take the stand that "education [should be] on a non-segregated basis and that no relief other than that will be acceptable [in future cases]" (quoted in Tushnet, 1987: 136).[3] Thus, the direct attack on segregated schools was launched. The task was to get a court ruling directly on the constitutionality of segregation itself. To reach a decision favorable to black interests would require that the Court consider the realities of inherent inequalities not easily presented through usual legal evidence.

The vehicle for the Court's ruling was a suit filed by Oliver Brown and 12 other parents who sought to enjoin enforcement of a Kansas statute that permitted, but did not require, cities of more than 15,000 residents to maintain racially segregated schools. Similar suits challenging denial of admission of black pupils to schools with white students under statutes requiring or permitting racial separation were filed in South Carolina, Virginia, and Delaware. These suits were combined for purposes of a Court decision (see Kluger, 1975; H. A. Bullock, 1967: 231–234).

Combining a tested legal strategy, objective facts about segregation, and social scientific arguments about the effects of segregation, the plaintiffs presented a case that led the U.S. Supreme Court in 1954 to declare, ". . . in the field of public education the doctrine of 'separate but equal' has no place. Separate educational facilities are inherently unequal" (*Brown* v. *Board of Education,* 1954: 495).

Implementing *Brown*

After the Court handed down this momentous opinion, euphoria reigned among the victorious attorneys. Thurgood Marshall was reported in the *New York Times* to speculate that it might take "up to five years" for segregation to be eradicated, but "by the time the 100th Anniversary of the Emancipation Proclamation is observed in 1963, segregation in all its forms [will be]

---

3. Recent research by Champagne (1987) has examined the amicus briefs filed by the solicitor general of the United States in desegregation cases. This examination reveals that the Justice Department attorneys were usually ahead of the NAACP in advocating major changes in desegregation and other race-related issues. Champagne's analysis implies that the role of the federal bureaucracy in school desegregation is even greater than the one expressed later in this chapter.

eliminated from the nation" (quoted in Cruse, 1987: 25–26). Exactly how this was to eventuate was unclear, at least to the Court. When it delivered its decision, the Court scheduled reargument on whether the remedies of the newly declared unconstitutional situation should be applied immediately or gradually (*Brown* v. *Board of Education* 1954: 495–496). To Marshall, the answer was clear: "Now after all of this shit—no valid reason for delay—no hope that time would help" (quoted in Tushnet, 1987: 166).

The Court, however, did not agree with Marshall. When the Court issued its implementation decree in 1955 (*"Brown II"*), it rejected precipitous change. The guidelines directed district court judges to place responsibility for desegregation on local school officials, to require prompt initiation of desegregation programs, to be reasonable but firm in allowing extensions of time, and to ignore local segregationist feelings as excuses for delay. District judges were to retain jurisdiction to assure progress with "all deliberate speed." Subsequent efforts proved to be "nine parts deliberation and one part speed" (Rodgers and Bullock, 1972: 69–81).

The first decade after *Brown* produced massive resistance countered only by the federal courts and then unevenly (Muse, 1961; Gates, 1964; Peltason, 1971; Rodgers and Bullock, 1972: 69–81). Data showing the percentage of black students in desegregated schools leave little doubt as to the victors. In 1965, 10 years after *Brown II,* Texas led the southern states with 7.8 percent of its black students attending schools with whites; Alabama, Arkansas, Georgia, Mississippi, and South Carolina failed to reach the 1 percent mark (Dye, 1969: 18–19).

Several reasons exist for a lack of progress during this decade (see also Rodgers and Bullock, 1972: 74–81). First, the Court failed to take a definitive stand in its implementation decrees. By using phrases such as "all deliberate speed," "at the earliest possible date," and "good faith," the Court provided too much room for interpretation by opponents of desegregation. Thus, the South found *Brown II* to be less objectionable than many had feared; Florida's legislators applauded when the *Brown II* decision was read to them; and Georgia's governor Ernest Vandiver was quoted as saying, "I think the Supreme Court in some small measure attempted to correct an obnoxious decision" (Muse, 1964: 27).

Tactics were quickly devised to circumvent the spirit of *Brown* (see Peltason, 1971: 93–134). New rules were promulgated by legislatures and school boards to maintain segregation. Alabama, Virginia, and Georgia passed legislation forbidding local school boards to desegregate. "Freedom of choice" plans were devised that presented the facade of compliance. A typical freedom of choice plan required parents to complete a form expressing their preference for the school within the system each child would attend. Such plans resulted in either token or no desegregation, because blacks feared exposing their children to the dangers and tensions of being pioneers in school desegregation. Where the fears of black parents were overcome, whites used trivial errors in the completion of the choice forms or suddenly discovered "overcrowding" at the school a black had requested as a rationale to deny the request. Private schools sprang up, often in buildings that had been public schools but were "sold" by the local school boards for nominal fees. Each of these actions prompted a new series of time-consuming suits, briefs, motions, hearings, decisions, and appeals. The resources and ingenuity devoted to avoiding desegregation were truly amazing. At one point, for example, the attorneys for the New Orleans school board asked that an injunction against them be set aside because the plaintiffs had not proved that they were black (Peltason, 1971: 126)! Such obviously ill-fated actions still required time to process and consumed resources, of which the school boards had more than the black plaintiffs.

Closely related is another reason for the lack of progress: the reluctance of the United States district courts to act. District judges found the burden of applying *Brown* passed to them. The result was an uneven application of the law. While judges like Frank M. Johnson, Jr. (M.D., Alabama), pressed ahead, refusing to let the Court's "authority and dignity . . . be bent and swayed by such politically-generated whirlwinds" (*In re Wallace,* 1959: 121), octogenarian Judge T. Whitfield Davidson lectured the black plaintiffs in the 1959 Dallas case concerning the white man's "right to maintain his racial integrity" (quoted in Peltason, 1971: 119) before striking down the Dallas school board's plan to desegregate by 1973 because of its rapidity. The Fifth U.S. Circuit Court of Appeals, which heard most desegregation appeals, also found itself inefficacious in establishing uniform standards (see Rodgers and Bullock, 1972: 78). By March 1961, for example, the decisions of the district judges hearing the Dallas, Texas, school desegregation case had already been reversed six times by the court of appeals (Peltason, 1971: 122).

Third, the Court found itself far ahead of the other two branches of government. President Eisenhower, except for momentary action in Little Rock, avoided executive involvement in civil rights (Peltason, 1971: 46–50). His official position was: "The President would not make any assumption that the judicial branch of government is incapable of implementing the Supreme Court's decision" (quoted in Peltason, 1971: 50). Not only did the legislative branch fail to support the courts, but also almost all southern members of Congress signed the infamous "Southern Manifesto" denouncing the Court's decision (Lewis, 1965: 39).

Fourth, black citizens were not active in any consistent manner, particularly in areas where discrimination was the worst. The lack of activity was not without good reason, however. As noted earlier, black parents were understandably reluctant to offer their children as "guinea pigs" in a hostile environment. Furthermore, those so bold as to do so were frequently subjected to physical and economic intimidation. Organization efforts were often not forthcoming either. Lawsuits, the tactic required in that milieu, cannot be used as a focal point to build a mass movement. They do not generate the excitement of protests, are expensive and time consuming, require enforcement even if victory is won, and can easily become mired in complex technicalities (Peltason, 1971: 99–105; Rodgers and Bullock, 1972: 80–81).

A new era in the civil rights struggle was ushered in by the enactment of the 1964 Civil Rights Act (see Orfield, 1969). The legislative branch thereby shifted some desegregation responsibilities to what was then called the Department of Health, Education, and Welfare (HEW) and provided that department with a potent, but little-noticed, tool—the authority to terminate federal funds to any recipient practicing racial discrimination. This power, combined with increased federal support for education through the Elementary and Secondary Education Act of 1965, provided a major lever in the desegregation struggle. This era was characterized by efforts by both the courts and the bureaucracy. Even as HEW entered the fray, the courts retained and gained jurisdiction over many districts.

The Department of Health, Education, and Welfare initially issued guidelines calling for only a very general assurance of nondiscrimination. This inadequate standard reflected both a widespread underestimation throughout the government of the effort required to achieve desegregation and a general predisposition to rely on the good faith of local officials. As noted earlier, freedom of choice plans were soon devised that satisfied HEW and provided token desegregation. HEW gradually increased its pressure on districts, and the courts provided new ammunition (Orfield, 1969; Panetta and Gall, 1971).

In 1968 HEW decided that "freedom of choice" plans were no longer adequate. Two months later the Supreme Court specifically ruled against nonproductive "freedom of choice" plans (*Green* v. *New Kent County School Board,* 1968). A year later, in *Alexander* v. *Holmes* (1969), the Court refused to tolerate further delay in the desegregation process. The Court stated clearly:

> . . . continued operation of racially segregated schools under the standard of "all deliberate speed" is no longer constitutionally permissible. . . . The obligation of every school district is to terminate dual school systems at once and to operate now and hereafter only unitary systems . . . within which no person is to be effectively excluded from any school because of race or color.

Using these cases, the enforcement agencies made gains in spite of recalcitrance by local officials who awaited the payoff in President Nixon's "southern strategy" (Panetta and Gall, 1971; Rodgers and Bullock, 1972: 88–97).

The impact of *Alexander* v. *Holmes* was intensified in 1969 by a shift in enforcement strategy. Instead of threatening a cutoff of federal funds, which often disadvantaged blacks and which many districts were willing to surrender as a cost of maintaining the status quo, the new Office for Civil Rights within HEW simply turned cases over to the Justice Department for litigation. Districts were given the choice: comply or be sued. Although this move was widely seen as a fulfillment of President Nixon's southern strategy to slow down or stop the move toward unitary schools, the Justice Department's intentions were revealed when it filed suit against 81 Georgia districts and that state's department of education (*United States* v. *Georgia,* 1969). The suit threatened to eliminate state funding for segregated districts, a threat too grave to ignore, and quickly brought recalcitrant districts into compliance (Rodgers and Bullock, 1976a). This technique was used to complete the desegregation process in other southern states. Whereas only 32 percent of southern black students had been attending schools with whites during the 1968–69 school year, 79 percent of black students were by the 1970–71 school year.

Beyond the Letter of *Brown*

When the South came to have the most desegregated schools in the country, the focus moved northward to the major urban centers of black concentration. Major cases were litigated in Denver and Detroit, for example. Litigation also arose over the issue of whether or not the Office for Civil Rights was conscientiously performing its duties (*Adams* v. *Richardson,* 1972). More important, for our purposes, people became increasingly aware that desegregated schools were not necessarily providing equal educational opportunity across racial lines. Just because black and white students rode the same buses and entered the same buildings did not mean they took classes in the same rooms or were treated equally within those buildings. Chapter 1 presented the arguments for the importance of looking at such phenomena. In this section we outline the growing awareness of second-generational educational discrimination by public policy-makers.

Overt Second-Generation Discrimination

Rodgers and Bullock (1972: 94) provide lucid examples of overt second-generation discrimination practices, based on the findings of a report titled *The Status of School Desegregation in the South 1970,* which focuses on 467 school districts that desegregated in the fall of 1970. They note, for example, that in 123 of the 467 districts studied, children were segregated in the classroom. In some classes room dividers were installed; white children sat on one side of the room, blacks on the other. Segregated buses were used in 89 school districts. Where desegregated buses were used, policy required blacks to sit in the back of the bus.

A number of newly desegregated districts, 21, had segregated facilities such as lunchrooms, showers, and so on. Discrimination in extracurricular and social activities was also reported. In one district, for example, an invitation was required to attend the senior prom. No blacks were invited.

In many respects the use of such blatant second-generation discrimination practices represented the final overt response in newly desegregated schools to massive desegregation orders. The battle had been lost; southern school officials were forced to mix their students racially. Given the highly litigious nature of school desegregation, the use of clearly racist, overt second-generation discrimination practices to resegregate children decreased in frequency. They were patently discriminatory and invited further litigation. In many districts, however, the emphasis shifted. Room dividers were no longer needed to avoid cross-racial student contact. More subtle institutional policies including academic grouping and discipline have replaced these overt methods of second-generation educational discrimination.

Academic Grouping

Policy-makers have not been unaware of the potential problems of allowing educators to group or track students even when they use such putatively neutral devices as standardized tests to do so. The Emergency School Assistance Program regulations (C.F.R., Sect. 181.6(a) (4) (G)) specifically prohibits practices, "including testing," which promote racial isolation. OCR, in the process of administering the subsequent Emergency School Aid Act (ESAA), developed the standard of investigating districts where black enrollment in special education classes exceeded the proportion of black enrollment in the system by 20 percent (Bullock, 1976).

OCR has not been unique among policy-makers in recognizing the potential for mischief. The courts early on addressed the issue in the abstract and later did so directly. In 1957 the Fifth U.S. Circuit Court of Appeals noted that students might be "separated according to their degree of advancement or retardation, their ability to learn, . . . their health, or for any other legitimate reason, but each child is entitled to be treated as an individual without regard to his race or color" (*Borders* v. *Rippy,* 1957: 271). Later the same court reaffirmed the principle: ". . . there is no constitutional prohibition against an assignment of individual students . . . on the basis of intelligence, achievement or other aptitudes upon a uniformly administered program but race must not be a factor in making the assignments" (*Stell* v. *Savannah–Chatham County Board of Education*, 1964: 61–62). But the court avoided the issue in the case that was at hand. The premier case in which a court ruled tracking unconstitutional was *Hobson* v. *Hansen* (1967), involving the District of Columbia's schools. The federal district court found that where black children "are relegated to lower tracks based on intelligence tests largely standardized on white middle-class children, and there given reduced education, such disadvantaged children are denied equal educational opportunity." Not all tests, ability grouping, and tracking were banned; only those with racially discriminatory effects were prohibited.

Subsequently, the Fifth Circuit Court and its constituent district courts had numerous occasions to apply and refine this legal point. As these courts dealt with school districts in the process of desegregating, they forbade testing as a means of tracking students until desegregated school systems had been established (*Singleton* v. *Jackson Municipal Separate School District*, 1969; *United States* v. *Tunica County School District*, 1970; *United States* v. *Sunflower County School District*, 1970; *Lemon* v. *Bossier Parish School Board*, 1971; *Moses* v. *Washington Parish School Board*, 1971; *United States* v. *Gadsden County School District*, 1978). The burden of proof was placed on a school system to show "that its assignment method is not based on the present results of past segregation or that such system will remedy results of past segregation through better educational opportunities." Ability grouping in a previously segregated school district was prohibited "until district had operated as a unitary system without such assignment for a period sufficient to assure that underachievement of slower groups was not due to . . . prior segregation" (*McNeal* v. *Tate County Board of Education*, 1975).

The issue also arose in areas without a recent history of dual school systems. Perhaps the most notorious case of this ilk surfaced in California, where a district court initially held that if the plaintiffs could establish that IQ tests were the primary basis for placing students in EMR classes and that such classes disproportionately enrolled blacks, then the burden of proof would "shift to school district to demonstrate a rational connection between tests and purpose for which they were allegedly used." In this case blacks constituted 25.5 percent of the district's enrollment and 66 percent of all students in EMR classes, a sufficient disparity for the court to find a violation of law under provisions of the 1964 Civil Rights Act (*Larry P.* v. *Riles*, 1972).

Because the state of California did not remedy the problems after the court had issued a temporary injunction in 1972, the case returned to court and a subsequent decision was rendered in 1979. This time the court issued a more sweeping order. A permanent injunction on the use of intelligence tests for placement purposes was imposed, and the state of California was ordered to eliminate disproportionate placement of black children in EMR classes. The court's finding was based on the Rehabilitation Act of 1973, the Education for All Handicapped Children Act of 1975, Title VI of the 1964 Civil Rights Act, and the Fourteenth Amendment to the Constitution (*Larry P.* v. *Riles,* 1979). When this decision was appealed to the Ninth U.S. Circuit Court, the only part reversed was the finding of a violation of the Fourteenth Amendment (*Larry P.* v. *Riles,* 1984).

Disciplinary Measures

The use of disciplinary measures such as corporal punishment, suspension, and expulsion has been widespread in desegregated schools. Judged to be among the most positive attributes of teachers in schools is the ability to identify and separate disruptive students quickly (Redl, 1975).

Not surprisingly, blacks are disproportionately subjected to disciplinary measures. The burden of ''fitting in'' in desegregated schools is placed largely on black students. OCR's analysis of its 1973 data concludes that ''minority students are being kept out of school as a disciplinary measure more frequently and for longer periods of time than non-minority students'' (Office for Civil Rights, 1975). Peter Holmes, then OCR director, admitted that ''just a cursory examination of our data suggests the probability of widespread discrimination in the application of disciplinary sanctions.'' However, the first five OCR compliance reviews which focused on discipline concluded without finding noncompliance (Office for Civil Rights, 1975: 72; *In the Matter of the Board of Education of Cook County, Georgia,* 1972).

The courts have been ambivalent in cases raising this issue. The Fifth U.S. Circuit Court, in a Birmingham case, held that even if the offense were real, racially discriminatory discipline is unconstitutional. It found that ''discipline . . . cannot be made an instrument of racial discrimination . . .'' (*Woods* v. *Wright,* 1964: 375). Other early cases, however, found no racial discrimination in discipline (*Stevenson* v. *Board of Education of Wheeler County, Georgia,* 1970). A major case finding racial discrimination in disciplinary measures is *Hawkins* v. *Coleman* (1974). Judge Hughes found racism to be the major cause of a pattern of disproportionate black suspensions in the Dallas, Texas, school system. She specifically ordered the system to ''put into effect an affirmative program aimed at materially lessening 'white institutional racism' in district.'' But that case was soon declared moot, and the issue of disproportionate racial patterns in discipline seldom arises. More commonly, disciplinary action taken after a black student walk-out (e.g., *Dunn* v. *Tyler Independent School District,* 1971; *Black Students, etc., ex rel Shoemaker* v. *Williams,* 1970) or focused on a single individual (e.g., *Black Coalition* v. *Portland School District No. 1,* 1973) is litigated. The legal issues are joined in terms of procedural due process, and the overall pattern of discipline is ignored. Still discipline cannot be couched in educational terms as easily as ability grouping or tracking, and thus may be a promising area for those interested in exploring second-generation discrimination practices.

The Inevitability of Second-Generation Discrimination

The nature of the policy process is such that a perceptive analyst might have been able to anticipate the development of second-generation educational discrimination. The process of public policy-making is complex, involving several stages including problem identification, agenda setting, policy formulation, policy adoption, and program implementation (Anderson, 1984). Policy winds its way through this process at a rate and on a path determined by who is involved (or omitted) in the process and how those involved interact. Before linking second-generation educational discrimination to the policy process, an outline for analyzing the range of participants and the interaction process is presented.

To analyze the range of participants in policy-making, Redford (1969: 83–131) presents three levels of politics to categorize policy outputs—micropolitics, subsystem politics, and macropolitics. Micropolitics involve action by individuals, individual businesses, or communities acting in direct self-interest. Subsystem politics involve the interaction of congressional committees, administrative agencies, and interest groups. Macropolitics involve the broadest range of participants. These politics occur when the public and a large number of public officials, including the president, the Supreme Court, and the Congress, get involved in policy-making. Over time policies may move between these three levels of politics, and the difference in actors at each level of politics implies different policy outputs.

Rourke (1984) presents a clear explanation of policy-maker interaction, the bureaucratic politics model. Those who seek to influence the bureaucracy to shape policy and its implementation have four points of access: interest groups or clientele, Congress, the presidency, and individual experts. The number and combination of these actors who participate in policy-making determine the level of politics from which the policy will be produced, the nature of the policy, the independence of the bureaucracy in forming its own policy, and the power of the bureaucracy to implement the policy. If individual experts are the sole source of inputs, interpersonal politics within the bureaucracy produce policy. If Congress and interest groups are interjected, subsystem politics produce policy. If the president becomes active, macropolitics produce policy.

The specifics of policy may become more vague at each higher level of politics. Goals may be widely supported, but tactics become a point of disagreement. For example, equal educational opportunity is a goal that few oppose, but disagreement exists on its definition and the method of achieving it. As the definitions of goals become more vague, the discretion that bureaucracy has in policy formation increases. The inability of the various participants to agree on tactics results in an abdication of such responsibilities to a bureaucratic agency. When this occurs, subsystem politics and/or micropolitics may determine the actual shape of the general policy delineated in the macropolitical arena. Thus in the politics of policy-making, the tactics of implementation are inextricably intertwined with the preceding stages in the policy process.

How does second-generation educational discrimination relate to the policy process? If we keep in mind the different levels of politics and the bureaucratic politics model while looking at efforts to provide equal educational opportunity, we should have a clearer understanding of the sources of second-generation discrimination and the potential for amending the policy that permits second-generation discrimination. Second-generation discrimination is a natural product of continuing racial prejudice combined with a policy inadequate to deal with the task of providing equal educational opportunity. The sources of second-generation discrimination lie in the desegregation effort.

The struggle to provide equal educational opportunity began with individuals bringing suits in order to have this opportunity at the local level (e.g., access to graduate and professional schools). Over time the courts were convinced that their first definition of equal educational opportunity, separate-but-equal schools, was inappropriate because the equal part was normally missing. With the *Brown* decision the courts redefined equal educational opportunity as synonymous with desegregation. The courts continually redefined "desegregated" schools, but the question of whether desegregated schools necessarily provided equal educational opportunity was seldom raised. Thus, the major underlying assumption of how to define a goal that later became a national policy occurred in response to micropolitical demands.

When Congress passed the 1964 Civil Rights Act with strong pressure from President Johnson, civil rights had clearly jumped to the macropolitical level. While many macropolitical actors supported equal educational opportunity, few agreed on the method to achieve it. By this time, however, desegregated schools were considered to be the means to equal educational opportunity. Enforcers and opponents of desegregation plans wrangled over how to desegregate rather than whether desegregation actually produced equal educational opportunity.

As time passed, the federal subsystem level asserted control over the enforcement policy for equal educational opportunity. Presidential interest waned, though not completely. Individual suits continued, but they were no longer seen as the most efficient vehicle for achieving the goal. So even though the policy for equal educational opportunity lapped over into the macropolitical and micropolitical levels, it was centered at the subsystem level.

The controversial nature of the issue prevented any simple subsystem arrangements. Presidential support for the bureaucratic enforcers, an important tool in bureaucratic politics, started strongly under Johnson, waned somewhat as the Vietnam War occupied presidential attention, and dissipated under Nixon. Congressional relations were not of the classic subsystem style: an agency interacting with a few members of Congress from a concerned and supportive committee. Instead, bureaucratic enforcers had frequent interaction with hostile members of Congress, whose districts were affected by equal educational opportunity policy. Similarly, interest-group pressure came from both supporting and opposing groups. To complicate matters further, supportive groups were often the more vociferous in their demands for accelerated enforcement.

Amid this maelstrom of subsystem political activity, policy was formed to add muscle to the civil rights legislation passed by Congress. The priorities were clear to bureaucratic enforcers, because the macropolitical system had accepted the micropolitical system's definition of equal educational opportunity as synonymous with desegregation. All sources of bureaucratic power were mobilized in a massive, if sometimes halting, effort to desegregate southern schools. People within the bureaucracy were dedicated professionals who became experts at dealing with recalcitrant local officials to produce maximum desegregation. Upper-level bureaucrats exhibited considerable political acumen in maintaining presidential, congressional, and interest-group support to generate the fuel for additional bureaucratic efforts and to help create an environment conducive to policy implementation. These actors provided support for the enforcement machinery vis-a-vis others who demanded government resources, and eventually they helped generate a climate of resignation to, if not acceptance of, desegregation.

Indeed, the administrative achievement of dismantling southern dual school systems is a powerful example of how skillful bureaucratic politics can generate the power to achieve a bureaucratic goal. However, the evidence suggests that equal educational opportunity is still unachieved and that the agencies which accomplished so much are ill-equipped to fight another large-scale war successfully.

Often lost in the examination of equal educational opportunity policy is the reality that states and localities also have both macropolitics and subsystem politics. The state governor, state legislature, and state courts form a state's macropolitical system. In the South this system strongly resisted desegregation and provided strong support for local subsystems (composed of the school board, school administrators, and local parent groups) to resist desegregation. With the *United States* v. *Georgia* (1969) court case, state macropolitical systems were interjected into the desegregation policy process, and local school boards were isolated and faced sanctions from both the federal and state subsystems. Desegregation then came quickly. Once desegregation, the defined goal, was accomplished, control over educational policy gradually reverted to the local policy subsystem.

The local policy subsystem has dynamics similar to those of national policy subsystems. Administrative agencies need to acquire political support from their environment to continue operating (Rourke, 1984). For school administrators, political support means support from the school board and local parent groups, particularly those white middle-class parent groups with resources. Given professional norms that support the use of academic grouping and discipline, school systems could then seek political support from parents and school boards by resegregating the school system. Resegregation has been possible through second-generation discrimination only because equal educational opportunity was defined as desegregation rather than the provision of a learning environment that permits both black and white access to all educational facilities in a multiracial context.

The rise of second-generation educational discrimination, then, was quite predictable given the existent political forces and the definition of the policy problem. The history of black education reveals that each time educational policies are changed, efforts are made to limit the access of blacks to equal educational opportunity. When schools were initially provided for blacks, unequal funding subverted the goal of equal educational opportunity. When the Supreme Court ordered desegregation, freedom of choice and overt methods of resistance prevented mixing the races. When desegregation was finally forced by a combination of court rulings and administrative actions, some attempt to subvert the policy should have been expected. Second-generation educational discrimination or some similar phenomenon, therefore, was eminently predictable.

Two broad propositions are warranted in view of the discussion above. First, the definition of the policy problem determines the limits of the implementation effort. Once the policy problem was defined in terms of desegregating southern schools, the limits of effective enforcement efforts were likewise defined. The desegregation-enforcement machinery was able to muster enough force to achieve the first goal, but the energy soon dissipated. Too many sources of bureaucratic power, both inside and outside of the organization, believed that the mission had been accomplished. The stage was set for second-generation problems unforeseen in the original problem definition and for difficulties in moving the desegregation effort northward.

Second, the political level at which the policy problem is defined determines the likelihood of the policy effectively dealing with the problem. Because equal educational opportunity was defined first at the micropolitical level, it was less probable that problems such as second-generation discrimination would be considered. The micropolitical level saw desegregation as a federal effort;

academic grouping and discipline were professional techniques applied to nonracial problems and, thus, not part of the problem.

Defining equal educational opportunity in terms of desegregation meant that other forms of racial discrimination in the schools would probably be side-stepped. Although courts have considered second-generation discrimination, they have not made a definitive ruling on the order of *Brown*. Problem definition at the micropolitical level sealed the inevitability of second-generation discrimination. Providing equal educational opportunities, like other policy problems, is normally more complex than envisioned at the micropolitical level.

The existence of second-generation discrimination indicates the importance of problem definition for policy implementation and evaluation. With the problem of unequal educational opportunity between races seen in terms of dual school systems in the South, a policy was implemented which dealt relatively effectively with that problem. If, however, the problem is cast in terms of removing all manifestations of racial discrimination from the educational system, this policy would have to be evaluated less favorably.

Summary

This chapter has explored the evolution of policies for equal educational opportunity for black citizens in the United States. Blacks were initially denied access to almost all education prior to the Civil War. After the Civil War segregated educational facilities were maintained under a policy of separate but equal. The education provided both in the North and the South was almost always separate but rarely ever equal. Desegregated schools became the solution to equal education opportunities after court decisions and lengthy implementation activities. The quest for equal educational opportunity, however, continues while second-generation educational discrimination techniques are used to resegregate schools and deny blacks the educational opportunities afforded to whites. By focusing on the local politics of education, the remainder of this book will examine why the quest failed.

3 Black Representation in Educational Policy-Making Positions

Education policies are determined by school boards, administrators, and teachers. Who holds these decision-making positions is important; because equal education policies greatly influence the life's chances of students. The representation of blacks in education policy-making is a function of the political process in local communities. That process is the focus of this chapter.

Representation and what it means for one individual to represent another are frequently discussed in political science (Pitkin, 1967; Kuklinski, 1979). The key distinction in the literature is between "passive representation" and "active representation." Passive representation is concerned with determining if representatives have the same demographic characteristics as the represented. Often such comparisons are made at a collective level rather than directly between individual representatives and their constituents (Weisberg, 1978). One such comparison might be between the percentage of black representatives in a legislature and the percentage of black voters in the population. Hanna Pitkin (1967) characterizes such treatments of representation as descriptive representation.

Implicit in the study of passive representation is the idea that it leads to other forms of representation. One need not make this assumption to study passive representation. Passive representation can be defended in and of itself in terms of equity and equal access to positions of influence. Political positions and occupation of them should be equitably distributed among races and ethnic groups—a piece of the pie–patronage view of representation.

Despite this logical defense for passive representation, most scholars seek to link passive representation with active representation. Representation, according to Pitkin (1967: 67), should not focus on "being something rather than doing something." Representation, she contends, should be viewed as one person "acting in the interests of the represented" (p. 209). Eulau and Karps (1977: 235) extend Pitkin's active view of representation. A representative may be considered to be acting in the interests of the represented in one of four ways. First, the representative can make decisions consistent with the policy preferences of the represented; this is known as *policy congruence*. Second, the representative can secure individual benefits for the represented (e.g., an exemption from a regulation)—known as *service responsiveness*. Third, the representative can seek benefits for his or her constituency that benefit the entire constituency (e.g., a pork barrel project)—*allocative responsiveness*. Fourth, the representative can take actions that build constituency trust and general support for the representative—*symbolic representation*.

Any of these might be considered active representation on the part of a representative. Because this study is concerned with policy outputs, we will examine only the first form of active representation—policy congruence. Service responsiveness, allocative responsiveness, and symbolic representation are still important to the process of representation, but their discussion is beyond the scope of this research.

If active representation is defined as representatives acting in the policy interests of the represented, how might passive and active representation be linked? Two methods of linkage have dominated the literature—the electoral linkage and the socialization linkage. The electoral linkage assumes that representatives wish to remain in office. Traditionally representatives have had a choice between two roles: a delegate role, which implies that a representative will vote consistently with constituent wishes regardless of his or her own views, *and* a trustee role, which implies that a representative will vote according to his or her conscience (Eulau, et al., 1959; Miller and Stokes, 1963; applied to school boards, Mann, 1974)[1] If representatives fear the loss of their positions through electoral defeat, a rational representative would act as a delegate.

The electoral linkage has two limitations for the analysis of policy responsiveness. First, many elected positions do not have particularly competitive elections, and as a result, some representatives have little fear of electoral defeat (Prewitt, 1970). Second, using elections to enforce representatives' responsiveness has little utility if one wishes to examine the representative behavior of nonelected individuals such as bureaucrats.[2]

1. Eulau and his associates' work also specified a third role, a politico who takes a position somewhat in between a delegate and a trustee. On the utility of these roles see Hedlund and Friesema, 1972; and Friesema and Hedlund, 1974.

2. One could tie electoral sanctions to bureaucrats if the unit of government were to operate under a patronage system. In such a system, an electoral defeat would remove both the elected officials and the bureaucrat. Alternatively, if elected officials had significant ways to reward or punish bureaucrats, the electoral threat could then be extended to the bureaucracy. The concept of overhead democracy (Redford, 1969) is one such proposal, and the Civil Service Reform Act of 1978 was presented as a way at the national level to achieve greater bureaucratic responsiveness to the wishes of elected officials.

The alternative linkage between representatives and the represented is the socialization model. The socialization model of representation is most developed in the arguments for representative bureaucracy (Long, 1952; Levitan, 1946; Mosher, 1968). According to advocates of representative bureaucracy, a bureaucracy (or any other institution) is representative to the extent that the social origins of the representatives mirror the social origins of the represented (Mosher, 1968).

The linkage between social origins (passive representation) and policy congruence requires several steps. Policy congruence suggests that a representative acts as the represented would act if the represented could somehow participate in the process and make the decisions. One way such policy congruence is ensured is if the representatives and the represented share the same political attitudes and values (Uslaner and Weber, 1983; Meier and Nigro, 1976).

To achieve congruence in political attitudes, then, requires that both the represented and the representatives be subjected to the same influences on their political attitudes. The political socialization literature (Dennis, 1968) argues that socialization patterns are related to demographic origins, race, sex, social class, religion, and so on. A representative bureaucracy, then, which mirrors the social origins of the population should share the population's socialization experiences, have similar political attitudes, and therefore make policy decisions similar to those that the populace would make if it were to participate in all decisions (Meier and Nigro, 1976).

Unfortunately for the socialization theory of representation, social orgins do not predict political attitudes particularly well. Meier and Nigro (1976: 465) have found that eight demographic origin variables were able to explain only 2–9 percent of the variance in the policy attitudes of adult federal bureaucrats. Why social origins are not a good predictor of political attitudes (and, in turn, policy congruence) is explainable. Socialization is nothing more than a learning process; as such it does not suddenly cease at age 21 but continues throughout one's life (Brim and Wheeler, 1966: 17). Simply by serving as a representative, therefore, an individual will have different socialization experiences from other individuals. For bureaucrats, as opposed to elected officials, the bureaucracy itself performs some additional socialization that can overwhelm many preexisting attitudes. (Meier and Nigro, 1976: 466; Miles, 1978; Romzek and Hendricks, 1982).

The socialization linkage survives, however, in certain specific situations. The demographic origin that remains the best predictor of attitudes and is likely to reinforce adult experiences is race (Free and Cantril, 1967). As Alan Monroe (1975: 87) contends, ". . . race constitutes the greatest social cleavage in America, at least as far as political opinions are concerned." In a bureaucratic context, Mann's (1974: 310) survey of school administrators found minority administrators twice as likely as white administrators to see their roles as delegates or politicos rather than trustees. The socialization linkage of representation, therefore, will be appropriate to this study if policy indicators that can be directly linked to race are used.

This chapter examines the descriptive representativeness of three groups of individuals—school board members, school administrators, and teachers. In each case the linkage between passive and active representation is somewhat different. For school board members, the most likely linkage is from elections (but see Prewitt, 1970). Because high-level school administrators serve at the pleasure of the school board but lower-level administrators are isolated from this direct electoral pressure, the linkage for administrators is likely a combination of elections and socialization. For teachers, protected by tenure, union contracts, or civil service rules, the representation linkage operates through socialization. This chapter examines only passive representation; active representation is covered in chapter 4.

School Board Representation

Levels of Minority Representation

Minority representation in urban governments has generated a substantial body of literature that guides this present effort. Both city councils and school boards have been examined to determine if they are representative of blacks in a passive sense. Representation has been measured in two ways. The initial definition was based on something called the representation index. The representation index is simply the percentage of the representatives that are black divided by the percentage of the population that is black (Subramaniam, 1967). This index has some valuable characteristics. It equals 1.0 when blacks attain the level of representation that is warranted by their population percentage. When blacks are underrepresented, the index is less than 1.0; and when blacks are overrepresented, the index exceeds 1.0.

The representation index is a useful measure, and we will use it in the following chapter; but it has one significant flaw. When the black population is small, any black representation at all often results in extremely large numbers that distort the index. Engstrom and McDonald (1981) have discovered one way to avoid the problem of extreme values.[3] If one uses the percentage of seats on the school board held by blacks as the dependent variable in a regression

3. Susan MacManus (1978) has a second proposal: to subtract the percentage of black representatives from the percentage of the black population. We agree with Engstrom and McDonald in their criticism of this approach. More important, however, is the fact that the Engstrom and McDonald (1981) regression approach allows one to examine the seats-population relationship with multiple controls simultaneously and in a relatively easy manner.

and the percentage of blacks in the population as the independent variable, then the regression slope provides a "representation index" estimate that is less affected by extreme values resulting from a small black population.

In such a regression, if the intercept is close to zero, the slope can be interpreted similarly to the representation index: A slope of 1.0 means that blacks hold exactly the percentage of seats that their population warrants. A slope of less than 1.0 indicates underrepresentation, and a slope of greater than 1.0 indicates overrepresentation.

To provide a comparative context for our results, past research in this area merits noting. The techniques discussed here were applied first to city council elections. Engstrom and McDonald (1981: 347), studying 239 large central cities, found a regression coefficient (or slope) of 0.593, meaning that blacks held only 59.3 percent of the city council seats that one would expect, given their population. This regression finding is fairly consistent with representation indices calculated by Robinson and Dye (1978) for this same set of cities and by Taebel (1978) for 166 cities.[4]

For school boards, black representation is significantly better than it is for city councils. Using the Engstrom-McDonald approach, Meier and England (1984: 400) found a slope of 1.20 for 89 large central-city school districts. This slope indicates that blacks had 20 percent more seats on school boards than their population warranted. This regression estimate compares favorably with school board representation indices calculated by Robinson and England (1981: 498) and Welch and Karnig (1978: 166). Robinson and England found a representation index of 0.96 for 173 school districts; Welch and Karnig's index was 1.06 for the 43 largest school districts. Because both Robinson and England and Welch and Karnig used the black population percentage for the entire city rather than the school district, their estimates lack some precision.[5]

The seats-population regression for our group of school districts is shown in table 3.1. Because the intercept of this regression is not significantly different from zero, the representational interpretation of the slope is possible. This slope (1.002) shows that blacks have almost exactly the same number of school board seats as their population percentage would suggest. In short, black representation in these large urban school districts is proportionately almost perfect.

4. Robinson and Dye had an index of 0.5 for all cities and an index of 0.6 for those cities with a black population of 15 percent or more. Taebel found an index of 0.558 limited to those cities with a black population large enough to be a majority in a single district if elections were held by district and all blacks lived in a single district.

5. School districts usually have boundaries different from those of the city in which they are located. The exception to this general rule is the dependent school districts. Meier and England (1984: 395, n. 4) report that the correlation between the percentage of blacks within the school

Table 3.1. Black Representation on School Boards: The Impact of Black Population

Independent Variable	Regression Coefficient	t-score
Black population (%)	1.002	19.02*

F = 368.77
r^2 = .69
Intercept = –0.351
N = 170

*p < .05

Representation and Political Reform

Perhaps no aspect of black representation on the local level is more controversial than electoral structure. As part of the reform of urban governments in the early twentieth century, an effort was made to take politics out of city government. Elections were held at times different from national elections, many elections were nonpartisan, and city manager government and at-large elections were introduced (Lineberry and Fowler, 1967). If anything, the reform movement was more successful with school districts than it was with cities. Independent school districts were created to sever the political ties of cities from the schools. Virtually all school district elections became nonpartisan, and the overwhelming majority began to use at-large districts. The separation of partisan politics from education was completed by hiring a professional administrator to run the schools.

Many individuals have judged certain impacts of these urban reforms to be detrimental to minorities. Especially visible is the harmful effect of at-large elections. By electing representatives at-large rather than from districts, a candidate must attract a majority of votes from the entire school district rather than from a smaller election district, or ward. Because blacks are often highly segregated in urban areas, at-large elections often mean a citywide white majority, whereas ward elections would have at least some election districts with a black majority.

Using representation indices, virtually every study has found that at-large elections limit minority access to city councils and school boards. For city councils, Karnig (1976: 229) has found a representation index of 0.77 for ward

districts and the percentage within the cities in which these districts are located was .94. In general, the percentage of black population is higher in these school districts than it is in the city, so the Robinson-England and Welch-Karnig results are likely to be underestimates.

elections and 0.46 for at-large elections. Robinson and Dye (1978) have found a ward representation index of 0.80 and an at-large index of 0.42. Engstrom and McDonald, using the regression approach, estimate representation at 0.994 for ward elections and 0.495 for at-large elections.[6] Several others (see Davidson and Korbel, 1981) have also addressed this question, and only two studies (MacManus, 1978; Cole, 1974) contend that at-large elections do not limit black representation.[7] In both cases, these anomalies can be explained. Cole used a limited number of cities in New Jersey, and MacManus used a representation-difference measure and introduced multiple controls.[8]

School district findings are similar. Using 75 school districts with a minimum 15 percent black population, Robinson and England (1981: 498) report a representation index of 0.82 for ward systems and 0.59 for at-large systems. School districts may also appoint members to the school board when the district is a dependent school district. The Robinson-England index for appointive systems is 1.01. The Robinson and England findings are contradicted by Welch and Karnig's (1978) findings; Welch and Karnig find a ratio of 0.84 for pure ward systems and 1.15 for at-large systems. Given the use of city rather than school district population data in both these studies, conclusions based on these studies would be premature. Meier and England (1984: 400), using the Engstrom-McDonald regression approach, find an index of 0.98 for ward elections, 0.69 for at-large elections, and 1.10 for appointive systems.

The most appropriate way to estimate simultaneously the impact of selection plans on black representation is to estimate a single equation that multiplies the percentage of black population by the type of selection plan (Engstrom and McDonald, 1982).[9] Such a regression is presented in table 3.2. Each of

6. These scholars also estimate impacts for mixed election plans, that is, plans that elect some council members at-large and others by district. Because the mixed form is rare for school districts, we will not report these measures.

7. Several studies treat the selection plan–representation relationship as a longitudinal one. These studies, including Helig and Mundt, 1983, Mundt and Helig, 1982, and Davidson and Korbel, 1981, look at cities that change their election procedures from at-large to district elections. In all three cases, the authors find a large increase in black representation after the change to district elections.

8. MacManus, in fact, finds pure at-large systems reduce black representation by 9 percent and pure district elections restrict it by 3.4 percent.

9. A dummy variable (coded 1 or 0) is set up for each selection system (ward, at-large, appointed). These dummy variables are then multiplied by the percentage of black population.

We follow the operationalization used by Engstrom and McDonald, even though we object to their use of it. Essentially the correct way to determine if selection plan and black population interact to affect black representation is to predict black representation with black population, selection plans, and an interaction effect in the same equation (see our criticism in Fraga, Meier, and England, 1986). Engstrom and McDonald assume an interaction without testing to see if the interaction interpretation is superior to the noninteraction approach. In neither this case nor the

Table 3.2. Black Representation on School Boards: The Impact of Selection Plan

Dependent Variable: Percentage of black representation

Independent Variable	Regression Coefficient	t-score
Ward system × black population (%)	1.02	14.24*
Appointive system × black population (%)	0.95	13.00*
At-large system × black population (%)	1.00	13.15*

F = 112.00
R^2 = .67
Adjusted R^2 = .66
N = 170

*$p < .05$

the slopes in that equation can be interpreted as being similar to the slope in table 3.1. The results are somewhat surprising. For ward elections, blacks receive approximately 2 percent more seats than the population percentage would indicate (slope = 1.02). At-large elections result in perfect representational parity, and appointive systems result in about 5 percent underrepresentation.

Because the three slopes are not significantly different from each other, this implies that selection plans have no influence on the election of blacks to school boards. This topic merits fuller discussion. We shall return to the discussion of the impact of at-large elections after we estimate a more complete equation for black representation. By completing this estimate first, we can be sure that findings are not spurious simply because some politically important variable has been omitted.

The Politics of Black School Board Representation

In chapter 1 we argue that black school board representation is a function of five variables. Two of these variables—black population and selection plan—have already been introduced. The other three variables are black resources, white poverty, and region. Black resources are needed for political mobilization. Because the level of mobilization necessary for voting, and thus for electing school board members, is relatively low, we have operationalized black

case of city council elections (see Engstrom and McDonald, 1982: fn. 6) does the interaction add significantly greater predictive power. Because the Engstrom and McDonald approach has become the new conventional wisdom, we will follow that approach rather than continue to be a voice in the wilderness.

resources as the percentage of blacks in the school district who graduated from high school. White poverty is, of course, our indicator of the Giles-Evans-Feagin power thesis, which argues that the white establishment will also seek to isolate themselves from poor whites (Giles and Evans, 1985, 1986; Feagin, 1980). Region, operationalized as a dummy variable for the South, is a surrogate for a variety of factors that distinguish the South from the rest of the nation, including history, political culture, and past public-policy decisions.

Table 3.3 presents the results of the five-variable regression of black school board representation. The results are consistent with our theoretical expectations. Ward elections result in a 10 percent overrepresentation of blacks on school boards. At-large elections appear to have no effect on black representation, resulting in parity representation. Appointive systems result in 2 percent overrepresentation. The difference between these slopes, however, is not statistically significant.

Black resources improve representation; for each 1 percent increase in blacks with high school diplomas, black representation on school boards increases by 0.10 percent. White poverty also increases black representation, although the relationship is not statistically significant. For each additional 1 percent of whites living in poverty, black representation increases by 0.26 percent. This finding gives some credence to the Giles-Evans-Feagin power thesis that class as well as race must be considered in discrimination. Finally, the southern

Table 3.3. Determinants of Black Representation on School Boards

Dependent Variable: Percentage of black school board members

Independent Variable	Regression Coefficient	t-score
Ward system × black population (%)	1.10	14.75**
Appointive system × black population (%)	1.02	13.66**
At-large system × black population (%)	1.00	12.84**
Black education (%)	0.10	1.65*
White poverty (%)	0.26	1.33
Southern region	−4.33	2.65**

$F = 63.20$
$R^2 = .70$
Adjusted $R^2 = .69$
Intercept $= -7.18$
$N = 170$

*$p < .10$
**$p < .05$

region is significant. Southern districts on the average have 4.33 percent fewer blacks on their school boards than northern districts.

The predictive level of the equation in table 3.3 is good for both this type of research and for social science research in general. The set of independent variables can explain 70 percent of the variation in black school board representation. Unfortunately, these results are not as impressive as they seem, because population alone explains 69 percent of the variance.

Another Look at Selection Plans

The argument relating at-large elections to detrimental impacts on minorities starts from an assumption that the minority group under consideration is in a voting minority, that is, has fewer than 50 percent of the votes. Because our concern is with black representation, not black representation when it is in the minority, we did not make this assumption. Accordingly, we did not eliminate from the analysis those school districts with black majorities. This inclusion may well affect the impact of at-large elections, because when blacks have a voting majority, at-large elections should actually favor blacks.

Two possible definitions of black majorities are possible. One is the standard definition in terms of people residing in the school district (i.e., more that 50 percent of the people residing in the district are black). Using such a definition might not be appropriate in this case, because school board elections have extremely low turnout. Taebel (1977: 157) has found that only 4.6 percent of eligible voters cast ballots in Texas school board elections; Minar (1966: 824) has estimated 8.7 percent turnout in 48 Illinois school districts.[10] A school district with less than a majority of black residents might well have a majority of black voters if large numbers of white voters do not go to the polls.

What factors might increase black turnout relative to white turnout? Interest in the election has been shown to be a major factor in increasing black turnout (Wolfinger and Rosenstone, 1980: 8).[11] Black candidates, for example, increase the salience of an election for blacks and are associated with higher levels of black turnout (Abney, 1974; Pettigrew, 1976). Although a variety of factors influence individuals to vote (Verba and Nie, 1972), in a school board election perhaps the greatest motivating factor is having children in the

10. Milton (1983) has found much higher turnout in Florida school board elections. Unfortunately this finding is marred by several limitations. First, Florida has partisan school board elections, and the elections are held on the same day as other primary elections are held. Such scheduling will artificially stimulate turnout. Second, the author used rolloff as a measure of turnout, so that one knows the level of school board turnout compared with turnout for other elections but does not know the absolute level of school board turnout.

11. Generally blacks vote less often than whites (Wolfinger and Rosenstone, 1980: 90); but when individuals' ages and education are controlled, blacks actually have a higher turnout rate than whites.

school system. An individual without children or with children in a private school system has little reason to take the time to vote in a school board election.[12] In the only study of individual voters in school board elections, Taebel (1977: 158) has found 52.1 percent of the voters had children in the school system.[13]

This argument implies that, as white students leave a public school system, the school district electorate will attain a black voting majority sooner than it will attain a black residential majority. Table 3.4 is an attempt to estimate when a black voting majority in a school district becomes likely. Using black district population to predict black school enrollment reveals that black school enrollment is approximately 38 percent higher than black district population. Solving the regression equation for a simple black school-district majority indicates that, when a school district has approximately 34 percent black population, it will have a black student majority.

To illustrate how at-large elections might help black majorities, table 3.5 reveals the school board composition of the 21 school districts with a potential for black voting majorities (i.e., more than a 34 percent black population). In most of these cases blacks have more school board seats than their

Table 3.4. Impact of Black Population on Black School Enrollment

Dependent Variable: Percentage of black school enrollment, 1986

Independent Variable	Regression Coefficient	t-score
Black population (%)	1.38	35.13*

F = 1233.79
r^2 = .88
Intercept = 3.19
N = 169

Note: Black population must be 34 percent to produce a black school enrollment >50 percent.
*$p < .05$

12. One possible reason an individual without children in the school system chooses to vote is that he or she wants reduced taxes. Generally such individuals have few ways to express themselves in regular school board elections. They would be more likely to vote in school bond elections or budget referenda.

13. A total of 31.2 percent were employees of the school district and 22 percent stated that they were friends of a candidate. Some voters could, of course, be in more than one of these categories. Taebel (1977: 160) has found that more than 70 percent of the voters either had children in school or were employees of the district.

Table 3.5. Black Representation in School Districts with a Potential for Black Voting Majorities, by Type of Selection Plan

District	Black Population (%)	Black Seats (%)
Ward System		
Compton Unified, Calif.	73	86
Oakland Unified, Calif.	47	56
St. Landry Parish, La.	40	20
Caddo Parish, La.	38	33
Greensboro, N.C.	35	28
Appointive System		
Baltimore, Md.	55	55
Richmond, Va.	51	56
Jackson, Miss.	47	40
Dougherty County, Ga.	43	28
Chicago, Ill.	40	45
Philadelphia, Pa.	38	22
Norfolk, Va.	35	42
At-large System		
Newark, N.J.	58	55
Orleans Parish, La.	55	60
Camden, N.J.	53	55
Flint, Mich.	41	44
Dayton, Ohio	36	56
Little Rock, Ark.	36	28
Cincinnati, Ohio	35	42
Mixed Systems		
District of Columbia	70	88
Bibb County, Ga.	39	40

population would indicate regardless of the selection plan that is used. The results suggest a reestimation of the equation in table 3.3 using only those school districts where blacks do not have a voting majority.

To estimate the impact of selection plans on black minority representation, we reestimated the equation in table 3.3 using only those districts with less than a 34 percent black population.[14] This regression clearly shows the detrimental impact of at-large elections on the representation of black minorities. Ward election systems result in about a 1 percent overrepresentation of blacks on the school board (see the reduced model in table 3.6). Appointive systems underrepresent blacks by about 8 percent, and at-large elections produce a 16 percent underrepresentation. Although the resulting difference of 17 percent in representation is not quite statistically significant, it is consistent with past findings on the detrimental impact of at-large elections on the electoral fortunes of black minorities.

Representation of Black Administrators

The literature on policy-making has frequently demonstrated that administrators exercise policy-making discretion just as elected officials do (Rourke, 1984). Because discretion exists, the theory of representative bureaucracy argues that the representativeness of administrative elites is politically important. Educational policy is one area where administrators have been successful in defining many of the decisions they must deal with as being technical and of a nature that requires their particular area of expertise (Tucker and Zeigler, 1980). School boards are not full-time positions, so much day-to-day decision-making and many of the policy proposals are left to school administrators.

Although no one has examined the representativeness of school administrators, the literature on representative bureaucracy provides extensive data on the composition of other bureaucracies. Meier and Nigro's (1976: 462) study of the higher civil service at the federal level has found that administrative elites were "predominantly white, male, well-educated professionals from upper middle class urban families." Blacks held only 4.9 percent of the leadership positions in the federal bureaucracy, producing a representation index of 0.392. Examining city-level positions, Dye and Renick (1981: 478) found black representation indices of 0.45 for administrative jobs and 0.51 for professional positions. Analyzing both city and state government jobs, Henderson and Preston (1984: 38) found representation ratios of 0.69 for administrative jobs and 0.86 for professionals.

Blacks do much better in gaining access to school administrative positions than they do in regard to other higher-level administrative positions. Our group of school districts have 20.4 percent black administrators, resulting in a representation index of 0.73 when black students are used as the comparison base (see table 3.7). Because black students are a much larger percentage than

14. To avoid a misspecified model, we have provided a reduced model, deleting the insignificant variables.

black school district residents, the more appropriate comparison is to school district residents. In that case, using the regression method of estimation, the representation index is 0.96, showing only a 4 percent underrepresentation of blacks in school administrative positions.

The process by which black administrators are hired is related to the politics of the school district. In table 3.6 we related black access to school board seats to selection-plan structure, black resources (population and education), white poverty, and region. With minor alterations, black administrators should also be a function of these same forces (see chapter 1). Because selection plans do not appear to have any direct effect on the way administrators are hired, selection plans will be deleted from this model. In its place, we will use the percentage of black school board members as a predictor variable.

Black elected officials have frequently been related to the subsequent access of blacks to administrative positions in city government. Eisinger (1982a: 390) has found that the presence of a black mayor is positively related to increased levels of black employment. Dye and Renick (1981: 481) have concluded, "The single most important determinant of black employment in ad-

Table 3.6. Determinants of Black Representation on School Boards when Blacks Are in the Minority

Dependent Variable: Percentage of black school board members[a]

	Full Model		Reduced Model	
Independent Variable	Regression Coefficient	t-score	Regression Coefficient	t-score
Ward system				
× black population (%)	1.04	9.22*	1.01	9.56*
Appointive system				
× black population (%)	0.96	6.02*	0.92	5.88*
At-large system				
× black population (%)	0.86	6.82*	0.84	6.94*
Black education (%)	0.07	1.04		
White poverty (%)	0.30	1.44		
Southern region	−4.81	2.72*	−5.44	3.26*
F	18.01		26.28	
R^2	.44		.43	
Adjusted R^2	.41		.41	
N	146		146	

[a]When the percentage of black population > 1 and < 34.
*$p < .05$

Table 3.7. Representation Ratios for Black and White Administrators and Teachers[a]

	Blacks		Whites	
	Mean	Standard Deviation	Mean	Standard Deviation
Administrators				
1986	0.73	0.62	1.70	1.88
Teachers				
1968	0.81	0.60	1.28	1.05
1969	0.72	0.39	1.36	1.22
1970	0.73	0.38	1.32	1.17
1971	0.72	0.36	1.40	1.26
1972	0.73	0.46	1.36	1.21
1986	0.68	0.76	1.66	1.36

Note: All differences between blacks and whites are significant at .0001 or less.
[a]Using black student enrollment as the comparison base.

ministrative positions in cities is the percentage of blacks elected to city councils.[15]

The five-variable model predicting black administrators does fairly well, accounting for 86 percent of the variance in black school administrators (see the full model in table 3.8). Black education, white poverty, and region do not have a statistically significant impact on black school board administrators. This cursory glance at table 3.8 suggests that black school administrators may well be a function of only black population and black members on the school board.

To determine if this is true, a second regression equation was run using only these two variables (see the reduced model in table 3.8). The results of the reduced model confirm the implications of the full model. Using only black population and black school board members results in a level of prediction ($R^2 = .85$) within 1 percentage point of the five-variable model. The slope for black population suggests that blacks attain approximately 79 percent of the school administrative posts that one would expect given their population. The more important finding is revealed by the slope for school board members. For each additional 1 percent of the school board seats held by blacks, an ad-

15. Similar results have been found for Hispanics by Dye and Renick (1981) and for women by Saltzstein (1983).

Table 3.8. Determinants of Black Representation among School Administrators

Dependent Variable: Percentage of black school administrators

	Full Model		Reduced Model	
Independent Variable	Regression Coefficient	t-score	Regression Coefficient	t-score
Black population (%)	0.81	12.19*	0.79	13.37*
Black school board members (%)	0.23	4.44*	0.24	4.99*
White poverty (%)	−0.06	0.47		
Black education (%)	−0.01	0.19		
Southern region	−1.20	1.14		
F	192.12		483.99	
R²	.86		.85	
Adjusted R²	.85		.85	
Intercept	2.80		1.30	
N	168		168	

*p < .05

ditional 0.24 percent of school administrators will be black. Phrased slightly differently, if one of five school board members is black, we would expect that district to have an additional 5 percent black administrators compared with districts without any blacks on the school board, all other things being equal.

The reduced model in table 3.8 strongly suggests that blacks on the school board are able to create opportunities for other blacks in administrative positions. Such a finding makes sense, because school board members hire the superintendent (who may or may not be black). In continued interaction with the superintendent, black school board members can express interest in affirmative action programs or other efforts to attract or promote black administrators. School board members may not directly do any hiring, but they have numerous opportunities to influence the superintendent or other administrators who do the actual hiring.

Black Teachers

Representative bureaucracy has generally been concerned with higher-level administrative positions, because these administrators are more likely to make policy decisions. The representativeness of lower-level positions, the street-level bureaucrats (Lipsky, 1980), is also important for several reasons. First, discretion is often vested throughout the bureaucracy. Teachers, the implementing-level bureaucrats in a school system, must actually apply decisions made by administrators and policies passed by the school board. Second, contact between lower-level administrators and clients is often facilitated if the administrators are representative of the clients. Black teachers, in short, should have a greater understanding of the problems of black students, because these teachers may have encountered many of the same problems when they were students (Silver, 1973). Third, a representative bureaucracy at lower levels implies the openness of the government to all individuals. Black teachers in this manner serve as role models to black students, illustrating to young blacks that such aspirations are attainable.

In general studies of representative bureaucracy have found blacks to be well represented at lower levels of the bureaucracy. In city bureaucracies Dye and Renick (1981: 478) have found black representation indices of 0.44 for protective services (police and fire departments are often resistant to hiring minorities; see Preston, 1977: 512), 0.86 for office personnel, and 1.87 for service personnel. Examining all state and local employees, Hutchins and Sigelman (1981: 81) report a mean representation ratio of 1.34. At lower levels of state and local bureaucracies, Cayer and Sigelman (1980: 447) report minority representation indices of 1.42 for welfare workers, 1.61 for hospital workers, 2.32 for housing workers, 1.46 for transportation workers, and 2.18 for sanitation workers. Using 1981 data for city and state governments, Henderson and Preston (1984: 38) find black representation indices of 1.03 for technicians, 0.90 for protective services, 2.52 for paraprofessionals, 1.45 for clerical workers, and 2.63 for maintenance workers. Hall and Saltzstein (1977: 866), on the other hand, find a representation index of only 0.42 for all employees of 25 Texas cities. Data from the federal level have revealed a representation index of 1.33 for all employees, but minorities were concentrated at the lower grade levels (Hellriegel and Short, 1972: 854). In the only study of black teachers to date, Meier (1984: 255, n. 4) has found that black teachers in 89 large urban school district were overrepresented by 16 percent.

Black teachers have done moderately well at attaining teaching positions in these urban school districts. In 1986 the representation index (using the regression approach) for black teachers was 1.13 when compared with district population, but only 0.64 when compared with student enrollment. As table 3.7 reveals, the black teacher index in comparison to black student enrollment has actually dropped from 0.81 in 1968 to 0.68 in 1986. The drop is not the result of a decline in black teachers; black teachers in these districts have increased by a modest 3 percent since 1968. Rather this trend is a function of black student enrollment growing at a faster rate than black teachers are acquiring positions. This trend in black teachers merits some further discussion, and we will return to the topic after our investigation of the determinants of black teacher representation.

Again we hypothesize that the proportion of black teachers in a district is the result of the same set of forces used to predict black administrators—black resources (population and education), black school board members, white poverty, and region. In addition, because teachers are hired by administrators, we also hypothesize that black school administrators are positively related to the proportion of black teachers (see chapter 1).

Table 3.9 reveals an interesting pattern of relationships for black teachers. The full model explains 90 percent of the variation, but three variables—white poverty, black education, and black school board members—are not statistically significant. The lack of significance for the last-mentioned variable is consistent with the view that board members should not interfere in personnel decisions (Mann, 1974: 312). As a result, these three variables were dropped from the equation; and the coefficients were reestimated.

The reduced model in table 3.9, estimating black teacher representation as a function of black population, black representation among school administrators, and southern region, predicts as well as the equation in the full model. Fully 90 percent of the variation in black teacher representation can be explained by these three variables. Each 1 percent of black population predicts that the school district will have an increase of 0.64 percent in black teachers, a figure strikingly close to the representation index in table 3.7. Black

Table 3.9. Determinants of Black Teacher Representation

Dependent Variable: Percentage of black teachers

Independent Variable	Full Model		Reduced Model	
	Regression Coefficient	t-score	Regression Coefficient	t-score
Black population (%)	0.62	7.78*	0.64	8.79*
Black school board members (%)	0.03	0.71		
Black school administrators (%)	0.42	6.20*	0.44	6.82*
White poverty (%)	0.11	1.05		
Black education (%)	0.00	0.09		
Southern region	3.53	3.84*	3.26	3.94*
F	252.78		508.70	
R^2	.90		.90	
Adjusted R^2	.90		.90	
Intercept	−4.49		−3.21	
N	167		167	

*$p < .05$

school administrators, in turn, have a significant impact on hiring black teachers.[16] For each additional 1 percentile increase in black administrators, the number of black teachers increases by 0.44 percentiles. Finally, southern region is significant; southern school districts have an average of 3.26 percentiles more black teachers, all other things being equal.

Recruiting Black Teachers

The relative lack of change in the mean number of black teachers in these districts (3 percent) should not be taken to suggest that the portion of black teachers in all districts has been stable. In fact, the percentage of black teachers has changed dramatically in some districts. If one subtracts the percentage of black teachers in these districts in 1968 from the percentage in 1986 to get a change measure, we find a mean of 3.2 percent, but a standard deviation of 7.3. This large standard deviation and the range of this variable (-21.9 to 46.8) suggest substantial variation in these districts' ability to attract and retain black teachers.

Between 1968 and 1986 the relative proportion of black teachers remained fairly constant, but black teachers were redistributed among school districts. The relatively small increase in black teachers may well be a function of the successes of the civil rights movement. Teaching was one of the few professions open to blacks in the early part of this century. Because the South maintained segregated school systems, blacks had numerous opportunities to teach in all-black schools. The black institutions of higher education such as Fisk, Morehouse, and Tuskegee trained numerous black teachers who were then employed in segregated black schools. Few other upwardly mobile occupations were open to blacks.

As a result of the federal government's attempt to break down racial discrimination in hiring, numerous other professions have become open to blacks. Young blacks can now get into law school, business school, medical school, and other avenues of professional training. The higher relative salaries in these professions may explain why the proportion of black teachers has remained fairly constant over the last 18 years. Blacks who 40 years ago might have become teachers are now entering business or earning professional degrees (see Alston, 1988: 2-3).

To examine the redistribution of black teachers among these school districts, we need to speculate why black teachers would be attracted to one school district rather than another. The chance for upward mobility is one likely explanation. Black teachers will probably prefer to teach in a school district that pro-

16. Freeman (1977) has found that black voters led to more black teachers in southern states but was unable to specify how this process took place. Our results suggest that votes result in more black board members, who in turn hire black administrators, who in turn hire black teachers.

vides them with greater opportunities for professional advancement. Two indicators of attractive districts will be used—district wealth and district size. The former should be related to facilities and salaries; the latter should be related to opportunities for promotion. A related opportunity for upward mobility might be social mobility, the ability to move to a community more congenial to black professionals. Two indicators of social mobility will be used—percentage of black college graduates and southern region. The former should indicate communities with a large black middle class; the latter is a surrogate for the myriad forces that resulted in the massive black migration to the North.

Finally, one might suggest that the ability to attract and retain black teachers is similar to the determinants of black teacher representation. Black school administrators might be more successful in persuading black teachers to work for their district. Similarly black teachers might be attracted to a district with a large number of black school board members.

These six variables were used to predict the change in the percentage of black teachers from 1968 to 1986 (see the full model in 3.10). The results of this analysis show only two factors significantly related to changes in black teachers—black school administrators and southern region. Enrollment, district wealth, black college graduates, and black school board members had no impact on attracting black teachers.

The equation for changes in black teachers was then reestimated as a two-variable model with black school administrators and southern region. The results in the reduced model in table 3.10 show nearly the same level of explained variance as the six-variable model. All things being equal, a northern district can be expected to gain 5.03 percentiles more black teachers than a southern district. In addition, for each additional 1 percent of administrators who are black, a school district is able to increase its black teacher contingent by 0.26 percentiles. We should note that these gains are from a 1968 base, so these figures essentially represent changes over an 18-year period.

Summary

This chapter has examined black representation for urban school districts. We have found that blacks have attained representational equity in terms of school board seats and near representational equity in terms of administrators and teachers. The politics of representational equity are more revealing. Access to school board seats is affected by black population as it interacts with the type of selection plan (as expected, at-large elections limit black representation), by black resources (education), and southern region.

Representation for black administrators is a function of black population plus black representation on school boards. Representation by black teachers is determined by region, black representation among school administrators, and the

Table 3.10. Determinants of Successful Recruitment of Black Teachers

Dependent Variable: Percentile change in black teachers, 1968–86

Independent Variable	Full Model		Reduced Model	
	Regression Coefficient	t-score	Regression Coefficient	t-score
School district size (enrollment)	0.00	0.51		
Black college graduates (%)	0.10	0.97		
Black school administrators (%)	0.22	3.93*	0.26	8.45*
Black school board members (%)	0.05	0.96		
District wealth (median family income)	0.00	0.38		
Southern region	−4.64	4.84*	−5.03	5.38*
F		15.84		46.04
R²		.38		.37
Adjusted R²		.36		.36
Intercept		−1.49		−1.24
N		162		163

*$p < .05$

percentage of black population. The changes in black teacher proportions over the last 18 years have been a function of region (as teachers moved north) and the proportion of black administrators.

The core linkages of black representation are fairly simple. Ward elections, ample black resources (population and education), and the northern region produce greater black representation on school boards. Black school board representatives (along with black population) are able, in turn, to increase the number of black school administrators. Black school administrators (along with black population and the northern region) then are able to increase the number of black teachers. In terms of representation, therefore, a developmental sequence exists where school board representation leads to administrative representation, which in turn leads to black representation among teachers.

4 The Politics of Second-Generation Discrimination

Chapter 3 addresses passive black representation for school boards, administrative positions, and teaching jobs. The key question of representation is, to what extent does passive representation translate into active representation? In more concrete terms, does having black school board members, black administrators, and black teachers have any impact on educational policies that affect black students? Our theory in chapter 1 argues that academic grouping, discipline, and educational-outcome actions are uniquely suited to measure the impact of black representation on public policy.

The analysis in this chapter proceeds in three steps. First, several tables illustrate that blacks are adversely affected by academic grouping and discipline and in educational outcomes. Second, an argument is made that such racial differences on these measures result from discrimination against black students. These actions form the core of what is termed second-generation educational discrimination. Third, the measures of second-generation discrimination will be linked to our political theory of educational policy. Discrimination will be tied to black representation, black political resources, white poverty, region, and district size in a multivariate explanation.

Differential Impact of Educational Policies

Desegregated or partly desegregated schools can be resegregated[1] by limiting contact between black and white students and by limiting the access of black students to quality education. In chapter 1 we argue that resegregation can be accomplished by a variety of means including academic grouping and discipline. No study can examine all the nuances of resegregation in a multischool context. This study is limited by the data collected by the Office

---

1. By resegregated we mean a decreased level of interracial contact. We do not mean that such contact is completely eliminated.

for Civil Rights. OCR's data-collection requests vary from year to year. Some data are collected for several years and then dropped from subsequent surveys. Other data are added, such as information on sex-segregated classes, as new laws (e.g., Title IX) change the nature of OCR's enforcement function. Finally, some data are never gathered.

Data limitations will restrict our analysis to three general types of activity—academic grouping, discipline, and educational outcome. Academic grouping includes placement in classes for the educable mentally retarded (EMR), the trainable mentally retarded (TMR), and the gifted. Discipline includes the use of corporal punishment, suspensions, and expulsions. Educational outcome focuses on graduating from high school and dropping out of school.

As a result of data limitations, some aspects of resegregation cannot be studied at all. First, OCR does not collect curriculum-tracking information other than that for sexual stereotyping.[2] In the best of all possible worlds, data would be available on placement in vocational tracks and college-prep tracks as well as intermediate tracks. Second, we have no information on how teachers encourage or discourage individual students. One need not totally isolate a student to deprive him or her of access to educational opportunities. Discouragement by a teacher that does not appear in our categories as discipline or academic grouping might be equally effective. Third, OCR collects no information on how well students are performing in classes other than whether or not they graduate.[3] Although objective test scores, be they national achievement tests or state competency tests, have numerous limitations, access to such information would reveal a great deal about the quality of education that individual students receive.

2. They collect data on enrollment in industrial arts programs and home economics programs by sex and for sex participation in athletics. If the industrial arts were to include categories for enrollment by race, this would provide an indicator of tracking. Unfortunately, the industrial arts data are collected only by sex.

3. The National Assessment of Education Progress (NAEP) project does collect censuslike information and has developed a reliable student-performance data base that allows for a national overview of what American students know and can do (see Pratt, 1983; Forbes, 1985; Lapointe, 1984; Ortiz, 1986; Applebee, Langer, and Mullis, 1986; National Academy of Education, 1987). Generally referred to as the nation's report card, NAEP assessments are based on representative samples of children 9, 13, and 17 years of age. In addition to performance scores on tests, NAEP collects and analyzes some background data about students, their families, and their schools. If this data were collected at the school district level, then the NAEP could move beyond a descriptive account of national student-performance trends to an invaluable source of information that could be merged with other data bases (such as the OCR data used in the present study). Such a merged data base could be used to link student achievement to measures of second-generation discrimination. The national level of aggregation, however, prevents the NAEP from being an essential tool in the hands of policy analysts.

Academic Grouping

EMR Classes. Of the various special-education classes including classes for the trainable mentally retarded, specific learning disability classes, and seriously emotionally disturbed children, EMR classes have the greatest potential for discrimination. EMR classes have the fewest restrictions on entry. Placement in classes for the seriously emotionally disturbed, in contrast, are subject to more checks in that these classes are smaller and the burden of proof to place a child in such a class is greater.

To determine the degree of differential assignment to EMR classes and other policies, a representational index similar to the one used by Finn (1982) has been constructed. The index assumes that black students should be assigned to various classes or punished in approximately the same proportion as their student numbers. For EMR classes the index is calculated by dividing the proportion of the district's black students in EMR classes by the proportion of all students who are in EMR classes.[4]

To illustrate, assume a school district has 100 students, 20 black students and 80 white students. This district has an EMR class of 6 students; 2 of the EMR students are black. Calculations reveal that 10 percent of all black students are in the EMR classes while 6 percent of all students are in the class. The EMR representation ratio for this district would be 10 percent divided by 6 percent, or 1.67. This section of chapter 4 is concerned only with differential assignment to classes; we do not argue that such assignments are the result of discrimination. That argument is presented in later sections of the chapter.

The representation ratio for class assignments has the same characteristics that it has for political representation. If blacks are assigned to EMR classes in the same proportion as everyone else in the student body, the representation ratio will be 1.0. Ratios above 1.0 will indicate proportionately more blacks are in EMR classes, and ratios below 1.0 will indicate proportionately fewer blacks in EMR classes. An index of 1.20, for example, reveals that blacks have 20 percent more students in EMR classes than one would expect, given the overall assignment pattern of students to EMR classes.

The representation ratios for EMR classes are shown in the top panel of table 4.1. The findings of this table are consistent with past literature (see

4. This measure is also known as the odds index, because it states the odds that a black student will be in an EMR class relative to that student's random chance of being in an EMR class. This is the same measure used by Finn (1982: 330) with two exceptions. Finn uses the black and white student population as a base for comparison, and we use the total student body (that is, Finn's measure uses the proportion of black students relative to total black and white students rather than to total students including blacks, whites, and other minorities). In addition, Finn uses a log transformation of his index. We use a similar transformation where the index is used in regression equations, but we do not use it in descriptive tables, because the odds index is more interpretable than the logged index.

Table 4.1. Policy Representation Ratios for Blacks and Whites, by Academic Grouping

	Blacks		Whites	
	Mean	Standard Deviation	Mean	Standard Deviation
Placement in EMR Classes				
1973	2.25	1.09	0.65	0.20
1974	2.24	1.16	0.67	0.24
1976	2.25	1.23	0.67	0.22
1978	2.23	1.13	0.66	0.21
1980	2.14	1.02	0.68	0.22
1982	2.03	0.81	0.68	0.22
1984	1.95	0.83	0.68	0.24
Placement in TMR Classes				
1973	1.42	0.79	0.88	0.21
1974	1.34	0.64	0.87	0.19
1976	1.29	0.65	0.90	0.23
1978	1.29	0.66	0.90	0.21
1980	1.30	0.60	0.93	0.26
1982	1.41	1.50	0.94	0.23
1984	1.23	0.48	0.94	0.24
Placement in Gifted Classes				
1976	0.43	0.40	1.31	0.56
1978	0.52	0.72	1.35	0.56
1980	0.38	0.27	1.39	0.56
1982	0.38	0.26	1.46	0.51
1984	0.45	0.30	1.42	0.53

Note: All differences between blacks and whites are significant at .0001 or less.

chapter 1) and are not surprising. For each of the seven years, the black EMR ratio equals or exceeds 1.95; blacks are overrepresented in EMR classes by anywhere from 95 to 125 percentage points. Comparing the EMR ratios for blacks and whites reveals significant differences between the black ratio and the white ratio for every year.

In this and other examinations of differential assignments, one should remember that the tables show the means for a large number of school districts. As means, the figures mask substantial variation. In 1984, for example, the black EMR ratio ranged from a low of 0.54 to a high of 5.45. In many school districts, therefore, representation ratios greatly exceed the mean.

The final observation about the top panel of table 4.1 concerns the trend over time. Placement in EMR classes has been an interest of OCR since 1973; in fact, OCR once specifically defined a black EMR ratio of more than 1.20 as cause for concern (C. S. Bullock, 1976). In recent years, the black EMR ratio has decreased slightly. This finding is consistent with Gartner and Lipsky's (1987: 373) recent analysis of the implementation of the Education for All Handicapped Act of 1975; they present evidence showing that the number of children labeled mentally retarded has decreased since passage of the act. They argue that the decline is a function of the stigmatizing nature of the EMR label and of allegations of discrimination in EMR placements. While the trend is encouraging, the low point of the trend (1984) still overrepresents blacks by 95 percentage points.

TMR Classes. Classes for the trainable mentally retarded are for individuals more retarded than those in EMR classes.[5] The average school district has a TMR enrollment of less than 0.4 percent of its student body, approximately one-fourth the size of its EMR class enrollment. Given the smaller classes and the greater burden of proof to assign a student to a TMR class, we would expect that the differential assignment of blacks to TMR classes would not be as great as the differential assignment of blacks to EMR classes.[6]

The middle panel of table 4.1, showing the differential assignment ratios for TMR classes, reveals exactly this pattern. Although blacks are not assigned to TMR classes in as large proportions as they are to EMR classes, blacks are overrepresented in TMR classes by 23–42 percentage points. In each case the difference between the black TMR ratio and the white TMR ratio is statistically significant at the .0001 level.

The trend pattern for TMR classes is interesting. White ratios show a slightly increasing trend to within 6 percentage points of parity by 1984. Blacks, on the other hand, show some minor fluctuation; but the general level of assignments remains the same. The reason that white ratios can increase while black ratios stay the same is that Hispanic students, Asian students, and other students not classified as "white" or "black" are also placed in these classes.

Gifted Classes. Classes for gifted children are at the top of the educational spectrum. Access to gifted classes, oriented to college preparation or specialized in areas such as the performing arts, science, or humanities, is access to the best quality education that a district provides. In some districts such classes

5. Definitions of student eligibility for EMR and TMR classes vary greatly by state and school district. See Heller, Holtzman, and Messick, 1982: 24.

6. This is an inference based on the assumption that assignments have an element of discrimination in them. If IQ tests alone were used to assign black students to TMR classes, then the black TMR ratio would greatly exceed the black EMR ratio (see Heller, Holtzman, and Messick, 1982).

serve as an incentive to participate in magnet school programs; and in others they are special, restricted classes within a school.

According to table 4.1 (bottom panel), blacks have much less access to gifted classes than whites. An access ratio of 0.45 in 1984, for example, indicates that blacks were underrepresented by 55 percentage points in classes for the gifted. Whites, in comparison, are three to four times more likely than blacks to be enrolled in gifted classes. These differences between whites and blacks are statistically significant at the .0001 level.

The lack of black access to gifted classes is underscored by a slight trend. The proportion of white enrollments in gifted programs has increased slightly over the time period of study. The black ratio has shown more fluctuation but has generally decreased over the same time period.[7]

Discipline

Similar to academic grouping, much disciplinary action is not reported to OCR. The most frequent form of discipline is probably a verbal reprimand or being sent to the school principal. Three disciplinary procedures are reported to OCR—corporal punishment, suspensions for one day or more, and expulsions.

Corporal Punishments. In theory corporal punishment is the least severe of the disciplinary actions reported to OCR. The use of corporal punishment is highly controversial. Parents have filed lawsuits against schools whose staff members have struck their children, and discussions of corporal punishment are often heated. Although nine states have banned corporal punishment, current estimates are that 1.5 million students receive some form of corporal punishment every year (Baker et al., 1987).[8]

The corporal punishment ratios in table 4.2 show that black students are from 74 to 86 percentage points overrepresented in receiving corporal punishment. The corporal punishment ratios for blacks are approximately twice as high as the white ratios, and the differences between these ratios are statistically significant at the .0001 level. The trends for these variables show a slight reduction of the differences. Black ratios dropped by 0.05 in eight years, while white ratios increased 0.04 during the same time period.

Suspensions. An intermediate step in the discipline process, whether or not a district allows corporal punishment, is suspension. Many districts, in fact, require suspension before an administrator takes the extreme step of expelling

7. Whites may be making gains at the expense of Asian students in some districts. Asian students tend to be highly overrepresented in gifted classes, especially Asian students who are not recent immigrants.

8. In 1988 Nebraska and Wisconsin passed legislation that affected the conditions under which corporal punishment could be used.

Table 4.2. Policy Representation Ratios for Blacks and Whites, by Disciplinary Action

	Blacks		Whites	
	Mean	Standard Deviation	Mean	Standard Deviation
Corporal Punishment				
1976	1.86	0.92	0.80	0.24
1978	1.83	1.16	0.84	0.24
1980	1.74	0.77	0.85	0.20
1982	1.74	0.81	0.87	0.40
1984	1.81	0.88	0.84	0.31
Suspensions				
1973	1.85	0.76	0.74	0.26
1974	1.76	0.66	0.78	0.20
1976	1.88	0.72	0.76	0.18
1978	1.75	0.58	0.81	0.15
1980	1.62	0.52	0.84	0.20
1982	1.54	0.40	0.83	0.16
1984	1.59	0.46	0.82	0.18
Expulsions				
1971	3.71	4.11	0.60	0.39
1972	4.15	4.90	0.52	0.35
1973	3.35	2.79	0.52	0.38
1974	2.70	1.72	0.70	0.97
1976	2.78	1.96	0.64	0.47
1978	2.70	1.81	0.61	0.41
1980	2.34	1.57	0.67	0.46

Note: All differences between blacks and whites are significant at .0001 or less.

a student. OCR collects data on the number of students who are suspended for one day or more during the school year.

The suspension ratios that appear in the middle panel of table 4.2 are remarkably similar to the corporal punishment ratios. Depending on the year, a black student is between 54 and 88 percentage points more likely to be suspended than the average student. White students, on the other hand, are about 20 percent less likely to be suspended. The differences between the black suspension ratios and the white suspension ratios are statistically significant for all years.

Although the overall trend for black students is somewhat unclear, in the most recent eight-year period (1976–84) black suspension ratios dropped by 0.29. Over the same time period white suspension ratios rose about 0.06. This pattern is similar to the trend for corporal punishment, though the drop in ratios is slightly greater for suspensions. Such trends, however, are modest; they represent gradual changes in the discipline ratios rather than fundamental shifts in action.

Expulsions. The capital punishment stage of school discipline is expulsion. Students who remain behavior problems after other corrective measures fail or who commit serious offenses are likely to be expelled. The severity of expulsion is recognized by school administrators; the districts in our sample had 10 suspensions for every expulsion.

The Office for Civil Rights gathered data on expulsions (the first measure of second-generation discrimination gathered) from 1971 until 1980, when the agency omitted expulsions from the data-request form. Of all the data reported here, those for expulsions are perhaps the least reliable, because many school districts did not report expulsion data to OCR. Despite these data problems, the comparison of black students to white students is striking.

Black students are disproportionately expelled (see the bottom panel of table 4.2). In any given year a black student is between three to eight times more likely to be expelled than a white student. Differences of this magnitude are, of course, statistically significant. Even more apparent from the ratios table is the trend in expulsions. Unlike other variables that experience only moderate trends, the black expulsion ratio dropped from 3.71 (an overrepresentation of 271 percent) in 1971 to 2.34 in 1980. The white ratio at the same time experienced a modest increase.[9]

Educational Outcome

The bottom line for educational systems is the quality of education that a school district provides. Measuring educational quality is both difficult and controversial, as recent efforts to implement competency-based testing have revealed. The only measures of educational quality gathered by OCR are indirect ones. Graduation rates were gathered for five years, and dropout rates were collected for 1976 only.

Graduation Rates. Graduation from high school is what policy analysts term a policy outcome rather than a policy output. Policy outputs are policies that

9. OCR's decision to no longer collect expulsion data cannot be defended. Expulsions are the most serious form of discipline, and the form most likely to eliminate a student from school completely. In addition, expulsions are much more focused on black students than suspensions or corporal punishment. If the objective is to monitor the discriminatory actions of school districts, the decision not to collect expulsion data is a serious mistake.

decision-makers can directly affect. That is, decision-makers can directly affect the number of students in an EMR class or the number of suspensions issued. High school graduation rates are dependent on a wide variety of factors in addition to the policies discussed here. Such a policy outcome is affected by the home environment, a student's individual ability and motivation, the interaction between a student and teachers, as well as a wide variety of school-district policies. In fact, with the pressures for social promotion, high school graduation rates are probably less related to quality education today than they have been in the past.

Table 4.3 (top panel) shows the high school graduation ratios for our school districts. The pattern is familiar though not as extreme as the pattern for other policy variables. Blacks are underrepresented in graduation rates by 12–20 percentage points, and whites in turn are overrepresented by 8–14 percentage points. All differences between the races are statistically significant at .0001.

Again in the case of high school graduates a gradual trend exists. From 1976 to 1984 the black graduation ratio increased from 0.80 to 0.88. White graduation ratios have similarly increased from 1.08 to 1.12. The difference between blacks and whites remained much the same; the level of graduation for each, however, increased.

Dropout Rates. The converse of high school graduation rates is the dropout rate. Because OCR gathered dropout data for only a single year, no trend analysis can be done. The figures for 1976 (see the bottom panel of table 4.3) show the familiar pattern. Blacks have a dropout ratio of 1.12, or 12 percent

Table 4.3. Policy Representation Ratios for Blacks and Whites, by Educational Outcome

	Blacks		Whites	
	Mean	Standard Deviation	Mean	Standard Deviation
High School Graduates				
1976	0.80	0.31	1.08	0.24
1978	0.82	0.22	1.12	0.16
1980	0.81	0.20	1.14	0.18
1982	0.86	0.19	1.13	0.17
1984	0.88	0.19	1.12	0.17
Dropouts				
1976	1.12	0.36	0.95	0.18

Note: All differences between blacks and whites are significant at .0001 or less.

above average; whites have a dropout ratio of 0.95, or about 5 percentage points below the norm.

Differential Assignments as Discrimination

Thus far we have reported differences between blacks and whites for a variety of educational indicators, but have avoided the question of discrimination. Academic grouping and discipline have been part of the educational system for a long time and clearly predate desegregation.[10] Such practices exist even in schools that have only white students. Two justifications other than discrimination have been offered for the use of academic grouping and discipline (Eyler, Cook, and Ward, 1983: 127). First, policies of academic grouping and discipline reflect professional norms in education concerning the best way to run school systems. Academic grouping is supported by the argument that only when students are grouped by ability can the brightest students be challenged and the less able students get the special attention they need.[11] Using this logic, "resegregation is necessary in order for each child to attain the highest level of achievement" (Eyler, Cook, and Ward, 1983: 127). Similarly discipline, including corporal punishment, suspensions, and expulsions, is part of the school administrator's duty to maintain a school environment where learning is possible. If students from a certain group are disciplined in greater numbers, this may reflect that group's greater behavior problems.

The second possible reason for academic grouping and disciplinary action can be termed the cross-pressure thesis. School officials are subjected to pressures not only from parents but also from state and federal governments. Courts or the Department of Education may mandate desegregation. The federal government may also require bilingual education, special education, or special programs for the economically and educationally disadvantaged. Implementing such programs will result in some students (many of them minority students) being pulled out of regular classes to meet federal or state mandates. Thus, conflicting policy mandates will result in resegregation.

Even though actions consistent with both justifications will still result in some resegregation of school systems, the intent is to assist disadvantaged students not to hinder them. The assertion of discrimination implies that a school district is, in fact, hindering the student's education by such practices. Terming such

10. Whether ability grouping and discipline predate discrimination is another question. Ability grouping techniques were developed at about the same time that school populations became more diverse with the advent of more universal education. There are reasons to suspect that ability grouping techniques have always had an element of social-class bias.

11. This assumes that advanced classes and special education classes actually improve the performance of students in these classes. See chapter 1 for our critical evaluation of the impact of these classes on performance.

practices discrimination, however, does not necessarily mean that discrimination is the intention. Teachers, administrators, and school board members might well be pursuing normal educational practices or accommodating conflicting mandates and inadvertently discriminate against black students. When discriminatory practices are part of the norms and institutional structure of an organization, decision-makers may be unaware of any discriminatory impact (Feagin and Feagin, 1986: 31).

This section argues that, whether or not such practices have been implemented with the intention of discrimination, some evidence exists that is consistent with discrimination. Further, this evidence is clearly not consistent with the proposition that academic grouping and discipline are simply good educational practices.

The Consistency of Results

The first argument for using the term *discrimination* in regard to the practices under discussion is the pattern of consistency. If discrimination were the underlying cause of actions studied in this chapter, we would expect that black students would be underrepresented in those policies that reflect positively on a student (assignment to gifted classes and graduation) and overrepresented in policies that reflect negatively on a student (assignment to EMR and TMR classes, corporal punishment, suspensions, expulsions, and dropouts).

Tables 4.1 through 4.3 compare black students and white students on eight different policy ratios for as many as seven years. There are 44 comparisons. In every case where the policy reflects positively on a student, black students are underrepresented. In every case where the policy reflects negatively on a student, black students are overrepresented. In all 44 cases the differences between blacks and whites are statistically significant at the .0001 level. Such consistency does not prove that the policies are discriminatory; but given such a clear pattern, one should be skeptical about claims that academic grouping and discipline are merely good educational practices.

The Intercorrelations

If the policy ratios in tables 4.1 to 4.3 reflect nothing more than good educational practices or conflicting mandates, then many of the policies should be unrelated to each other. To be sure, suspensions and expulsions should be related; and a relationship definitely exists between dropouts and graduates. But no apparent reason exists why placement of blacks in EMR classes should be related to the absence of blacks in gifted classes. Neither should corporal punishment be related to placement in EMR or TMR classes.

If the policy measures reflect some element of discrimination, a predictable pattern should result. All indicators that reflect positively on students (gifted classes and graduates) should be positively related to each other, and all indicators that reflect negatively on students (EMR and TMR classes, corporal punishment, suspensions, expulsions, and dropouts) should also be positively related to each other. In addition, correlations between positive actions and negative actions should be negative.

The pooled correlations between the policy ratios are shown in Table 4.4; intercorrelations between indicators for each individual year are reported in Appendix A. Of the 28 correlations in table 4.4, 27 are in the direction predicted by the discrimination hypothesis. Only one correlation, the .29 correlation between dropouts and graduates, is inconsistent with the discrimination hypothesis; and that counterintuitive correlation is based on a single year. The probability that 27 of 28 correlations would be in the predicted direction if the actual pattern of relationships were random is less than .0001.[12]

Even examining the intercorrelations for individual years shows an equally overwhelming pattern (see appendix A). Of the 112 intercorrelations for the seven different survey years, 103 are in the direction predicted above. The probability of such a pattern is less than .0001.[13] Of these 103 correlations in the predicted direction, 64 are statistically significant at the .05 level. None of the nine correlations in the unexpected direction are statistically significant.

Some individual correlations in table 4.4 merit discussion. If the policies do not reflect any element of discrimination against blacks, then a correlation of .38 between EMR classes and suspensions is difficult to explain. Similarly the inverse relationship between suspensions and gifted classes is difficult to defend. Further consideration of the correlation table would reveal several other relationships that do not make sense if the policy indicators simply reflect unrelated actions designed to implement good educational practices.

Clustering of Measures

A more comprehensive way to view the interrelationships of the policy indicators is via factor analysis. Rather than examining the factor structure for each individual year, only the factor structures for 1976 and 1984 will be discussed. These two years were selected because 1976 has the largest number of indicators collected by OCR and our most recent data are for 1984. The results for these two years are similar to the results for the other five years. The discrimination hypothesis predicts that actions that positively affect black

12. This probability is estimated using the binomial probability distribution. The t-score associated with the present case comparing it with a random distribution is 4.91.

13. Again, this probability is estimated using the binomial probability distribution. In this case the t-score is 9.80, which would translate to an astronomically low probability if a large t-table were used to get a precise estimate of the probability.

Table 4.4. Pooled Intercorrelations for Policy Variables

	Expulsions	Corporal Punishment	Suspensions	Gifted Classes	EMR Classes	TMR Classes	Graduates
Corporal punishment	.38	×					
Suspensions	.41	.47	×				
Gifted classes	−.17	−.09	−.21	×			
EMR classes	.40	.35	.38	−.48	×		
TMR classes	.10	.02	.09	−.35	.42	×	
Graduates	−.12	−.09	−.11	.16	−.26	−.04	×
Dropouts	.24	.28	.39	−.08	.30	.00	.29

students (e.g., graduation and gifted classes) will be negatively loaded on the first factor, whereas actions that negatively affect black students (e.g., EMR and TMR classes, dropouts, punishments, suspensions, and expulsions) will be loaded positively on the first factor.[14]

In 1976 the eight policy indicators load on the first factor exactly as expected (see the top panel of table 4.5).[15] High school graduates and gifted classes both load negatively, whereas EMR classes, TMR classes, suspensions, corporal punishment, expulsions, and dropouts load positively. This core factor explains 33 percent of the variance common to all eight indicators.

Although 1984 contains only six of the eight indicators of second-generation discrimination, the factor pattern (also shown in table 4.5) is similar to 1976. Again both graduates and gifted classes load negatively. Suspensions, corporal punishment, EMR classes, and TMR classes load positively. Explaining 35 percent of the common variance, the loadings are precisely those predicted by the discrimination hypothesis.

14. More precisely the discrimination hypothesis predicts that these two sets of indicators will load in opposite directions. The negative actions will load positively, because there are more negative actions than positive ones.

15. Wainscott and Woodard (1988) argue for two dimensions for second-generation discrimination. We find their argument atheoretical. We have specified how the individual variables will load on a single factor, and we have confirmed those loadings with actual results. Whether or not more than one factor can be extracted from a set of indicators is not a relevant question. Up to eight factors can be extracted from a set of eight indicators. The common use of eigenvalues of greater than 1.0 to justify the extraction of additional factors has no logical support and about as much theoretical support as stepwise regression. The indicators reflect more than discrimination; by arbitrarily extracting additional factors and then arbitrarily rotating those factors, one can get a wide array of different results. Without any theoretical expectations for those results, such results border on gibberish.

Table 4.5. Factor Analysis of Second-Generation Discrimination Measures

| | Factor Loading | |
	1976	1984
Expulsions	.42	—
Corporal punishment	.77	.07
Suspensions	.80	.56
Gifted classes	−.64	−.69
EMR classes	.87	.81
TMR classes	.19	.55
Graduates	−.22	−.59
Dropouts	.14	—
Eigenvalue	2.67	2.11
Percentage of variance	33.00	35.00

Is the Level of Activity Sufficient?

One final counterargument to the pattern of results presented thus far is that the actions we are discussing are hardly sufficient to resegregate a school system (see Wainscott and Woodard, 1988). TMR classes, this argument goes, are fairly small; suspensions are rare; expulsions are even rarer, so the number of students that can be separated from each other is fairly small.

Table 4.6 presents the average percentage of the student body affected by discipline and academic-grouping actions. These figures at first glance support this argument. In 1984, the average district placed only 0.38 percent of its students in TMR classes and only 1.41 percent in EMR classes. Gifted classes on the average made up only 4.36 percent of students. Academic grouping, therefore, can affect only a small percentage of the students in a school district and cannot have the massive impact necessary to resegregate the school system. A similar argument could be made for discipline. Although corporal punishment did affect 4.57 percent of students in the average school district in 1984, and 7.38 percent of the students were suspended, only 0.61 percent of students were actually expelled in 1980 (the last year for which data on expulsions were available).

This argument on the totality of impact of these programs has two major flaws. First, it assumes that the indicators presented here are the sum total of academic grouping and disciplinary actions. Academic grouping has numerous forms other than gifted classes and special-education classes. Other types of classes are segregated by ability, including efforts to track students into vocational programs and college-prep programs. Finley (1984: 234) has

Table 4.6. Percentage of Students Affected by School Actions

	Expulsion	Suspension	Corporal Punishment	Assignment to Special Classes		
				EMR	TMR	Gifted
1971	0.14	—	—	—	—	—
1972	0.16	—	—	—	—	—
1973	0.22	4.94	—	1.56	0.32	—
1974	0.29	5.33		1.61	0.34	—
1976	0.13	5.17	4.67	1.61	0.35	1.72
1978	0.12	5.38	4.81	1.56	0.37	2.46
1980	0.61	6.75	5.01	1.50	0.37	2.92
1982	—	7.29	5.46	1.51	0.37	3.67
1984	—	7.38	4.57	1.41	0.38	4.36

even found ability grouping of high school English classes that were partly segregated by race. The academic grouping measures presented here are only the tip of the iceberg in terms of segregation via grouping. Similarly, not all forms of discipline are monitored by OCR. Noncorporal punishment is not recorded. Whether suspended or expelled students return to school is not recorded. Selective discipline can have impacts far above the 0.61 percent of students who are expelled.

Second, inspecting only the means of these categories seriously underestimates the total impact that such policies can have. Although the average school system expelled only 0.61 percent of its students in 1980, one school system expelled 12.56 percent. The maximum values for the other variables also reveal activities with a massive potential impact. In 1984 the maximum value for suspensions was 22.18 percent, the maximum value for corporal punishment was 19.5 percent, for EMR classes 4.21 percent, for TMR classes 1.06 percent, and for gifted classes 16.7 percent. If one looks only at black students, the maximum percent affected in 1984 jumps to 9.8 percent in EMR classes, 30.3 percent corporally punished, and 46.9 percent suspended. In some districts, therefore, just these academic-grouping actions and disciplinary sanctions are sufficient to resegregate an entire school system.

The four arguments presented here—the consistency of the policy ratios, the intercorrelations, the factor analysis, and the percentage of students affected by these actions—do not prove that every act of academic grouping or discipline is nothing more than discrimination against black students. That is not our purpose. Our intent is to suggest that some, though by no means all, academic grouping and discipline can be attributed to discrimination. That a pattern similar to the one revealed here could occur without some discrimination is virtually impossible to believe. We have presented at least four partial tests, and in each case we have found patterns consistent with discrimination. We are convinced that an element of second-generation discrimination exists and that these measures of academic grouping and discipline reflect it. Even if a conclusion of discrimination were not supported, a systematic pattern of educational policies with deleterious impacts on black students has been revealed.

The Politics of Second-Generation Discrimination

Our political theory of second-generation discrimination, presented in chapter 1, argues that five variables affect second-generation discrimination against black students. First, black political representation should mitigate the amount of second-generation discrimination. Although one could argue that representation on the school board (Meier and England, 1984) and among school administrators might affect policies that involve second-generation discrimination, the person most likely to affect them, through direct decision-making, is the teacher. The teacher makes the initial assessment of a student's ability and likely is the first person to interact with a student in terms of discipline.[16] The actual measure is the percentage of black teachers in the school district. As noted in chapter 1, the percentage of black teachers is used rather than a teacher-representation index, because the teacher percentage reflects the probability that a black student will come in contact with a black teacher.

Second, black resources should limit the amount of second-generation discrimination against black students. In communities with ample black political resources, blacks can exert political pressure on the school district and voice their objections to certain policies.[17] Two measures of black political resources are used. The first is the percentage of blacks in the district who have graduated from high school. The second is the ratio of black median family income to white median family income. The latter measure is an attempt to assess the level of black resources compared with the level of white resources.

Third, social class should affect second-generation discrimination. We have argued that the power thesis of Giles, Evans, and Feagin applies to second-generation discrimination. In this view, discrimination against black students

16. We tried other models of second-generation discrimination that compared the impact of teachers, administrators, and school board members. Such models are greatly affected by collinearity, but a pattern is evident. That pattern reveals that the strongest impact of the three sets of actors on these policies is teachers. Because this finding is consistent with our theory, we will include only measures of black teachers in our models.

17. Education and income can be considered a resource whether blacks exert pressure on the school district as a group or as individuals pressing individual claims.

is a function of both race and social class. In districts with large numbers of lower-class whites, lower-class white students will suffer similar discriminatory actions. The result will be that, in districts with large lower-class white populations, discrimination against blacks will be mitigated. The specific indicator is the percentage of the white population with an income below poverty level.

Fourth, southern region should be positively associated with levels of second-generation discrimination. Region is clearly a surrogate variable for factors that cannot be measured in other ways. In this case region likely represents some element of past policy actions, political culture, mass political attitudes, and historical patterns of discrimination. The indicator is a dummy variable coded 1 for the states that have maintained *de jure* segregated schools.

Fifth, district size should be negatively associated with levels of second-generation discrimination. The larger a school district is, the more likely that school district is to be professionalized. Greater levels of professionalization should result in greater awareness of the problems of black students and greater recognition that something like second-generation discrimination is possible. The indicator of district size is the total school enrollment

The dependent variables are the eight policy ratios introduced in this chapter, with one small alteration. An examination of the distribution of these variables revealed that several are skewed by extreme values. Extreme values can distort a regression by giving too much weight to an extreme case. To avoid this problem, a log transformation of each indicator was used. The log transformation changes the interpretation of the result somewhat in that regression slopes now refer to percentage changes in the dependent variable rather than one-unit changes (Tufte, 1974: 113–128).

To avoid unwieldy tables, the analysis of this chapter examines the last four years of the policy variables under consideration. Four time points will be sufficient to determine if the pattern is consistent across years or the result of idiosyncratic one-year fluctuations. The regressions for the remaining years appear in Appendix A (tables A.10 through A.14). In every case the regressions in Appendix A are consistent with those presented in this chapter.

EMR Classes

The political model of second-generation discrimination works fairly well for placement of blacks in EMR classes (see table 4.7). In every case but two (district size in 1982 and 1984) the regression slopes are in the expected direction. In addition, the level of explained variation ranges from 49 percent to 55 percent, a fairly high level compared with past studies of second-generation discrimination (see Meier and England, 1984).

The strong role of black teachers in mitigating the placement of black students in EMR classes is demonstrated by these equations. For each 1 percentile in-

Table 4.7. Placement of Black Students in EMR Classes: Multivariate Regressions

Dependent Variable: Black EMR ratio

	Regression Coefficients			
Independent Variable	1978	1980	1982	1984
Black teachers (%)	−0.66**	−0.70**	−0.65**	−0.62**
White poverty (%)	−1.93**	−1.04**	−1.03**	−0.84**
Black education (%)	−0.38**	−0.33**	−0.19**	−0.13
Black-white income ratio	−5.89	−15.41	−26.61**	−74.51**
Southern region	11.04**	10.73**	5.37**	4.52*
District size (in thousands)	−0.0118	−0.0019	−0.0010	0.0009
F	28.48	24.37	26.13	24.49
R^2	.53	.49	.55	.54
Adjusted R^2	.51	.47	.53	.52
N	158	159	136	131

*$p < .10$
**$p < .05$

crease in black teachers, the black EMR assignment ratio declines by about 0.66 percent (range 0.62–0.70). The relationship is statistically significant, and the value of the regression coefficients is remarkably stable.

Black resources also have a strong impact on reducing the assignment of blacks to EMR classes. The pattern of relationships for black education and the black-white income ratio suggests that some modest collinearity between these measures makes interpretation difficult. When one indicator has a significant relationship, the other usually does not. To illustrate, in 1980 each 1 percentile increase in blacks with high school diplomas resulted in a 0.33 percent decrease in the black EMR ratio. Similarly in 1982 an increase of 1 in the black-white income ratio resulted in a 26.6 percent decrease in the black EMR ratio. The large value of the income ratio regression coefficient should not come as a surprise because a change of 1 in the income ratio would essentially increase black income by 100 percent of white income while white income remains constant. A more likely impact is that a 1 percentile increase in the black-white income ratio will result in a 0.27 percent decrease in the black EMR index.

Black placement in EMR classes is also associated with white poverty. In school districts with higher percentages of whites living in poverty, blacks are more equitably represented in EMR classes. Three of the coefficients are generally the same size, suggesting that a 1 percentile increase in white poverty will result in a 1 percent decrease in the black EMR ratio. This finding is consistent with our theory that social class operates in such districts to place lower-class whites in EMR classes rather than blacks.

As expected, the southern region has a positive impact on the EMR ratio. It increases the black EMR ratio between 4 and 11 percent. All four coefficients are statistically significant. Finally, district size, although negatively related (as predicted) to black EMR assignment ratios, is not statistically significant.

TMR Classes

Because TMR classes are a more "severe" classification than EMR classes, inappropriately placing a black student in a TMR class is more difficult. As a result the predictive level of a "political" view of TMR assignments should not be as high as the levels for EMR classes. The model explains between 14 percent and 31 percent of the variation in TMR ratios, depending on the year (see table 4.8). While 20 of the 24 relationships are in the predicted direction, the number of significant relationships is fewer than for EMR classes (12 versus 17).

Of all the relationships in table 4.8, the most consistent are again those for black teachers. All four are statistically significant and show that black teachers are able to reduce the assignment of black students to TMR classes. In general,

Table 4.8. Placement of Black Students in TMR Classes: Multivariate Regressions

Dependent Variable: Black TMR ratio

Independent Variable	Regression Coefficients			
	1978	1980	1982	1984
Black teachers (%)	−0.27**	−0.27**	−0.33**	−0.15*
White poverty (%)	−1.16**	−0.28	−0.34	−1.48**
Black education (%)	−0.47**	−0.22*	−0.28*	−0.32
Black-white income ratio	20.81	−4.46	−4.82	−8.21
Southern region	11.44**	15.67**	8.25*	2.39
District size (in thousands)	−0.0141	−0.0040	−0.0056	0.0046
F	7.43	9.67	3.09	4.75
R²	.26	.31	.14	.21
Adjusted R²	.22	.28	.10	.17
N	136	137	120	113

*p < .10
**p < .05

a 1 percentile increase in black teachers results in about a 0.3 percent decrease in the black TMR ratio.

The other reasonably consistent impact on TMR assignments is the southern region. Southern school districts, all things being equal, assign a higher percentage of black students to TMR classes. The estimate is that an increase of between 2.4 percent (for 1984) and 17.0 percent (for 1976; see Appendix A, Table A.11) in the black TMR ratio is associated with southern districts.

Black resources are not as strongly associated with TMR assignments as they are for EMR assignments. Higher levels of black education are consistently associated with lower levels of black student TMR assignments, and three coefficients are significant. None of the relationships for the black-white income ratio is significant; and one of the relationships is not in the predicted direction.

White poverty again appears to reduce the size of the black TMR ratio. In 1978 and 1984 significant coefficients suggest that a 1 percentile increase in white poverty is associated with a bit more than a 1 percent decrease in black TMR assignments. The other coefficients remain in the predicted direction but are no longer significant. Finally, school district size has no impact on TMR assignments.

Gifted Classes

The political model for gifted classes performs fairly well. It accounts for 38–44 percent of the variance in black assignments to gifted classes. All 24 relationships are in the predicted direction, and 23 of them are statistically significant (see table 4.9).

Black teachers are again the strongest predictor of black access to gifted classes. Greater numbers of black teachers result in more black students assigned to gifted classes. The relationship between black teachers and gifted classes varies modestly over time. In 1984 a 1 percentile increase in black teachers is associated with a 0.59 percent increase in the black gifted class ratio.

Black resources also affect black student assignments to gifted classes. All four coefficients for black education are significant, but the actual size of the impact varies too much for a consistent estimate. The black-white income ratio is more consistent. A 1 percentile increase in the black-white income ratio is associated with a 0.56–0.74 percent increase in black student access to gifted classes.

School districts with more white poverty also assign more black students to gifted classes. The four significant coefficients suggest that a 1 percentile increase in white poverty results in a 1.6–2.8 percent increase in the black gifted class ratio. The southern region in turn reduces the black gifted ratio by 11.5–18.9 percent, depending on the year. Finally, large districts are

Table 4.9. Placement of Black Students in Gifted Classes: Multivariate Regressions

Dependent Variable: Black gifted class ratio

Independent Variable	Regression Coefficients			
	1978	1980	1982	1984
Black teachers (%)	0.58**	0.71**	0.84**	0.59**
White poverty (%)	2.73**	1.64**	1.64**	2.84**
Black education (%)	1.29**	0.45**	0.55**	0.36*
Black-white income ratio	59.00*	59.47**	74.07**	55.69**
Southern region	−14.82**	−18.87**	−16.52**	−11.48**
District size (in thousands)	0.0150	0.0391*	0.0739**	0.0377*
F	16.82	14.92	16.84	15.22
R²	.42	.38	.44	.43
Adjusted R²	.40	.35	.41	.40
N	144	154	136	130

*p < .10
**p < .05

associated with a larger black gifted class ratio, exactly what would be expected if we can believe the larger, more professionalized school systems engage in less second-generation discrimination.

Corporal Punishment

Our political theory of second-generation discrimination predicts the incidence of corporal punishment only moderately well. The model explains between 26 and 34 percent of the variation in the black corporal punishment ratio (see table 4.10). Only half of the coefficients are in the direction predicted by the theory, and only seven are statistically significant.

The strongest determinant of corporal punishment is the percentage of black teachers in the district. Black teachers are able to reduce the overrepresentation of black students among the corporally punished. A 1 percentile increase in black teachers is associated with about a 0.6 percent decrease in corporal punishment ratios for black students. All four coefficients are statistically significant.

Black resources are the only other variable consistently related to black corporal punishment ratios. The black income ratio is associated with a reduction in the black corporal punishment ratio. Although three of the income ratio coefficients are negative, none of these is significant. Black education is unrelated to corporal punishment ratios for black students.

Table 4.10. Corporal Punishment of Black Students: Multivariate Regressions

Dependent Variable: Black corporal punishment ratio

Independent Variable	Regression Coefficients			
	1978	1980	1982	1984
Black teachers (%)	−0.59**	−0.63**	−0.64**	−0.46**
White poverty (%)	−0.25	−0.48	−0.12	−0.32
Black education (%)	0.00	−0.10	0.03	−0.03
Black-white income ratio	−10.38	−22.65	−9.31	30.30*
Southern region	−3.10	−2.99	−3.70	−4.44
District size (in thousands)	0.0298	0.0404*	0.0394*	0.0431
F	10.60	7.53	9.01	7.66
R²	.32	.26	.34	.33
Adjusted R²	.29	.23	.30	.29
N	141	136	112	101

*p < .10
**p < .05

Although none of the relationships for white poverty and the southern region is significant, a pattern should be noted. Contrary to expectations, all four coefficients for southern region are negative, indicating that corporal punishment in the South is less biased toward blacks.[18] Larger districts are also associated with more corporal punishment for blacks, again contrary to theoretical expectations.

Suspensions

The modest predictive pattern of the political theory of second-generation discrimination is repeated for the black suspension ratio. The political model is able to explain between 28 and 34 percent of the variation in the suspension ratio (see table 4.11). Fifteen of the 24 relationships are in the direction predicted by the theory; 10 of those relationships are statistically significant.

Once again the strongest predictor of black suspensions is the percentage of black teachers. The more black teachers a school district has, the lower the black suspension ratio is. All coefficients are statistically significant. A

18. Our colleague Theodore P. Robinson suggests that a large number of black principals in all-black schools became vice-principals in the desegregated schools after black schools were closed. Vice-principals are traditionally the individuals in charge of discipline. Although we have no data to substantiate this claim, it appears plausible.

Table 4.11. Suspension of Black Students: Multivariate Regressions

Dependent Variable: Black suspensions ratio

Independent Variable	Regression Coefficients			
	1978	1980	1982	1984
Black teachers (%)	−0.53**	−0.54**	−0.47**	−0.41**
White poverty (%)	0.03	−0.69**	0.52	0.09
Black education (%)	0.01	−0.30**	−0.10	−0.05
Black-white income ratio	−36.74**	−25.16*	−63.47**	−11.44
Southern region	−4.21*	−2.80	−2.51	0.37
District size (in thousands)	−0.0001	0.0042	0.0156	0.0137
F	12.99	11.77	8.87	8.03
R²	.34	.31	.29	.28
Adjusted R²	.31	.28	.25	.25
N	160	164	139	131

*p < .10
**p < .05

1 percentile increase in black teachers is associated with about a 0.5 percent decrease in the black suspension ratio.

Similar to the pattern for corporal punishment, the only other important variable is black resources. Again of the two black resource indicators, the black-white income ratio is the more important. Higher ratios of black to white income are associated with lower black suspension ratios. Although three relationships are statistically significant, the coefficients vary too much to make a single estimate of impact. Black education produces a single statistically significant relationship in 1980, when a 1 percentile increase in black high school graduates resulted in a 0.3 percent decrease in the black suspension ratio.

For the remaining variables, the pattern of relationships can be characterized as inconsistent. White poverty has one statistically significant relationship in the expected direction, but the other three relationships are not in the expected direction. The southern region produces two relationships in each direction, and district size is unrelated to the black suspension ratio.

Expulsions

Expulsions are the most serious form of discipline a school district can administer. Students are generally expelled only after both informal and formal methods of discipline such as corporal punishment and suspensions have been used. The political model of expulsions initially works only modestly well, but over time the predictive ability improves to a moderate level of 43 percent (see table 4.12). Although only 14 relationships are in the predicted direction, many in the direction not predicted are close to zero and, therefore, can be discounted.

Although the model of black student expulsions does not resemble those for other forms of discipline until 1980, the percentage of black teachers is consistently the strongest determinant of the black student expulsion ratio just as it is for other forms of discipline. A 1 percentile increase in black teachers is associated with a 0.65–0.97 percent decrease in the black expulsion ratio. The relationships are statistically significant.

Black resources are not as good a predictor of expulsions as they are of suspensions and corporal punishment. Black education is not significantly related to expulsions, and only for 1978 and 1980 is the black-white income ratio significant. In 1980 an increase of 1 percentile in the black-white income ratio resulted in a 0.5 percent decline in the black expulsion ratio.

Both white poverty and school district size are unrelated to the black expulsion ratio. The most interesting relationship in table 4.12 is that for the southern region. In 1974, southern school districts expelled proportionately more black students but by 1978 expelled proportionately fewer. The relationship is statistically significant by 1980, when southern school districts had a black expulsion ratio of 10 percent less than northern districts, all other things be-

Table 4.12. Expulsion of Black Students: Multivariate Regressions

Dependent Variable: Black expulsions ratio

	Regression Coefficients			
Independent Variable	1974	1976	1978	1980
Black teachers (%)	−0.65**	−0.71**	−0.97**	−0.74**
White poverty (%)	−0.22	−1.18	1.28*	−0.58
Black education (%)	0.09	0.25	0.24	−0.08
Black-white income ratio	13.07	−46.68	−93.47**	−52.55*
Southern region	6.93	0.35	−2.04	−9.98**
District size (in thousands)	0.0024	−0.0058	0.0266	0.0230
F	3.77	6.64	9.50	7.11
R^2	.22	.28	.43	.34
Adjusted R^2	.16	.24	.39	.29
N	87	110	82	89

*$p < .10$
**$p < .05$

ing equal. This finding is consistent with the impact for southern school districts in tables 4.10 and 4.11. In recent years southern school districts have used proportionately less corporal punishment and fewer suspensions and expulsions against black students. The pattern of second-generation discrimination in southern school district appears to be different from that in northern districts. Although southern districts are more likely to rely on academic grouping, they are less likely to use discriminatory disciplinary practices.

High School Graduation

High school graduation is a result of a wide variety of educational policies, individual efforts, family variables, and other forces. The political model, based as it is on the concept of second-generation discrimination, should not be strongly linked to a measure that is influenced by so many other factors. The modest results of the political model (see table 4.13) are somewhat predictable then. The political model is able to explain between 23 and 30 percent of the variation in black graduation ratios. Despite this low level of prediction, 16 of the 24 relationships are in the predicted direction, and 12 of these are statistically significant.

Once again black teachers are a strong force in affecting the black-white graduation ratio. School districts with larger percentages of black teachers consistently have higher proportions of black students who graduate from high

Table 4.13. Black High School Graduates: Multivariate Regressions

Dependent Variable: Black graduation ratio

Independent Variable	Regression Coefficients			
	1978	1980	1982	1984
Black teachers (%)	0.14**	0.17**	0.18**	0.15**
White poverty (%)	0.98**	0.56**	0.80**	0.73**
Black education (%)	−0.14*	−0.24**	−0.09	−0.19**
Black-white income ratio	27.86**	33.81**	28.43**	25.37**
Southern region	2.13	2.67	0.41	1.80
District size (in thousands)	0.0059	0.0111	0.0125	0.0115
F	8.01	11.01	6.74	7.93
R^2	.24	.30	.23	.28
Adjusted R^2	.21	.27	.20	.24
N	161	164	139	131

*$p < .10$
**$p < .05$

school. This relationship increases modestly over time; by 1982 a 1 percentile increase in black teachers results in a 0.18 percent increase in the black student graduation ratio.

Black resources form a confusing pattern with the black graduation ratio. All four relationships for black education are negative, three of those are statistically significant (albeit barely). No logical reason exists why communities with better-educated blacks would have school systems graduating fewer blacks from high school. This finding must be treated as an anomaly until a logical explanation is found. The black-white income ratio, on the other hand, performs as expected. All four relationships are in the predicted direction, and all are statistically significant.

Neither southern region nor school district size (except for 1980) is related to black graduation ratios. White poverty, on the other hand, has a strong and consistent relationship with black graduation rates. School districts with a large percentage of white poverty have a larger proportion of blacks who graduate from high school. In districts then where numerous whites suffer from many of the same economic disadvantages experienced by the blacks, the class biases of the educational system affect greater numbers of the white students. This white class relationship in turn appears to benefit the districts' black students.

Dropouts

Because dropout rates are closely linked to graduation rates, our expectations for the political model are low for the dropout ratio just as they were for the ratio of high school graduates. In the only year for which OCR gathered dropout data, the political model explains a mere 16 percent of the variation in the black dropout ratio (see table 4.14).

The modest relationships for dropouts can be summarized quickly. The strongest predictor, albeit a weak one, of the black dropout ratio is the black-white income ratio. An increase of 1 percentile in the black-white income ratio is associated with a 0.58 percent decline in the black dropout ratio. The only other significant relationship is for black teachers. A 1 percentile increase in black teachers results in a 0.14 percent decline in the black dropout ratio. The other coefficients are not significantly different from zero.

The Political Model: A Summary

The political model of second-generation discrimination works best for academic grouping. The black EMR ratio is available for seven different time periods (including the three shown in Appendix A), and six political variables result in 42 predictions concerning relationships. In 40 of the 42 cases, the direction of the relationship for the black EMR ratio is in the predicted direction. Thirty-one of those relationships are statistically significant. The two relationships in the direction not predicted are not significant (both for district size).

Table 4.14. Black Dropouts: Multivariate Regression for 1976

Dependent Variable: Black dropout ratio

Independent Variables	Regression Coefficients
Black teachers (%)	−0.14*
White poverty (%)	0.03
Black education (%)	−0.04
Black-white income ratio	−58.61**
Southern region	−3.61
District size (in thousands)	0.0414

F = .4.92
R² = .16
Adjusted R² = .13
N = 162

*p < .10
**p < .05

Similar though not quite as impressive results were found for TMR classes. Thirty-five of the 42 relationships (83 percent) are in the predicted direction, and 21 are statistically significant. The seven relationships in the direction not predicted are not significantly different from zero. For gifted classes, the excellent pattern of predictability continues. All of the 30 relationships are in the predicted direction, and 26 are statistically significant.

The political model has a moderate ability to explain variations in corporal punishment. The results are still good but not as close to prediction as they are for academic grouping. Sixteen of the 30 relationships for corporal punishment are in the expected direction, and five of those are statistically significant. Three relationships in the direction not expected (two for district size and one for income) are significantly different from zero.

The political model explains suspensions better than corporal punishment. Of the 42 predicted relationships, 28 are in the expected direction. Twenty of these are statistically significant. For expulsions, 23 of 42 relationships are in the predicted direction, and 11 are significant. Two relationships not in the predicted direction are statistically significant. One of these, the relationship for the southern region, may indicate a change in policies in southern schools.

The political model predicts educational outcome only modestly well. Of the 30 predicted relationships for high school graduates, 19 are in the expected direction, and 13 are statistically significant. In the most notable violation of the logic of the model, three of the relationships in the direction not expected (all for black education) are significant. For the one measure of black dropouts, three of the six relationships are in the predicted direction. Two of these are significant, and none of those in the direction not predicted is significantly different from zero.

Overall, the results of the model must be considered fairly good. Over several different years and eight different indicators of second-generation discrimination, 194 of the 264 relationships are in the predicted direction. The probability that 73.5 percent of the relationships would be in the predicted direction on a random basis is astronomically low. Fully 48.1 of the relationships (127) are statistically significant. In only eight cases are relationships in the direction not predicted significantly different from zero, and in one of those cases the change in direction can be explained.

Another way to assess the impact of the political model is to examine the individual predictive variables. Without a doubt the single best predictor of second-generation discrimination is the percentage of black teachers. In all 44 of the cases, higher percentages of black teachers are associated with lower levels of second-generation discrimination. In 43 of the cases, the coefficients are statistically significant.

The second best overall predictor of second-generation discrimination is the black-white income ratio. In 39 of the 44 cases the income ratio produces a relationship in the expected direction, and 22 relationships are significant. Higher black-white income ratios are associated with lower levels of second-generation discrimination.

White poverty is the third best predictor of second-generation discrimination. Our indicator of class impact, white poverty, produces 34 of 44 relationships in the predicted direction and 20 statistically significant relationships. Higher levels of white poverty result in lower levels of second-generation discrimination against black students.

The southern region, our surrogate for a variety of education differences by region, is the next best predictor. Twenty-seven of the 44 relationships for region are in the predicted direction, and 21 are significant. Southern schools have had higher levels of second-generation discrimination against blacks. The significant relationship in the direction not predicted (expulsions) may reflect changes in the use of discipline in southern schools.

Black education, a measure of black political resources, has a mixed pattern of impact. Twenty-seven of the 44 relationships are in the direction not predicted, and only 16 are statistically significant. In addition, three relationships for black education are significant in the direction not predicted. In general higher levels of black education result in lower levels of second-generation discrimination, but the generalization sometimes does not hold.

Finally, district size has no real impact on second-generation discrimination. Only 22 of the 44 relationships are in the expected direction, and only

5 of the relationships are statistically significant (2 in the direction not expected). The safe conclusion is that district size has little if any impact on second-generation discrimination against black students.

Summary

This chapter has examined several aspects of what we have termed second-generation discrimination against black students. First, using representation ratios, we have examined the assignment of blacks to EMR, TMR, and gifted classes, the use of corporal punishment, suspensions, and expulsions to discipline blacks, and educational attainment represented by high school graduation rates and dropout rates. In every case, blacks are overrepresented in every category with a negative connotation and underrepresented in every category with a positive connotation. This pattern holds for every year the Office for Civil Rights gathered data.

Second, we have argued that this pattern results from discrimination. Discrimination is indicated by three sets of findings. The indicators, as just noted, are all in a direction consistent with discrimination. The intercorrelations among the policy indicators reflect a pattern that is predicted by a hypothesis of discrimination, which is true as well of the clusters produced by the factor analysis.

Third, we have examined the individual measures of policy using a political theory of second-generation discrimination. Second-generation discrimination is lower in districts with a large percentage of black teachers, with a black population with ample resources (especially the ratio of black to white incomes), with large numbers of poor whites, and in northern school districts. The greatest single influence on policies of second-generation educational discrimination is the racial distribution of the teaching faculty. The political theory of second-generation discrimination results in good predictive levels for academic grouping, moderate levels for discipline, and low levels for educational outcome.

5 The Consequences of Second-Generation Discrimination

Chapter 4 argues that academic grouping, discipline, and educational attainment have a common core that may be termed second-generation educational discrimination. Such discrimination against black students is related to a variety of political factors including representation among black teachers, black political resources, social class, and region. This chapter examines some consequences and impacts of second-generation educational discrimination. First, we probe the interrelationships between the various forms of second-generation discrimination. Second, an in-depth look at disciplinary practices asks if corporal punishment and suspensions have a deterrent effect. Third, second-generation discrimination is contrasted with desegregation. Fourth, we investigate the linkage between second-generation discrimination and declining white enrollments. Fifth, we examine the relationship between second-generation discrimination and declining black enrollments.

The Interrelationships of Second-Generation Discrimination

Acts of racial discrimination by academic grouping or discipline are not discrete events. They form a pattern of actions that limit the equal access of black students to the best education available in the school district. Discrimination in academic grouping produces inequalities in discipline, and both in turn can affect the ability of blacks to graduate from high school. The theoretical interrelationships of the second-generation discrimination measures are shown in figure 5.1. Our data set provides a unique opportunity to examine the linkages shown in this figure.[1]

The model in figure 5.1 should not be interpreted as a rigid deterministic model. We are not arguing, for example, that the only determinant of dispropor-

1. This is the first study to examine any of the interrelationships between the individual items of second-generation discrimination, except for Finn, 1982 (p. 355), which examines the relationship between black EMR ratios and black suspensions.

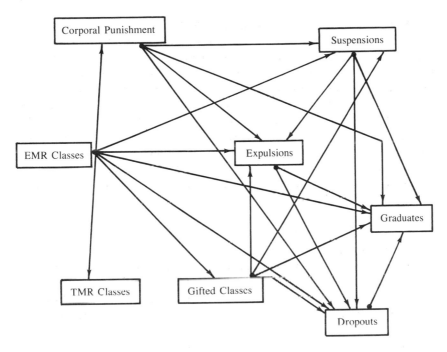

Figure 5.1. The Interrelationships of Second-Generation Educational Discrimination Measures: Preliminary Model.

tionate placement of blacks in TMR classes is the placement of blacks in EMR classes. A wide variety of factors affect placement in TMR classes, including the characteristics of the student and the teacher, funds for TMR classes, procedures used to classify students, emphasis on special education in the school district, and so on. Our interest is not in fully explaining black TMR enrollments; rather our purpose is to postulate a theoretical model of relationships that would exist if discrimination against black students were to underlie these actions. This theoretical model is then compared with the data to see if the data are consistent with the model. If the results are inconsistent with the model, then we will reject discrimination as a determinant. If the results are consistent with the model, then the hypothesis of discrimination will gain credibility.

TMR Classes

The second-generation discrimination model suggests that placement of blacks in TMR classes is a function of their placement in EMR classes. If EMR classes are used to separate out black students who might be behavior problems or more difficult to teach, then a large number of black students will be referred to EMR classes. Enrollment pressures on EMR classes require a response, because school districts do not have unlimited resources for this type of class. One way to ease some of the crowding in EMR classes is to shift some of the students from these classes to TMR classes.[2] If race is a consideration in initial assignments to EMR classes, then race is quite likely a reason to assign students to TMR classes, either initially or as the result of EMR pressures.

Table 5.1 shows the relationships between EMR and TMR classes from 1978 through 1984.[3] The relationships show remarkable consistency over the six-year period. School districts that disproportionately assign blacks to EMR classes also disproportionately assign blacks to TMR classes. Using the average of the four slope estimates, a 1 percent increase in the black EMR ratio is associated with a 0.39 percent increase in the black TMR ratio.

Gifted Classes

Gifted classes are at the opposite end of the educational spectrum from EMR and TMR classes. In theory, assignments to gifted classes should be unrelated to EMR assignments, because each type of class should serve a completely different type of student. Viewing academic grouping as a discriminatory process, however, suggests that discrimination in academic grouping will occur at all its levels. This view implies that districts with high black EMR enrollments will have low black gifted class enrollments.

Table 5.1. Relationship between Placements in TMR and EMR Classes

Dependent Variable: TMR class ratio

Independent Variable	Regression Coefficients			
	1978	1980	1982	1984
EMR class ratio	0.35*	0.46*	0.44*	0.31*
F	23.11	45.37	16.91	15.37
r^2	.15	.25	.13	.12
N	137	136	118	114

*$p < .05$

2. A student who actually belongs in an EMR class, for example, might be designated as not able to master the work in a class for educable mentally retarded. Such a student might then be inappropriately shifted to a class for the trainable mentally retarded.

3. In all cases we have used the log transformation of the racial ratios. This procedure results in a more explicable interpretation of the coefficients and is consistent with the analysis in the previous chapter. It is also consistent with the work of Finn (1982).

The relationship between the black enrollment ratio for EMR classes and the black enrollment ratio for gifted classes is presented in table 5.2. A strong, reasonably consistent, negative relationship exists. A 1 percent increase in the black EMR ratio is associated with a 0.75–1.18 percent drop in the black gifted class ratio. Averaging the coefficients produces our estimate that a 1 percent increase in black EMR enrollments is associated with a 0.92 percent decline in black gifted class enrollments.

Corporal Punishment

In our theory of second-generation discrimination, we argue that negative academic grouping of black students will be associated with the increased use of discipline against black students. Because corporal punishment is the first of the disciplinary procedures likely to be used, it should be related to only the first academic grouping measure, placement in EMR classes. When EMR enrollments are controlled, in fact, no relationship exists between corporal punishment and placement in either TMR or gifted classes. Our model hypothesizes a simple positive relationship between the black EMR ratio and the black corporal punishment ratio.

The association between corporal punishment and EMR classes is depicted in table 5.3. For three of four years, school districts with higher black EMR ratios also have higher black corporal punishment ratios. Using the four regression coefficients to estimate the impact's magnitude suggests that a 1 percent increase in the black EMR ratio is associated with a 0.29 percent increase in the black corporal punishment ratio.

Suspensions

Figure 5.1 implies that suspensions are a function of corporal punishment plus placement in EMR classes and exclusion from gifted classes. The linkage bet-

Table 5.2. Relationship between Placements in Gifted and EMR Classes

Dependent Variable: Gifted class ratio

| Independent Variable | Regression Coefficients | | | |
	1978	1980	1982	1984
EMR class ratio	−0.75*	−0.87*	−1.18*	−0.86*
F	25.64	48.54	63.56	46.24
r^2	.15	.24	.32	.27
N	144	153	134	129

*$p < .05$

Table 5.3. Relationship between Corporal Punishment and Placement in EMR Classes

Dependent Variable: Corporal punishment ratio

Independent Variable	Regression Coefficients			
	1978	1980	1982	1984
EMR class ratio	0.43*	0.30*	0.42*	0.01
F	38.14	12.67	17.62	.01
r²	.22	.09	.14	.00
N	141	136	110	100

*p < .05

ween corporal punishment and suspensions is direct; both are forms of discipline. If black students are disproportionately corporally punished, we would also expect them to be disproportionately suspended. A student inappropriately placed in an EMR class or excluded from a gifted class will find school less challenging than it should be. The absence of challenge may well generate student dissatisfaction, which in turn will create behavior problems. Disproportionate black suspensions, then, can also result from inappropriate academic grouping.

The relationships between the black suspension ratio and ratios for corporal punishment, EMR classes, and gifted classes are shown in the full model in table 5.4. Although the pattern is not particularly consistent over time, it generally fits with the model of discrimination in figure 5.1. More suspensions of black students are strongly related to more corporal punishment of black students and more assignments of black students to EMR classes. More placements of blacks in gifted classes are negatively and weakly related to black suspension ratios. All things being equal, the averages of these coefficients indicate that a 1 percent increase in the black corporal punishment ratio is associated with a 0.38 percent increase in the suspension ratio; a 1 percent increase in the black EMR class ratio produces a 0.15 percent increase in the suspension ratio; and a 1 percent increase in the black gifted class ratio corresponds with a 0.03 percent decline in the black suspension ratio.

The weak relationship between gifted classes and suspensions suggests that the equations should be reestimated without gifted classes to determine if the inclusion is necessary. The reduced model in table 5.4 indicates that suspensions are a function of only EMR classes and corporal punishment. Although these estimates are more consistent than those in the full model, the predictive level of this model drops from 1 to 6 percentage points. The slightly superior

Table 5.4. Relationship between Suspensions and Other Second-Generation Discrimination Measures

Dependent Variable: Suspension ratio

Independent Variable	Regression Coefficients			
	1978	1980	1982	1984
Full Model				
Corporal punishment ratio	0.26*	0.43*	0.46*	0.35*
EMR class ratio	0.26*	0.14*	−0.03	0.23*
Gifted class ratio	0.02	−0.02	−0.11*	0.01
F	29.21	27.85	12.54	22.64
R^2	.42	.40	.26	.42
Adjusted R^2	.40	.39	.24	.40
N	127	128	109	99
Reduced Model				
Corporal punishment ratio	0.27*	0.39*	0.43*	0.34*
EMR class ratio	0.24*	0 14*	0.10	0.23*
F	38.45	35.66	16.41	33.13
R^2	.36	.35	.23	.41
Adjusted R^2	.35	.34	.22	.39
N	141	136	110	100

*p < .05

predictive ability of the full model, which includes gifted classes, indicates that it is a better view of the suspension process.

Expulsions

According to figure 5.1 the expulsion of black students is a function of disparities in both discipline and academic grouping. Inappropriate discipline is unlikely to have a positive effect on a student. Disproportionate black ratios for corporal punishment and suspensions should be positively related to black expulsion ratios. Negative academic grouping actions should affect expulsions the same way they affect suspensions. High black EMR class ratios and low black gifted class ratios should be associated with high black expulsion ratios.

The four-variable model of the black expulsion ratio is shown in the full model in table 5.5. A pattern is immediately apparent. Both gifted class assignments and corporal punishment are unrelated to expulsions. Whatever

Table 5.5. Relationship between Expulsions and Other Second-Generation Discrimination Measures

Dependent Variable: Explusion ratio

	Regression Coefficients		
Independent Variable	1976	1978	1980
Full Model			
Corporal punishment ratio	0.34	0.19	0.27
EMR class ratio	0.30	0.62**	0.10
Suspension ratio	0.10	0.15	0.75**
Gifted class ratio	0.01	0.01	−0.11
F	2.42	6.55	8.64
R^2	.15	.28	.33
Adjusted R^2	.09	.24	.29
N	61	72	75
Reduced Model			
EMR class ratio	0.41**	0.39**	0.24*
Suspension ratio	0.21	0.60**	0.89**
F	8.87	13.45	20.78
R^2	.14	.25	.32
Adjusted R^2	.13	.23	.31
N	112	83	90

*$p < .10$
**$p < .05$

impact these variables have on the black suspension ratio must be mediated though one of the other variables.

To provide a more parsimonious view of expulsions, the model was reestimated using only EMR classes and suspensions to predict the black expulsion ratio (see the reduced model in table 5.5). The superiority of the two-variable model can be seen by comparing the adjusted explained variation. In addition, the coefficients in the reduced model are more stable than those in the full model. Using the averages of these coefficients to estimate the overall relationship, a 1 percent increase in the black suspension ratio is associated with a 0.57 percent increase in the black expulsion ratio; and a 1 percent increase in the black EMR class ratio corresponds to a 0.35 percent increase in the black expulsion ratio.

Dropouts

Dropouts, according to the model in figure 5.1, should be positively related to corporal punishment, suspensions, expulsions, and EMR classes; they should be negatively related to gifted classes. Because the OCR gathered data on dropouts only for 1976, any assessment of dropouts is speculative. Only with several measures for different years can we be sure that consistent relationships exist.

Table 5.6 shows the relationships between the black dropout ratio and the various forms of academic grouping and discipline. As noted in the previous chapter, dropout rates have numerous causes, so high levels of explanation using a limited number of variables should not be expected. The predictive level of the model is modest, and only one significant relationship is found. A 1 percent increase in the black expulsion ratio results in a 0.12 percent increase in the black dropout ratio.

High School Graduates

The last variable in the internal model of second-generation discrimination is high school graduations. Denying blacks equal access to quality education can occur without affecting black graduation rates; the quality of education a black graduate receives can well be lower than the quality of education a white graduate receives. High school graduation ratios, therefore, reflect only one

Table 5.6. Relationship between Dropout Rates and Other Second-Generation Discrimination Measures, 1976

Dependent Variable: Dropout ratio

Independent Variable	Regression Coefficient
Corporal punishment ratio	0.09
EMR class ratio	0.19
Suspension ratio	−0.18
Expulsion ratio	0.12*
Gifted class ratio	0.05

$F = 2.45$
$R^2 = .18$
Adjusted $R^2 = .11$
$N = 61$

*$p < .05$

aspect of educational quality. Black high school graduation ratios in theory should be negatively related to black EMR ratios, black corporal punishment ratios, black suspension ratios, and black expulsion ratios. They should also be positively associated with black gifted ratios. Because dropout data were gathered for only one year, this variable was not included in the analysis.

The relationships in table 5.7 reveal a mixed but reasonably consistent pattern. Expulsions are unrelated to graduation rates. Although gifted classes generally do not affect graduation, they had a significant impact in 1984. Both corporal punishment and EMR assignments are negatively linked to graduation rates; in the case of EMR classes, three of the regression coefficients are significant. Finally, the unexpected positive relationship between suspensions and graduation rates is a result of collinearity among the independent variables.

The results of this examination of the interrelationships between the various forms of second-generation discrimination produce a less complex version of the model in figure 5.1. Figure 5.2 shows the interrelationships between second-generation-discrimination indicators for which consistent evidence exists. The coefficients in the figure are nothing more than the average regression coefficients generated by tables 5.1 through 5.7.

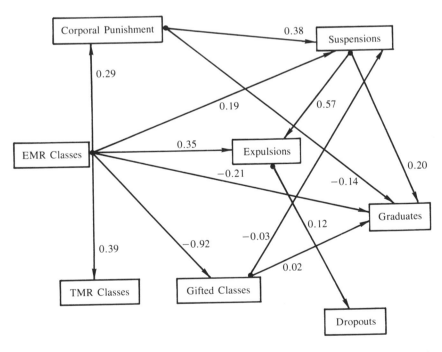

Figure 5.2. The Interrelationships of Second-Generation Educational Discrimination: Final Model.

Table 5.7. Relationship between High School Graduation Rates and Other Second-Generation Discrimination Measures

Dependent Variable: High school graduation ratio

Independent Variable	Regression Coefficients			
	1978	1980	1982	1984
Corporal punishment ratio	−0.34**	−0.12	−0.04	−0.07
EMR class ratio	−0.30**	−0.21**	−0.22**	−0.10
Suspension ratio	0.37*	0.14	0.24*	0.04
Expulsion ratio	0.05	−0.00	—	—
Gifted class ratio	−0.03	0.03	0.01	0.08**
F	4.18	2.61	1.54	3.28
R^2	.24	.16	.08	.12
Adjusted R^2	.18	.10	.03	.09
N	72	75	99	98

*$p < .10$
**$p < .05$

By following the linkages in this model, one can see how the various forms of second-generation discrimination are related. For example, the black suspension ratio is a function of the black corporal punishment ratio, the black gifted class ratio, and the black EMR class ratio. The figure is rather self-explanatory. What is striking about it is the crucial role that EMR classes play in the process. EMR ratios directly affect corporal punishment, suspensions, TMR classes, gifted classes, expulsions, and high school graduation rates; they indirectly affect dropout rates. If one is looking for the single best indicator of second-generation discrimination, the black EMR assignment ratio is it.

The Deterrent Effect of Punishment

Chapter 4 reveals that black students receive more corporal punishment, suspensions, and expulsions than do white students. Although we attribute such differentials to institutional second-generation discrimination, one counter argument to our position remains. Disciplinary practices are, of course, justified by reference to a school system's need to maintain an educational environment conducive to learning. If students cannot learn because individuals are disrupting the classroom, discipline is necessary. Racial differences in the frequency of discipline, therefore, might reflect differences in actual behavior.[4]

4. We have rejected this position. We find no evidence in the literature that the behavior of black students is appreciably different from the behavior of other students.

In such circumstances, these differences might be justified with the argument that discipline deters inappropriate behavior.

The deterrence theory of discipline holds that students should be disciplined frequently enough and visibly enough so that other students are deterred from unacceptable behavior. The deterrent impact of discipline is not necessarily on the student being disciplined (although one would hope that it has some impact), but rather on other students likely to engage in unacceptable behavior. If deterrence works, then one would expect a high frequency of discipline now to have an impact on behavior in the future.

The time-series nature of the data set permits us to test the deterrent effect of corporal punishment and suspensions. Corporal punishment, in theory, acts as a deterrent and reduces the number of suspensions or expulsions needed. Suspensions, in turn, also act as a deterrent and reduce the number of expulsions needed.

Testing the deterrent impact of discipline cannot be done simply by correlating corporal punishment in 1984 with suspensions in 1984. This correlation is positive (see above), suggesting that a third variable might be causing a difference between races in the frequency of both corporal punishment and suspensions. We contend that this third variable is discrimination, but for the sake of examining the deterrence theory we will assume that the level of behavior problems has an impact on both. If the level of behavior problems affects both corporal punishment and suspensions in 1984, then one way to control for the level of behavior problems is to control statistically for suspensions in 1982 (because they are also determined by the level of behavior problems). If corporal punishment acts as a deterrent, then one would expect a negative relationship between corporal punishment and suspensions when controlling for the previous level of suspensions.

Because the deterrence theory concerns the level frequency of discipline of all students rather than the racial disparity in its uses, our measurement of discipline must be changed. The level of corporal punishment is defined as the percentage of students that receive corporal punishment. Similar measures are calculated for suspensions and expulsions. To illustrate racial differences, percentages for both black and white students are used.

Deterrence: Corporal Punishment and Suspensions

If corporal punishment were to act as a deterrent and reduce suspensions, it could do so in two ways. First, corporal punishment could have an immediate impact on suspensions; that is, corporal punishment in 1984 would be negatively related to suspensions in 1984, controlling for suspensions in 1982. Second, corporal punishment might have a delayed impact, because corporal punishment and suspensions might convince other students to change their behavior. In this case, corporal punishment in 1982 would have a negative impact on suspensions in 1984 when suspensions in 1982 are controlled.

To test the immediate and delayed impacts, we will not use data for individual years. We will take full advantage of the time-series nature of the data set and use a pooled, longitudinal design. This process will produce a single estimate of deterrence for all years simultaneously.

The two models of corporal punishment's impact on suspensions are presented in table 5.8. A deterrent effect would be represented by a significant negative regression coefficient for corporal punishment. For both immediate impact and lagged impact, corporal punishment of blacks is negatively related to suspension of blacks, but the coefficients are insignificant. The results for white students are identical. Both sets of results contradict the hypothesis that corporal punishment deters suspensions.

Table 5.8. Impact of Corporal Punishment on Suspensions

Dependent Variable: Suspensions $_t$

Independent Variable	Regression Coefficients	
	Blacks	Whites
Immediate Impact		
Corporal punishment $_t$	−0.016	−0.018
Suspensions $_{t-1}$	0.345*	0.783*
F	88.51	357.10
R^2	.26	.59
Adjusted R^2	.26	.59
N	507	504
Lagged Impact		
Corporal punishment $_{t-1}$	−0.023	−0.019
Suspensions $_{t-1}$	0.711*	0.768*
F	196.84	259.17
R^2	.50	.57
Adjusted R^2	.50	.57
N	391	389

*p < .05

Suspensions Deterring Expulsions

Because corporal punishment is not permitted in nine states (Baker et al., 1987), the absence of a deterrent effect for corporal punishment might be the result of some districts not using this method of discipline. A second look at the question of deterrence without this limitation can be had by viewing suspensions as a deterrent for expulsions. Table 5.9 shows these deterrent equations for the immediate impact of suspensions and for the lagged impact. Again the results are totally inconsistent with the notion of deterrence. The immediate-impact equations show suspensions having no impact on expulsions for either white or black students. In terms of the lagged impact, a similar lack of impact on expulsions exists for both groups of students.

Both Suspensions and Corporal Punishment as Deterrents

Perhaps the deferrent effects of suspensions and corporal punishment are clear only when both are considered simultaneously. Although two variables that

Table 5.9. Impact of Suspensions on Expulsions

Dependent Variable: Expulsions $_t$

Independent Variable	Regression Coefficients	
	Blacks	Whites
Immediate Impact		
Suspensions $_t$	0.014	0.010
Expulsions $_t$	0.117*	0.050
F	2.17	.27
R^2	.02	.00
Adjusted R^2	.01	.00
N	189	164
Lagged Impact		
Suspensions $_{t-1}$	0.009	−0.010
Expulsions $_{t-1}$	0.115*	0.051
F	1.84	.25
R^2	.02	.00
Adjusted R^2	.01	.00
N	188	163

*$p < .10$

produce no relationships in simple regressions are unlikely to produce significant negative relationhips in a multiple regression, it is possible. Table 5.10
shows the immediate and lagged impact of suspensions and corporal punishment on expulsions. The immediate-impact equations show no impact for either
suspensions or corporal punishment on expulsions. The lagged-impact equations also show no significant relationships between suspensions or corporal
punishment and expulsions. These results are inconsistent with the deterrence
theory of discipline.

Overall, this effort to assess the deterrent effect of disciplinary practices
in schools has not produced supportive results let alone convincing results.
We began with the acceptance of an assumption consistent with the deterrence
theory (namely, that high frequency of discipline reflects high levels of inap-

Table 5.10. Impact of Other Disciplinary Measures on Expulsions

Dependent Variable: Expulsions $_t$

Independent Variable	Regression Coefficients	
	Blacks	Whites
Immediate Impact		
Suspensions $_t$	0.014	0.005
Corporal punishment $_t$	0.000	−0.001
Expulsions $_{t-1}$	0.159**	0.428*
F	1.72	1.20
R^2	.03	.02
Adjusted R^2	.01	.01
N	168	148
Lagged Impact		
Suspensions $_{t-1}$	−0.026	−0.046
Corporal punishment $_{t-1}$	0.001	0.007
Expulsions $_{t-1}$	0.775**	1.517**
F	2.41	2.23
R^2	.06	.07
Adjusted R^2	.04	.04
N	110	100

*p < .10
**p < .05

propriate behavior), yet not a single significant coefficient in the direction predicted by the deterrence hypothesis has been found. In many cases coefficients are not in the predicted direction for either black or white students.

In short, no evidence exists consistent with a hypothesis that in-school discipline acts as a deterrent to inappropriate behavior. This finding underscores the argument presented in the previous chapter that racial differentials in discipline are part of a process of second-generation discrimination. More frequent discipline against black students does not result in a future decline in discipline against black students. Neither is more frequent discipline against black students associated with improved performances by those blacks who remain in school (see table 5.7).

One final aspect of discipline as a form of deterrence merits brief attention. Bennett and Harris (1982) have suggested that discipline and dropouts are related in a manner opposite of what is normally supposed. We interpret discipline as a method of discouraging students, which results in more dropouts. Bennett and Harris (1982: 411) propose that maybe the reverse is true, that school officials encourage individuals who are behavior problems to drop out. This process, if true, would mean that school officials are seeking to lower discipline rates by removing their greatest behavior problems.

Unfortunately, the OCR data set gathered dropout data for only one year, 1976. Still, this information provides a limited view of whether or not increasing the number of dropouts can reduce future behavior problems. The approach is straightforward. The percentage of black dropouts is used as an independent variable to predict the percentage of black corporal punishment, suspensions, and expulsions for 1976 and all subsequent years. A negative relationship for 1976 would indicate that higher dropout rates have an immediate effect on the needed rate of discipline. Negative relationships for years 1978, 1980, 1982, and 1984 would show a delayed impact.

The dropouts-versus-discipline regressions are shown in table 5.11. The results are fairly consistent. Only a modest relationship exists between dropouts and subsequent suspensions, but that relationship is positive not negative. A small negative relationship exists between dropouts and corporal punishment, but this relationship is not statistically different from zero. Expulsions are generally unrelated to dropouts (except for a positive relationship in 1978). The evidence indicates that school officials cannot affect future discipline rates by encouraging students to drop out of school. Such advice might eliminate a few exceptionally troublesome students, but it will not solve a school's behavior problems. In addition, if discrimination plays a role in discipline and the advice to drop out, such action serves to perpetuate racial inequities in access to education.

Table 5.11. Impact of Black Dropouts on Subsequent Discipline of Blacks

Independent Variable: Percentage of black dropouts, 1976

Dependent Variables	Regression	t-score	R^2	N
Black suspensions (%)				
1976	0.77	3.84*	.11	119
1978	0.56	3.06*	.07	120
1980	0.49	2.18*	.04	121
1982	0.49	2.02*	.03	121
1984	1.55	6.94*	.35	93
Black corporal				
punishment (%)				
1976	−0.52	0.29	.00	102
1978	−0.91	1.23	.01	110
1980	−1.30	1.88	.03	102
1982	−0.94	1.40	.02	101
1984	−0.29	0.97	.01	93
Black expulsions (%)				
1976	0.00	0.00	.00	93
1978	0.08	2.04*	.06	73
1980	−0.01	0.00	.00	75

*p < .05

Desegregation and Second-Generation Discrimination

The use of academic grouping and discipline to resegregate classrooms has generally been associated with desegregation. Actions such as second-generation discrimination became visible in the South after southern schools were forced to desegregate in the late 1960s and early 1970s (Rodgers and Bullock, 1972; Children's Defense Fund, 1974; Smith and Dziuban, 1977; Eyler, Cook, and Ward, 1983; Trent, 1981). In the South such a linkage makes sense. Southern states maintained two separate school systems—one for blacks and one for whites. Until desegregation, second-generation discrimination techniques could not be used, because black and white students did not go to the same schools. Only after desegregation has it been possible for southern school districts to use second-generation discrimination to resegregate schools.

Second-generation educational discrimination, however, is not limited to southern school systems. At the present time, racial disparities in academic grouping, discipline, and educational outcomes occur in northern as well as southern districts. Although many northern school districts did, and some still do, maintain highly segregated school systems on a de facto basis, the level of segregation was not as complete as could be maintained with a *de jure* system. As a result, some racial mixing occurred in the urban North prior to desegregation efforts. Such a system means that northern school districts had the potential to use academic grouping and discipline to segregate students even before formal desegregation efforts were begun. Second-generation educational discrimination in this situation could occur simultaneously with segregation.

Any attempt at a systematic examination of the relationship between second-generation educational discrimination and desegregation is limited by lack of data. The Office for Civil Rights did not begin gathering data on second-generation discrimination until after most southern schools were desegregated. A full set of measures was not collected until 1976. This absence of data means that assessing the linkage between desegregation and second-generation discrimination can be done only indirectly.

If second-generation educational discrimination is used as a substitute for segregation, then we would expect that schools which experienced the greatest levels of desegregation would engage in the greatest second-generation discrimination against blacks (Finn, 1982: 353; but see Bickel, 1982: 190). In short, the relationship between school segregation and indicators of second-generation educational discrimination should be negative. For such a relationship to be examined, school districts must vary in the degree of desegregation.

The most common measure of school segregation is the Taeuber Dissimilarity Index (Taeuber and Taeuber, 1965), originally created to measure residential segregation. The Taeuber index measures the percentage of students that need to be moved from one school to another so that all schools in the district have the same racial distribution. An index of 100.0 means that a school district is completely segregated with no whites attending school with blacks. An index of 0.0 means that every school in the district has a racial distribution that exactly matches the districtwide racial distribution.

Table 5.12 shows the Taeuber indices for the school districts in our study. The impact of the desegregation movement of the late 1960s and early 1970s is evident, because the mean index dropped from 73.2 percent to 46.1 percent. The 1976 index reveals that the average district still had to move 46.1 percent of its students to attain perfect racial balance in all its schools. The table also reveals the tremendous variation in school segregation in the United States (standard deviation in 1976, 19.5). Schools ranged from an index of 11.0 percent (fairly well desegregated) to 91.9 (highly segregated) in 1976.

The correlations between the level of segregation in 1976 and measures of academic grouping and discipline are shown in table 5.13. Because our concern is with the use of academic grouping and discipline as a long-term method of resegregating schools, each of the second-generation measures is the mean black ratio for all the years the variable was measured. Using individual years

Table 5.12. Taeuber Indices of School Segregation for the Sample Districts

Variable	Mean[a]	Standard Deviation	Low	High
Segregation in 1968 (%)	73.2	15.4	33.6	97.4
Segregation in 1976 (%)	46.1	19.5	11.0	91.9
Change in segregation from 1968 to 1976 (%)	−27.1	21.2	7.9	−75.6

[a]The Taeuber index of segregation indicates the percentage of students that would have to change schools in order that all schools have the same racial distribution.

rather than the mean makes no difference in the results, because in all cases the direction of the relationships remains the same.

If academic grouping or discipline is being used to resegregate schools, we would expect to find a negative relationship between segregation and placement of blacks in EMR and TMR classes, and corporal punishment, suspension, and expulsion of blacks. In addition, we would expect to see a positive relationship between segregation and placement of blacks in gifted classes. Table 5.13 shows exactly this pattern.

The strongest relationships with segregation occur for two measures of academic grouping—EMR classes and gifted classes. Although the relationships between segregation and disciplinary measures are in the expected direction, they are not as strong as the academic grouping relationships. This suggests that academic grouping is more likely to be used than discipline to resegregate schools. This priority makes sense. Academic grouping can immediately separate one group of students from another. Discipline short of

Table 5.13. Relationship between Segregation in 1976 and Second-Generation Discrimination Measures

	Correlation Coefficient
EMR class ratio	−.30**
TMR class ratio	−.17*
Gifted class ratio	.33**
Expulsion ratio	−.16*
Suspension ratio	−.21**
Corporal punishment ratio	−.14*

*p < .10
**p < .05

expulsion does not effectively separate blacks from whites unless blacks subsequently drop out of school.

The relationship between segregation and both academic grouping and discipline is another piece of evidence that links academic grouping and discipline differentials to discrimination. If academic grouping and discipline were unrelated to discrimination, neither of these variables would be related to school segregation. The negative relationships between segregation and academic grouping and discipline do not prove discrimination, but the relationship is consistent with a discrimination hypothesis.

Declining White Enrollment

The declining level of white enrollment in urban schools, or as it is better known, "white flight," is one of the more controversial issues in urban education. A frequently expressed fear is that desegregation results in whites leaving the school system so that only black students remain, thus frustrating the intent of desegregation. This fear has caused what Willie and Fultz (1984: 164) call goal distortion. "A court order that gave local school authorities primary responsibility for developing plans *that protect the rights of blacks* was transformed into a primary responsibility to develop school desegregation plans *that are least offensive to whites.*" Goal distortion explains why early efforts to desegregate schools focused on voluntary desegregation strategies such as open enrollment, voluntary magnet schools, and majority to minority transfers.

Second-generation discrimination can be viewed as an effort by the local school system to make desegregation as tolerable to whites as possible. By grouping individuals by "ability," not only are whites separated from most blacks, but also middle-class whites are separated from lower-class whites. Disproportionate disciplinary practices in turn have a greater impact on black students and further limit interracial contact by pushing black students out of the educational system.

This section examines the relationship between second-generation discrimination and white enrollment decline. First, a brief literature review of the research on white flight is presented, providing an overview of the controversy. Second, a model of white enrollment decline is constructed. Third, measures of second-generation discrimination are added to the enrollment decline model to determine if academic grouping and disciplinary practices affect white enrollment levels.

Previous Research on White Enrollment Decline

The issue of white flight has been sensationalized by James S. Coleman, (Coleman, Kelly, and Moore, 1975a; Coleman, 1976, 1981). Essentially Coleman argued that a substantial desegregation effort (that is, a reduction of 20 or more in the Taeuber index would result in a 6 percent loss of white enrollment during the implementation year in those districts with 25 percent or more black student enrollment. Six percent is about double the white enrollment loss that had normally occurred in these districts (Morgan and England, 1984).

The "white flight debate" degenerated into a series of charges and counter-charges with individuals being labeled everything from racist to incompetent (Armor, 1978, 1980; Farley, Richards, and Wurdock, 1980; Marshall, 1979; Ravitch, 1978). Several studies disputed Coleman's findings (Farley, 1975; Pettigrew and Green, 1976; Bosco and Robin, 1974; Fitzgerald and Morgan, 1977). Often these studies focused on limitations in Coleman's methods, presenting a version of dueling statistics. After several years of academic disputes a consensus emerged that supported some of Coleman's original claims (Farley, Richards, and Wurdock, 1980). The consensus was that desegregation produced a white enrollment decline of 8–10 percent in the implementation year in school districts that were 35 percent or more black. Such losses were conditional on a variety of factors such as distance of busing, type of school, type of desegregation plan, local publicity, and so on (Welch, 1987).[5]

A Model of White Enrollment Loss

Our intent is not to participate in the debate over the determinants of white student enrollment; rather we are interested only in the relationship between white enrollment loss and second-generation discrimination. The model presented here does not intend to resolve the academic debates; we simply wish to incorporate as many possible determinants of white enrollment decline as our data set permits and then proceed with our own analysis.

Franklin Wilson (1985: 138), in his study of white enrollment decline, argues that "the policy implications of the impact of school desegregation can best be addressed by focusing on the long-term effects rather than on any implementation year effects that may be compensated for later." White enrollment fluctuates far more than one would expect; short-term declines are often compensated for by longer-term effects in the opposite direction (Wilson, 1985; England and Morgan, 1986). Such a view of white enrollment decline and policy impacts is similar to our own. Accordingly, we will not model white flight on an annual basis as is the custom in the literature, because this might produce misleading results. Our attempt will focus on long-term declines in white enrollment using the time period 1968–1986.[6]

5. The conditional nature of white enrollment loss is still controversial. Wilson (1985) in an elaborate pooled time-series model has not found that the type of desegregation plan affects white enrollment loss. His position on this issue has been criticized by Welch (1987).

6. To our knowledge, no other work has estimated white enrollment declines over such a long period of time. Normally the estimates are made annually for the years 1968 through 1976. The preponderance of estimates of this type is a function of the availability of data on enrollments, levels of segregation, and so on. The primary data set (of which part is used in our study) has become known as the Wilson-Taeuber data set, because it was compiled by Franklin Wilson and Karl Taeuber of the University of Wisconsin–Madison.

Our model begins by simply predicting white student enrollment in 1986 with white student enrollment in 1968. Both variables are subjected to a log transformation to eliminate problems of heteroscedasticity and extreme values. This initial model is consistent with the consensus approach used to model white enrollment decline (see Wilson, 1985; Welch, 1987).

That white enrollment has declined over this 18-year period is beyond dispute. The average white student enrollment for the school districts in this study dropped from 35,162 in 1968 to 19,672 in 1986, or 44 percent. Nowhere near all this decline is attributable to desegregation. White enrollments have declined for a variety of reasons, including the drop in birth rates, migration patterns from cities to suburbs, economic patterns, crime, and countless other factors.

To the basic model of white enrollment, we have added several additional variables. If these variables have negative coefficients in the resulting regression, this indicates that they increase the rate of white enrollment decline. Positive slopes indicate that the variables attenuate the rate of white enrollment decline.

The first variable is, of course, desegregation, measured as the change in the Taeuber segregation index from 1968 to 1976. Past studies have linked the amount of desegregation to the white student enrollment decline (Coleman, Kelly, and Moore, 1975b).[7] Since the early studies, measures of desegregation have become more sophisticated. Giles (1975) argues that a tipping point of 35 percent black exists; in districts greater than 35 percent black, desegregation will result in white out-migration (see also Wilson, 1985). To measure this conditional impact, we have created a dummy variable for those districts of more than 35 percent black. We have used both this variable and a second variable that is the interaction between desegregation and black enrollment (or the amount of desegregation multiplied by the black enrollment dummy variable). Such a procedure is consistent with previous work in this area (see Wilson, 1985).

White withdrawal from a school system, according to Giles and Gatlin (1980), is a function of both attitudes toward desegregation and the ability to act. With our current data set we cannot measure attitudes toward desegregation, but we can measure the opportunities that whites have to leave the public school system. White students who leave urban public schools, the research finds, do not usually transfer to suburban schools. Escaping students are far more likely to enroll in private schools. The opportunity to enroll in a private school is significantly limited by the availability of private schools. In a city without

7. Having segregation scores only up to 1976 is not as serious a problem as it seems. Very little planned desegregation occurred in the United States after 1976. Changes in this index after 1976 more likely reflect changes in school district demographics than the implementation of desegregation plans.

a developed private-school system, a white student may have no choice other than to remain in public schools. To tap this dimension, we have used the 1980 percentage of school-aged children enrolled in private schools.[8]

The existence of private schools alone does not determine whether students will leave a public school system. Private schools require tuition. Many individuals who would like to attend private schools may not be able to do so because they lack the financial resources. Our second measure of the capacity of whites to leave the public school system, then, is the white median family income.

The group power thesis (Giles and Evans, 1985, 1986; Feagin, 1980) introduced in our political theory of second-generation discrimination is also applicable here. Some white students might leave public schools, not because desegregation exposes them to black students, but because it exposes them to lower-class black students. To tap this social class–aversion view of white flight, the percentage of blacks with a high school education is used.

Finally, the southern region is associated with a decreased ability for whites to leave public schools (England and Morgan, 1986). Many southern school districts are large countywide districts that cover more than one incorporated area. In a countywide school district, moving to the suburbs is not an avenue of flight, because the school district includes the suburbs. To tap this and other unique southern educational patterns, a dummy variable for southern districts is included.

The regression model for white enrollment decline is shown in table 5.14. An initial look at the model reveals that two variables are not statistically significant, white median family income and black education (see the Full Model column). To avoid estimating a misspecified model, these two variables have been deleted; and the model has been reestimated (Reduced Model column). All coefficients in the reduced model are statistically significant and in the predicted direction. The model itself has a fairly good level of prediction with a coefficient of determination of .76.[9]

Academic Grouping, Discipline, and White Enrollments

If academic grouping and discipline can be used as techniques to limit white enrollment declines, we would expect positive relationships between actions that adversely affect black students and overall white enrollments. The measures

8. This measure includes both Catholic schools and other private schools in existence before desegregation. It also includes those schools that we affectionately refer to as Honky Christian academies, that is, schools that were established for the sole purpose of avoiding desegregated public schools.

9. Because it is not our intent in this modeling process to explain white flight per se, we will not discuss this model. The one interesting finding, though, is the finding for private school enrollment, because no one has ever included such a variable in a white flight model. The model shows that a 1 percent increase in private-school enrollments is associated with a 1.12 percent decline in white public-school enrollments.

Table 5.14. Determinants of White Enrollment Decline

Dependent Variable: Log (white enrollment in 1986)

| | Regression Coefficient | |
Independent Variable	Full Model	Reduced Model
Log (white enrollment in 1968)	0.89682*	0.88961*
Desegregation change (%)	0.00311*	0.00319*
Desegregation (%) × black enrollment (%)	−0.00462*	−0.00470*
Private-school enrollment (%)	−1.26967*	−1.12030*
White median family income	0.00001	
Black education (%)	−0.00163	
Southern region	0.12824*	0.14841*
F	52.74	74.21
R^2	.76	.76
Adjusted R^2	.75	.75
N	122	122

*$p < .05$

of academic grouping, discipline, and educational attainment are multiple-year averages, because our concern is with long-term rather than short-term impacts. To eliminate problems of heteroscedasticity, the academic grouping and discipline measures are subjected to a log transformation.

The regression coefficients resulting from the addition of black academic grouping and discipline ratios to the model of white enrollment decline are shown in table 5.15. A clear, consistent pattern exists for academic grouping. Districts that disproportionately assign blacks to EMR and TMR classes and disproportionately limit black assignments to gifted classes experience a smaller amount of white enrollment decline. Each relationship is statistically significant and in the predicted direction. Academic grouping procedures that separate blacks from whites attenuate white flight from the school district.

The relationship between discipline of black students and white flight is not quite as strong as the relationship between academic grouping of blacks and white flight. Although only the relationships for suspensions and corporal punishment are statistically significant, districts that disproportionately discipline black students, as predicted, have smaller declines in white enrollment. In addition, a higher black dropout rate is associated with smaller declines in white enrollment, and higher black graduation rates are significantly related to greater declines in white enrollment.

Testing the impact of academic grouping and discipline patterns on white enrollment decline suggests even stronger linkages of academic grouping and

Table 5.15. Impact of Second-Generation Discrimination Measures on White Flight

Dependent Variable: Log (white enrollment in 1986)

Independent Variable	Regression Coefficient[a]	t-score	R^2	F	N
EMR class ratio	0.750	7.29*	.84	98.54	122
TMR class ratio	0.407	3.38*	.19	69.08	120
Gifted class ratio	−0.291	5.73*	.81	84.25	122
Expulsion ratio	0.094	1.26	.77	60.95	116
Suspension ratio	0.364	2.53*	.77	65.78	122
Corporal punishment ratio	0.276	2.14*	.75	54.47	115
Dropout ratio	0.212	1.59	.76	58.47	120
Graduate ratio	−0.676	3.36*	.78	69.20	122

[a]Partial regression coefficients include controls for white enrollment in 1968, desegregation change, southern region, private-school enrollment, and the interaction of desegregation with the percentage of black enrollment
*$p < .05$

discipline to racial discrimination. The pattern found is consistent with a postdesegregation strategy to resegregate schools. Via administrative actions, school districts are able to translate a court-ordered policy intended to benefit black students into a policy that provides the least inconvenience to white students by reducing interracial exposure. School districts have been willing to trade off black access to equal education opportunities for continued white enrollments in the school system.

Declining Black Enrollments

Lost in the debate over white flight has been the phenomenon of decreased black enrollments. In our survey districts, the average black enrollment dropped from 19,671 in 1968 to 18,231 in 1986. Although the black enrollment decline of 7.3 percent is nowhere near the white enrollment decline of 44 percent, it does represent a significant demographic trend. In some districts the decline has been much greater; Los Angeles, for example, lost 28.4 percent of its black enrollment during this time period, and Baltimore lost 31.2 percent.

Black enrollment declines should not come as a surprise. The black birth rate has also dropped in the past 20 years, and black families follow many of the same migration patterns that white families do. As Katzman (1983) argues, black flight is probably caused by the same factors that produce white enrollment decline. The presence of black enrollment decline suggests that it is also linked to the relationship between academic grouping and discipline. If such actions motivate blacks to withdraw from the school system, the blacks that withdraw will likely be those with the ability to move or to send their children to private schools. As a result, a district might lose enrollments from the middle-class black community.

To determine if academic grouping and discipline affect black enrollments, a model of black enrollment decline similar to the white enrollment model was constructed with some modifications to reflect black interests rather than white interests. The basic model remains the same; the dependent variable is the log transformation of black enrollment in 1986. The independent variables are black enrollment in 1968 (to tap the decline), southern region, desegregation interacting with the percentage of black enrollment, black median family income, and black enrollment in private schools. The two last-named variables tap the capacity of blacks to leave the school system (see table 5.16).

The decline in black enrollments follows a different pattern from the decline in white enrollments. Only two of the variables are significant—previous black enrollments and southern region. Particularly interesting is the lack of relationship between black enrollments and the capacity to withdraw from the public school system and enroll in private schools. What we have found may be the absence of such a capacity. Private schools do not offer the same opportunity to blacks as they do to whites. In the North many private schools are Catholic, and most northern blacks are not.[10] In the South many of the private "Chris-

Table 5.16. Determinants of Black Enrollment Decline

Dependent Variable: Log (black enrollment in 1986)

| | Regression Coefficients | |
Independent Variable	Full Model	Reduced Model
Log (black enrollment in 1968)	0.806*	0.853*
Southern region	0.076*	0.060*
Desegregation (%) × black enrollment (%)	0.000	
Black median family income	−0.000	
Black enrollment in private schools (%)	0.672	
F	208.88	515.44
R^2	.90	.90
Adjusted R^2	.90	.89
N	122	122

*$p < .05$

10. We are aware from anecdotal evidence that some Protestant black parents send their children to Catholic schools in northern cities. We are also aware that some Catholic schools have made a concerted effort to attract black students by offering scholarships. The overall numbers involved, however, are fairly small.

tian'' schools were established to provide education for whites only. Only 5 percent of private school enrollments are black compared with 15 percent of public school enrollments (Taeuber and James, 1982: 134). In addition, black median family income is only 70 percent of white median family income. Large numbers of blacks may not have the financial capacity to move to the suburbs or to pay private-school tuition.

The black enrollment decline model was then reoperationalized using only previous black enrollment and southern region. This simple model suggests that black enrollment declines are more consistent across school districts than white enrollment declines. This supposition is further supported by the higher coefficient of determination (.90) for the simple model of black enrollment than for the more complex model of white enrollment (.76). This supposition also suggests that academic grouping and discipline might not affect black enrollment, because black students do not have any options to avoid discriminatory education practices.

The pattern of relationships between academic grouping, discipline, and black enrollments (table 5.17) is consistent with this interpretation. None of the relationships except the one for black graduates is statistically significant. This finding is probably just an artifact, because rising black graduation ratios should not decrease the level of black student enrollments.

Academic grouping and discipline, then, do not appear to affect aggregate black enrollments.[11] A school system that disproportionately assigns black students to lower-ability-group classes, limits black assignments to higher-ability-group classes, and disproportionately disciplines black student can induce more white students to remain in the school system. Because blacks lack the same capacity to leave the school system, they face a Hobson's choice of unequal education or no education.

Summary

This chapter has examined the implications of academic grouping and disciplinary practices. First, the interrelationships between the various forms of second-generation discrimination were examined. A model that assumes racial disparities result from discrimination was presented and a series of tests were made. The results are consistent with the discrimination model. Lower rates of black graduation are a function of higher rates of black corporal punish-

11. This is a different conclusion from the previous ones in the chapter, which argue that black academic grouping and punishment result in higher black dropout levels and lower black graduation rates. When examining the entire school system enrollment, the rate of dropouts becomes overwhelmed by the other factors that affect total student enrollment. The previous conclusion is still valid. Inappropriate black academic grouping and punishment do push some black students out of school. The numbers pushed out, however, are not as visible in overall enrollments as the impact of higher black birth rates and other factors.

Table 5.17. Impact of Second-Generation Discrimination Measures on Black Flight

Dependent Variable: Log (of black enrollment in 1986)

Independent Variable	Regression Coefficient[a]	t-score	R^2	F	N
EMR class ratio	0.07	0.60	.90	341.89	122
TMR class ratio	0.04	0.37	.90	328.73	119
Gifted class ratio	0.02	0.44	.90	341.36	122
Expulsion ratio	0.00	0.00	.89	313.17	116
Suspension ratio	−0.16	1.05	.90	344.26	122
Corporal punishment ratio	−0.04	0.36	.90	348.33	115
Dropout ratio	−0.12	0.90	.89	323.88	120
Graduation ratio	−0.84	4.67*	.91	410.86	122

[a]Partial regression coefficients include controls for black enrollment in 1968, and the southern region.

*$p < .05$

ment and EMR class placement and lower rates of gifted class placement. Higher black dropout rates are a function of higher rates of black expulsion. Higher rates of black expulsion are the result of higher rates of black suspension and EMR class placements. Higher rates of black suspension are a function of higher rates of black corporal punishment and placement in EMR classes and lower rates of placement in gifted classes. Higher rates of black corporal punishment and placement in TMR classes and lower rates of black placement in gifted classes are all a function of higher rates of black placement in EMR classes. The model is not only consistent with an underlying cause of discrimination, but it also underscores the crucial nature of EMR placements as the first step in the process of second-generation discrimination.

Second, disproportionate discipline of black students was examined to determine if it acts as a deterrent of future behavior problems. Despite using models that allow for both an immediate impact and a lagged impact, we find no evidence that disciplining students has any deterrent effect. This finding calls into question the common assumption that discipline's value is in convincing others not to engage in unacceptable behavior.

Third, the relationships between desegregation and measures of second-generation discrimination were examined. Our analysis finds that higher levels of desegregation are associated with higher levels of second-generation discrimination against black students. This finding is consistent with the often proposed, but rarely verified, contention that academic grouping and discipline are used to resegregate school systems after formal desegregation takes place.

Particularly noteworthy in this analysis is that academic grouping is more strongly related to desegregation than is discipline.

Fourth, white flight was modeled and linked to second-generation discrimination. Working under the assumption that school districts can use academic grouping and discipline to reduce the impact of desegregation on white students, we have found that second-generation discrimination does indeed reduce the level of white enrollment decline. Again academic grouping is a stronger factor than discipline in explaining white enrollment decline.

Finally, the question of black enrollment decline was examined. Black enrollment decline, however, is unaffected by racial disparities in academic grouping and discipline. This finding is explained by reference to lower black incomes and the racial distributions in private schools. Blacks simply have a lower capacity than whites to leave the public school system.

6 The Quest for Quality Integrated Education

More than 30 years after the Supreme Court's historic decision in *Brown* v. *Board of Education* neither the letter of the law—desegregation—nor the spirit of the law—integration—have been attained. With respect to school desegregation, as reported in chapter 5, Taeuber's index of dissimilarity in 1976 was a little less than 50, indicating substantial school segregation remained. More recently Jennifer Hochschild (1984: 33) has concluded, "In 1984 . . . we have the largest, most urban, and most heavily non-Anglo schools left to desegregate. . . . the South and border states have progressed; the Northeast has regressed."

If one looks beyond school district measures of segregation, the level of segregation increases, because classrooms are often more segregated than school systems. Segregating or resegregating schools through second-generation discrimination impedes the integration process. Integrated education seeks an educational climate where students of different races interact within and outside classrooms to learn in a multiracial environment. In such a climate, status is not based on race, class, or other factors related to race or class. Each student is afforded an equal opportunity to learn and to progress as far and as fast as ability merits.

Equal access to quality integrated education is the most important racial issue facing the United States today, because access to quality integrated education affects most other opportunities for racial discrimination. By denying educational opportunities to blacks, the political development of the black community suffers. As a result, the black community will be slower to develop a political infrastructure and to produce candidates for elective office. Without candidates for office and registered voters, progress toward political equality will be slow.

Economic equality is even more directly tied to educational equity than is political equality. Recent studies have demonstrated beyond any doubt that access to education is crucial for blacks to gain access to well-paying jobs (Smith and Welch, 1986). Positions associated with middle-class status—attorneys, government employees, physicians, accountants, teachers, and so on—simply cannot be attained without first obtaining the necessary education. At one time education was not as good an economic investment for blacks as it was for whites, because the quality of the education blacks received was inferior to that afforded whites. Although educational opportunities offered to blacks are still far from equal to those offered whites, the racial gap in education's contribution to income has been narrowed.

Education and the resulting economic opportunities are also related to gaining access to quality housing, good recreational facilities, and other elements of mainstream American life. We do not believe that elimination of discriminatory education practices will eliminate racial discrimination in all other areas of life. That, unfortunately, will not be the case. What equalizing access to quality integrated education does is eliminate justifications for not affording blacks equal treatment because they are not as well qualified as whites. If access to quality integrated education can be equalized, then discrimination in other areas of life will have to become more overt to be effective, because it can no longer hide behind reviews of qualifications and credentials. Overt discrimination, in turn, is easier to combat simply because it is open.

The Status of Equal Educational Opportunity

Equal educational opportunity is not a reality in the United States. Our study demonstrates that the education available to black students is not the same as the education available to white students. Rather than integrated education with equal-status individuals learning in multiracial environments, education is resegregated to provide education that is separate and unequal.

Students are resegregated in schools through the use of ability grouping, curriculum tracking, special education, and discipline. We have argued that academic grouping and discipline are not as they are often portrayed, that is, as simply good educational practices designed to benefit the student. Rather, ability grouping, curriculum tracking, and special education form the core of an institutionalized process of educational discrimination. Three empirical findings support the discrimination argument. First, racial differences in academic grouping in every case produce more black students in lower-level academic groups and fewer black students in higher-level academic groups. Black students are also far more likely to be disciplined than white students. Empirical research from education scholars substantiates the proposition that assignment to lower-level academic groups has a detrimental impact on the student so assigned.

Second, measures of academic grouping, discipline, and educational attainment cluster in a pattern that cannot be interpreted without reference to discrimination. Placement in classes for the educable mentally retarded, for example, is positively correlated with suspensions, corporal punishment, and expulsions. Placement in gifted classes is negatively correlated with actions designed to punish students. Such a pattern could exist only if academic grouping had something in common with discipline. The most logical explanation is discrimination against minority students.

Third, academic grouping, discipline, and educational attainment form a cohesive pattern. The key factor identified in the process is assignment to classes for the educable mentally retarded. School districts that assign more blacks to EMR classes consistently assign fewer blacks to gifted classes, use more discipline against blacks, and have more blacks drop out of school and fewer blacks graduate from high school. Hypothetically, a black student is first classified as an EMR student (or assigned to a low-achievement group in the regular classroom); that student is then discouraged by low-quality education and more discipline. With sufficient discouragement, the student withdraws from the educational system.

The sum total of the practices of academic grouping and discipline create an educational environment hostile to the concept of integrated education. Blacks are separated from whites into groups with lower status. Learning does not take place in integrated classrooms but rather in highly segregated classrooms that have the stamp of inferiority. The detrimental nature of these education practices merits the name second-generation educational discrimination.

One issue associated with second-generation educational discrimination that has not been resolved is the nature of intent. Do educators intend to discriminate against black students or is the discrimination institutional? From the perspective of the student, whether discrimination is intentional or institutional is irrelevant. Discrimination is equally harmful whether or not the intent is to discriminate.

One could argue that the patterns shown in this book result solely from institutionalized discrimination. Structures and procedures give an objective gloss to educational actions. Students are tested before they are assigned to special education classes; students must violate specific rules in order to be suspended. Individual educators are simply following procedures established by the school system and applied to all students regardless of race. Such an argument, even if correct, would not detract from our findings. If the discrimination is institutional (and we agree that some of it is), this does not excuse the discrimination. It simply means that those structures and institutions that foster discrimination need to be changed.

The other possibility is that the discrimination found exceeds that attributable to institutional biases. Teachers still exercise discretion in assigning students to academic groups and determining discipline. Some empirical research has shown racial biases in this discretion. Perhaps the most disturbing aspect of second-generation discrimination in this regard is the relationship with white enrollment decline. This study demonstrates that schools with higher levels of second-generation discrimination are able to limit their white enrollment losses over time. Although second-generation discrimination may be invisible to policy-makers, one of its manifestations is highly visible to parents. White parents can easily tell if their child is attending classes with only white students. Because second-generation educational discrimination increases the probability of such classes, discriminatory school districts retain a higher proportion of white student enrollments. We cannot demonstrate that school administrators have made conscious decisions to limit white flight by restricting black educational opportunities, but the pattern causes us great concern.

The Politics of Second-Generation Discrimination

Unlike most students of education, we have assumed from the outset that educational policy is a political process. Consistent with our assumption, we have constructed a political theory to explain the access of blacks to political positions and to link black representation to educational policy outputs. We have not explained all the variation in black student access to education; but we have explained a substantial portion, thus giving our political view of education credibility.

The first political step in obtaining equal access to education for the black community is to gain representation on the policy-making body, the school board. Black representation on school boards is affected by black resources (especially population), electoral structures, and region. Specifically, blacks are able to gain proportional or better representation in school systems that use district rather than at-large elections to select school board members. District elections are particularly helpful when blacks constitute a minority of the school district population. In addition, northern school districts elect significantly more black school board members than do southern school districts.

Step two in gaining political power in educational policy is achieving access to school administrative positions. Administrators not only implement school district policy, but they also have discretion in setting other policies and taking individual actions. Black access to administrative positions is affected by both black population (a resource) and black representation on the school board. As would be expected, a larger percentage of black school board members results in larger percentages of black school administrators.

Step three in gaining influence over educational policy is filling teaching positions with black teachers. The single most important influence in a student's educational career is the teacher. Teachers implement school policies and make the initial judgments about students that result in academic grouping or discipline. In addition, teachers maintain an educational environment that may either be supportive of learning or detrimental to it. Black teacher representation is a function of black population, black administrators, and region; it is not affected by social class or other black political resources. As expected, school districts with a greater black population, more black administrators, and northern locations have more black teachers.

The Impact of Teachers

In our political theory of second-generation educational discrimination, we argue that the level of discrimination can be explained by the levels of black resources and white poverty, school district size, region, and the percentage of black teacher representation. As it turns out, there is no empirical evidence that school district size is related to second-generation discrimination, however there is evidence for the other factors. The theory is able to explain academic grouping actions fairly well, discipline moderately well, and educational attainment only somewhat.

Each indicator affects some of the measures of second-generation discrimination. At times greater black resources (more educated blacks and a higher black-white income ratio) are able to reduce the incidence of second-generation discrimination against blacks. As blacks attain resources, they are able either to resist individual decisions or to place pressure on the school district collectively to reduce such actions. Social class also plays a role because second-generation discrimination also affects lower-class white students. In districts with larger percentages of lower-class white students, black students are less likely to be placed in lower academic groups or disproportionately disciplined. Southern school districts form an interesting pattern. As expected, southern districts have greater racial disparities in academic grouping. In some cases of discipline, however, the record in southern districts is equal to or better than that of northern districts.

The single most important factor for all forms of second-generation discrimination, however, is the proportion of black teachers. In school districts with larger proportions of black teachers, fewer black students are placed in EMR and TMR classes, more blacks are placed in gifted classes, fewer blacks are corporally punished, suspended, or expelled, and more blacks graduate from high school. The political process of education from school board elections through administrative hiring culminates in teachers implementing policies that reflect equal educational opportunities. Without the political action that results in more black school board members, which in turn produces more black administrators, who in turn hire more black teachers, second-generation discrimination against black students would be significantly worse.

Lessons for Policy Analysts

The findings of this study have implications for the study of public policy in general as well as the design of specific public policies. Two such implications are especially important. First, politics matter. Public policy analysts, particularly those who research educational policy, too often ignore the role that politics play in the determination of public policy. Such a view holds an unrealistic image of public policy as being determined either by environmental forces or by professional factors. In addition, the policy-analysis literature often portrays politics in a negative fashion and argues that many policies would work if it were not for the "illegitimate" impact of politics on program design. Our study illustrates that politics not only play a role in educational policy, but a positive role. Black students fare significantly better in those school districts where blacks have used the political system to gain access to policy-making positions.

Second, the definition of public policy problems has a major impact on the evolution of public policy. The quest for equal educational opportunities for blacks has been handicapped by the policy system's definition of equal educational opportunities. In an effort to eliminate segregated schools because they did not provide equal educational opportunities, equal educational opportunity was defined as desegregated schools. The simple mechanical process of school desegregation, however, has been insufficient to achieve equal educational opportunity for black students. While black students have been allowed to attend the same schools as white students, the education they have received in those schools has often been significantly different. Academic grouping and the selective use of discipline has resegregated schools and reduced the access of black students to equal quality education. By defining the policy problem as one of attaining desegregated education, the problem of second-generation discrimination was overlooked; and the objective of equal educational opportunities is yet to be attained.

Policy Recommendations

Herbert Simon (1969: xi) contends that social sciences are sciences of the artificial concerned "not with how things are but with how they might be." As students of public policy we endorse the latter half of that sentiment. To this point, we have been concerned only with how things are, with the analysis of black student access to equal educational opportunities. Our interests do not end with the empirical, however. We completely accept the goal of equal access to quality integrated education and support policy changes that contribute to creating a multicultural environment where students of all races are accorded equal educational opportunities. In quest of this goal we offer the following policy recommendations.

Replace At-Large Elections with Ward Elections

The evidence concerning at-large elections is overwhelming. At-large elections reduce the ability of black candidates to win seats on the school board in the vast majority of school districts where blacks constitute a minority of the population. At the present time, most school districts still use at-large election systems adopted during the progressive reform era. *At-large elections should be eliminated and replaced with a system of ward elections.*

Our preference is that individual school districts see the logic of ward-based elections and freely adopt such selection methods. Such action, however, is unlikely if past practices are any indication. The courts have dealt harshly in recent years with at-large elections, and they will continue to do so. Rather than subject each school district to an expensive court challenge regarding at-large election districts, a more rational policy would be national guidelines issued by either the Justice Department or Congress (as an amendment to the Voting Rights Act) clearly specifying the conditions acceptable for retaining at-large elections.

Local citizens in large metropolitan areas should be aware that ward elections benefit political and racial minorities regardless of race or political persuasion. White residents, if in the minority, benefit as much from ward-based elections as blacks do. In addition, in school districts undergoing demographic transitions, ward elections temper the abruptness of such transitions by according minority representation earlier and retaining the new minority representation longer.

Recruit More Black Teachers

The key to mitigating second-generation educational discrimination against black students is increasing the number of black teachers. In school districts with larger percentages of black teachers, black students are less likely to suffer disproportionate discipline, negative academic grouping, and dropouts, and more likely to enter gifted classes and graduate. A consistently strong relationship holds both across policy areas and across time.

Recruiting additional black teachers, however, is not as simple as it may seem. Our study of changes in teacher composition over time reveals that only two factors have effected an increase in the percentage of black teachers—more black school administrators and northern school districts. School districts can do little about the region of the country where they are located, but the proportion of black administrators is a manipulable variable.[1] In fact, increas-

---

1. Affirmative action plans in the South and the North may differ as a result of the distribution of teachers. In the South, where more black teachers reside, the need is to redistribute black teachers among the school districts. A southern school district should concentrate on programs which assure that blacks can compete for promotions. Northern districts, on the other hand, need to attract black teachers to employment.

ing the number of black administrators may be easier than increasing the number of black teachers. Increasing the number of black teachers requires some increase in the percentage of blacks who graduate with education degrees or inducing black teachers who have left the educational system to return. Increasing the number of black administrators is not as constrained, because administrators can be trained in many different disciplines, not just in education. Management ability is not a monopoly of schools of educational administration. Although school districts generally recruit only administrators from schools of educational administration and from within their own ranks, an aggressive school system could recruit black administrators from other public agencies or from the private sector. For most positions involved in running a school district, a degree in educational administration is not necessary.

Increasing the pool of black teachers will not be an easy task. If much of the nation had not maintained segregated school systems, the current pool of black teachers would probably be even smaller than it is. At one time blacks could aspire to few professions; teaching was among them. As the restrictions on black access to other professions declined, the attractiveness of teaching also declined. A young black student who 30 years ago would have considered teaching is now planning a career in law, accounting, or similar professions. In 1985, 30,000 college degrees were awarded to blacks, Hispanics, Asians, and American Indians in medicine, law, and engineering, while only 3,400 degrees in education were awarded to minorities (Alston, 1988: 2).

The decline in black teachers, as a result, is reaching crisis proportions. As older black teachers retire and younger blacks eschew teaching, the prospects for a representative teaching faculty diminish. In a single year from 1980 to 1981, the proportion of black teachers nationwide dropped from 8.6 percent to 7.8 percent (B. P. Cole, 1986: 327). The National Governors' Association projects that by 1995 only 5 percent of all teachers will be from minorities compared with 30 percent of the students (Alston, 1988: 1). An estimated 500,000 minority teachers will be needed to reach parity, but fewer than 50,000 will be produced.

Improvements to salaries and status in the teaching profession are intermediate goals that might attract more black students into teaching. More likely to succeed, however, are direct actions such as scholarships and loan-forgiveness programs tied to teaching. School districts might even raise private funds to endow scholarships for their own high school graduates and offer a teaching position on completion of college. Another promising effort is Los Angeles' effort to create a magnet school for future teachers in a predominantly black neighborhood.

The patterns are such, however, that relying solely on increased enrollments in educational schools will not produce acceptable results. We strongly urge states to reexamine their teacher-licensing programs to provide alternative ways for individuals to be certified as teachers. New Jersey's Provisional Teacher Program, for example, allows individuals without education degrees to become teachers. The program, although small, is a striking success. Provisional teachers in New Jersey not only score higher than regular teachers on the New Jersey subject area test but also have a significantly lower attrition rate (Schechter, 1987: 4, 10).

A related but somewhat different problem concerns the rise of teacher-competency testing. Many states have implemented such tests without verifying that test performance is directly related to teacher competence. Cooper's (1985) study of competency testing in 11 southern states documents the disproportionate impact of these tests on black teachers. Dometrius and Sigelman's (1988: 81) simulation of the Texas teacher-competency tests shows a similar negative impact.

Easing and even eliminating certification or competency-test requirements would be a major change in the direction teacher education has taken in recent years. We urge states to reevaluate their certification and testing procedures to ensure that they are valid measures of teaching quality and that they do not discriminate against minorities. Eliminating tests that are not valid is a drastic measure, but without attracting more blacks into teaching, prospects for greater access to equal integrated education are not promising.

Revitalize the Powers of the Office for Civil Rights

At one time the Office for Civil Rights was an aggressive policy-maker that played a fundamental role in desegregating southern school systems (Bullock, 1980). As a result of its aggressive actions and changing political conditions, many of OCR's powers have been restricted so that it currently is little more than a organization that collects data. *OCR should be given back its authority to cut off federal funds to discriminatory school districts and be encouraged to fight for integrated education. The mechanism for revitalizing the powers of OCR should be the legislative reestablishment of the guideline that over-representation of minorities by 20 percent in EMR classes and disciplinary procedures will trigger an OCR compliance review.*

Similarly, OCR is greatly handicapped by the *Adams* v. *Richardson* case (1972), requiring it to respond to all complaints rather than setting its own priorities for investigation. The *Adams* case requires OCR to expend its scarce resources on numerous cases with marginal significance. As a result little is done on major questions of segregation or resegregation. Without discretion to act, OCR has no promise of becoming an effective enforcement agency.

Given the probability that OCR will remain primarily a data-collection organization, substantial improvements could still be made. First, OCR should address the phenomenon of curriculum tracking. At the present time OCR collects information on some forms of academic grouping but not on any type of curriculum tracking. To be sure, tracking is more difficult to define than special education, but consistent definitions are still possible. What is needed is racial distributions on such tracking as college-prep classes, vocational or distributive education tracks, and general education tracks. Equally promising would be information regarding placement in levels of English and math classes, because such placements often then determine tracks.

Some information that OCR gathers could be used to examine curriculum tracking if the data were more complete. Information is gathered on enrollments in industrial arts classes, but this information is collected only by sex, not by race. If trade-offs between types of data gathered are necesssary, OCR would be well advised to include some additional information on tracking and less information on the forms of special education such as classes for the specific learning disabled, which do not show substantial racial disparities.

Similarly, after 1980 OCR ceased gathering data on expulsions. Given the finality of expulsions and the importance they hold for forcing black students out of school, data on expulsions are an absolute necessity. Although expulsion data appear to be less reliable than other data, their importance is far greater than that of, say, corporal punishment. We would know more about a school system with data on expulsions and no data on corporal punishment than if the reverse were the case.

Two other OCR items related to data-gathering merit mention. First, although we are sympathetic to the costs associated with the biennial OCR Elementary and Secondary School Surveys, all districts should be surveyed every two years. Only through all-district inclusive data-gathering methodology, employed only in 1976, can a true longitudinal data base be created for analysis. Second, in order to explain more fully the dynamics of second-generation discrimination, individual-level student data are required. Student achievement scores, economic status, family background, and so on, could then be correlated to academic grouping–discipline decisions.

Release the Data Gathered by the Equal Employment Opportunity Commission

Data on employment by race for both teachers and administrators are collected by the Equal Employment Opportunity Commission but are not made available to the public. Ostensibly EEOC refuses to release data to protect the rights of individuals who might be identified from the summary forms. Because these data are not available, scholars have so far been unable to examine the linkage between teachers and second-generation educational discrimination. Data aggregated at the school district level would not reveal any information about specific individuals and would greatly augment data bases on second-generation discrimination. *The EEOC should make provisions to release data aggregated by school district on the racial composition of teachers and administrators.*

Eliminate or Restrict Academic Grouping

We find the research on the impact of academic grouping convincing. Lower-level academic groups are actually harmful to the students placed in them, whereas higher-level academic groups show a mixed impact on student performance. *The most rational policy for a school district to follow is to eliminate academic grouping completely.* Federal and state programs that create financial incentives to separate students on the basis of ability (e.g., special education, compensatory education) should be redesigned so that such education takes place within the context of the regular classroom. Local school districts do not need financial incentives to engage in second-generation discrimination.

In a rational world, we would hope that both local educators and school board members would read the literature on academic grouping and conclude that its costs far exceed its benefits. Alternatives to segregating students by ability are readily available, easy to implement, and have been proven to be effective pedagogical tools for students with both lower and higher abilities. Generally these strategies are referred to as cooperative learning (Slavin, 1980, 1981, 1982, Slavin and Dickle, 1981) and require the mainstreaming of students across the full range of racial, ethnic, ability, and gender groups in classrooms.[2] Numerous types of cooperative-learning models are offered in the education literature, such as Teams-Games-Tournament (TGT), Student Teams–Achievement Divisions (STAD), Jigsaw, small-group teaching, and multiple-ability classrooms. Regardless of the particular manifestation used, cooperative-learning strategies foster school integration by allowing for multiple-ability instruction and equal status of students.

Despite the success of cooperative-learning strategies, we are not optimistic that academic grouping will disappear. Academic grouping even without strong research support has shown remarkable resilience. If academic grouping cannot be abolished, it should be restricted to as few students as possible.[3] In those school districts that retain academic grouping, elaborate procedures should

2. We recognize that mainstreaming is not a panacea. The research that compares the results of mainstreaming with traditional EMR classes does not show either form to have a distinct advantage (Heller, 1982: 273). Because academic grouping does not work any better than mainstreaming and because academic grouping creates inequalities for black students, we feel that mainstreaming is to be preferred to academic grouping until definitive research shows that students can learn better in separate classes. We also feel that teachers must be given sufficient resources to provide quality instruction for all students, including any support necessary for students with special needs.

3. Finn (1982: 341) has found that disproportionate black assignment to EMR classes correlates significantly with the size of the EMR program. Reducing the size alone should reduce the racial disparity in assignments.

be designed to protect the interests of the students. Each school district should hire an independent child advocate to examine and challenge decisions to place students in special education classes. Students should be evaluated by outside evaluators rather than by the district's own personnel to get an objective evaluation. This evaluation should rely heavily on tests of adaptive behavior and student performance and discount the use of IQ tests (Heller, Holtzman, and Messick, 1982: 62). In the evaluation process the burden of proof should be placed on the school to demonstrate that the student has been exposed to effective teaching techniques and has still not made progress (Heller, Holtzman, and Messick, 1982:68). If a student is placed in a special education class, the student should be reexamined at least every six months to determine if placement continues to be warranted. Finally, for all students placed in special education classes a contract between the school district and the parents should be drawn that specifies how long the student will remain in special ecucation and when the student can expect to be returned to regular classes.

Despite our recommendations concerning how to restructure EMR classes, we remain convinced that ability grouping, curriculum tracking, and special education should be eliminated or greatly restricted. Because academic grouping has negative racial impacts in terms of equal access to education, its proponents should have to demonstrate that it provides positive benefits before any academic-grouping programs are implemented. If no clear-cut benefits can be demonstrated, students should not be grouped by ability.

Restructure Disciplinary Actions

Disproportionate discipline of black students is a pressing concern, because discipline does not appear to meet the school districts' goals for using it: discipline does not deter inappropriate behavior. *Disciplinary actions that disproportionately affect minority students should be restructured so that discipline is not a mechanism for pushing students out of school.* Because OCR data contain only information on corporal punishment, suspensions, and expulsions, we will confine our remarks to those forms of discipline. Other forms of discipline can be approached with the same philosophy.

Corporal punishment serves no useful purpose. Schools that use a great deal of corporal punishment do not solve their behavior problems; the data show that the use of corporal punishment causes no decrease in the subsequent use of suspensions and expulsions. We could find no support for the idea that physical contact offers anything over and above other forms of discipline. Given its disproportionate impact on black students, therefore, we can find no justification for not eliminating corporal punishment completely. *Those states that have not banned corporal punishment should do so.*

Suspensions provide the wrong message for a student. A suspension tells a student that "incorrect" behavior will result in time away from school. Such discipline may well be perceived as a reward by a student who is not particularly interested in attending school. In addition, it provides that student with numerous opportunities for observing role models who are also not in school. Unless rigorously reinforced by parents, suspensions do not appear to be appropriate discipline.

The alternative is in-school suspensions (National Institute of Education, 1979; Williams, 1979). A suspended student, rather than being sent home, is required to attend school but is placed in a restricted study hall to serve the suspension. The suspension might also have some additional penalty in terms of work load. Such a policy serves to keep the student in school while the discipline is being administered.

The types of behavior that warrant suspension should also be reviewed. Ironically, in a large number of cases students are suspended for not attending classes. Only twisted logic can justify preventing students from attending class because they have previously failed to attend class. Attendance violations are not adequate grounds for suspension and must be purged from the list of offenses that can lead to student exit from the school system.

The topic of expulsion needs substantial research before definitive recommendations can be made. We know little about the reasons why students are expelled and how many students who are expelled eventually return to school. We do know that expulsion of black students is proportionately more frequent than expulsion of white students. Because expulsion is an admission by the school system that a student can no longer benefit from attending school, procedures for expulsion should be regularized with protections against arbitrary action.

Summary

We are under no misperception that the policy changes recommended here can be implemented easily. School systems are organizations that change slowly, if at all. Despite the massive research on academic grouping, for example, few schools have eliminated such programs. We would be pleased to see schools attempt to reform themselves. We are skeptical, however, that internal reform will occur without external pressure.

The primary source of external pressure on a school system comes from the political system. Federal government pressures on education have changed dramatically in the last 20 years. The federal government is much less likely to intervene in local school systems in order to seek equal access to education for all students. This unwillingness is tragic.

Without federal action, hopes for reform lie at the state and local levels. Again the solutions are political. Only by gaining access to policy-making positions—school board seats—can advocates of equal educational opportunity gain a forum to press their case. Even in such circumstances, results are difficult to obtain, because the professional nature of schools resists the intrusion of "political" influence. The crucial nature of our school systems in shaping future economic, political, and social opportunities, however, demands political intervention. More political action directed at the inadequacies of the educational system cannot help but be good for education. Nothing less than the future of equality in America is at stake.

Appendices

Bibliography

Court Cases

Index

Appendix A
Statistical Analysis

Table A.1. Policy Representation Ratios for Blacks and Whites: A Comparison of Sample School Districts with Known Universe[a]

	Sample	Universe
Gifted classes		
Blacks	0.37	0.35
Whites	1.44	1.46
EMR classes		
Blacks	2.06	2.17
Whites	0.68	0.62
TMR classes		
Blacks	1.40	1.42
Whites	0.94	0.95
Corporal punishment		
Blacks	1.73	1.54
Whites	0.86	0.85
Suspensions		
Blacks	1.55	1.54
Whites	0.83	0.83
Expulsions		
Blacks	2.10	2.00
Whites	0.68	0.70
Graduates		
Blacks	0.85	0.89
Whites	1.13	1.09
Dropouts		
Blacks	1.11	1.08
Whites	0.95	0.73

[a]Includes all districts in the United States.

Table A.2. Policy-Indicator Correlations, 1973

	Expulsions	Suspensions	EMR Classes
Suspensions	.29*	×	
EMR classes	.30*	.39*	×
TMR classes	.02	.14	.38*

*p < .05

Table A.3. Policy-Indicator Correlations, 1974

	Expulsions	Suspensions	EMR Classes
Suspensions	.46*	×	
EMR classes	.28*	.49*	×
TMR classes	.20	.26*	.48*

*p < .05

Table A.4. Policy-Indicator Correlations, 1976

	Expulsions	Corporal Punishment	Suspensions	Gifted Classes	EMR Classes	TMR Classes	Graduates
Corporal punishment	.04	×					
Suspensions	.20*	.48*	×				
Gifted classes	−.19	−0.17	−.40	×			
EMR classes	.21*	.32	.49*	−.38*	×		
TMR classes	−.06	.06	.19*	−.21*	.35*	×	
Graduates	−.01	.03	−.07	.03	−.03	−.04	×
Dropouts	.15	.27*	.45*	−.17	.40*	.20*	.05

*p < .05

Table A.5. Policy-Indicator Correlations, 1978

	Expulsions	Corporal Punishment	Suspensions	Gifted Classes	EMR Classes	TMR Classes
Corporal punishment	.37*	×				
Suspensions	.39*	.32*	×			
Gifted classes	− 06	.09	−.17*	×		
EMR classes	.38*	.33*	.30*	−.23*	×	
TMR classes	.15	.02	.18*	−.22*	.33*	×
Graduates	−.08	−.08	−.09	.21*	−.29*	.13

*p < .05

Table A.6. Policy-Indicator Correlations, 1980

	Expulsions	Corporal Punishment	Suspensions	Gifted Classes	EMR Classes	TMR Classes
Corporal punishment	.27*	×				
Suspensions	.39*	.39*	×			
Gifted classes	− .13	−.09	−.13	×		
EMR classes	.30*	.22*	.32*	−.37*	×	
TMR classes	.09	.15	−.01	−.33*	.45*	×
Graduates	−.03	−.08	−.13	.24*	−.24*	−.03

*p < .05

Table A.7. Policy-Indicator Correlations, 1982

	Corporal Punishment	Suspensions	Gifted Classes	EMR Classes	TMR Classes
Suspensions	.30*	×			
Gifted classes	.08	−.29*	×		
EMR classes	.22*	.45*	.49*	×	
TMR classes	.16	.07	−.10	.24*	×
Graduates	−.15	−.05	.35*	−.29*	−.04

*p < .05

Table A.8. Policy-Indicator Correlations, 1984

	Suspensions	Corporal Punishment	Graduates	TMR Classes	EMR Classes
Gifted classes	−.20*	−.01	.42*	−.34*	−.43*
Suspensions	×	.42*	−.26*	.04	.49*
Corporal punishment		×	−.02	−.06	−.03
Graduates			×	−.18*	−.40*
TMR classes				×	.27*

*p < .05

Table A.9. Percentage Distributions of Races in Sample Districts, by Policy Indicator

	Expulsions		Suspensions		Corporal Punishment		EMR Classes		TMR Classes		Gifted Classes		Graduates	
	B	W	B	W	B	W	B	W	B	W	B	W	B	W
1971	54.8	40.5	—	—	—	—	—	—	—	—	—	—	—	—
1972	57.0	38.9	—	—	—	—	—	—	—	—	—	—	—	—
1973	55.6	36.8	36.8	50.9	—	—	46.4	45.0	33.1	58.4	—	—	—	—
1974	48.0	42.7	34.9	54.7	—	—	44.2	46.8	31.3	60.2	—	—	—	—
1976[a]	48.3	45.4	36.8	53.2	34.9	55.8	44.2	46.7	30.8	60.1	12.8	80.5	19.5	71.0
1978	49.7	43.4	36.8	54.5	36.1	56.5	45.2	45.4	30.3	60.9	12.1	80.8	21.7	70.0
1980	46.2	45.7	35.3	54.4	33.9	57.1	44.3	44.9	31.1	58.5	11.1	80.1	21.7	70.0
1982	—	—	39.6	50.3	37.9	53.5	49.2	41.4	34.1	55.2	12.7	79.5	25.6	65.8
1984	—	—	47.0	42.2	45.4	46.1	54.9	34.4	39.3	49.5	17.9	72.9	32.6	56.4

B = blacks
W = whites
[a]For the category Dropouts in 1976 (the only year for which data were collected), the percentages are 25.0 for blacks and 64.2 for whites.

Table A.10. Placement of Black Students in EMR Classes: Multivariate Regressions

Independent Variable	Regression Coefficients		
	1973	1974	1976
Black teachers (%)	−0.64*	−0.65*	−0.69*
White poverty (%)	−1.54*	−0.79*	−1.11*
Black education (%)	−0.21*	−0.15	−0.16*
Black-white income ratio	−26.25	−57.27*	−46.26*
Southern region	8.98*	9.96*	11.08*
District size (in thousands)	−0.0013	−0.0005	−0.0040
F	20.88	20.32	25.87
R^2	.48	.45	.50
Adjusted R^2	.46	.43	.48
N	143	155	160

*p < .05

Table A.11. Placement of Black Students in TMR Classes: Multivariate Regressions

Independent Variable	Regression Coefficients		
	1973	1974	1976
Black teachers (%)	−0.34**	−0.25**	−0.29**
White poverty (%)	−0.38	−0.91	−0.94**
Black education (%)	0.07	−0.26*	−0.30**
Black-white income ratio	−10.61	−29.05	2.46
Southern region	15.53**	7.49**	17.01**
District size (in thousands)	−0.0004	0.0002	−0.0046
F	6.45	6.24	10.50
R^2	.26	.23	.30
Adjusted R^2	.22	.20	.30
N	116	130	135

**p < .05
*p < .10

Table A.12. Suspension of Black Students: Multivariate Regressions

	Regression Coefficients		
Independent Variable	1973	1974	1976
Black teachers (%)	−0.51**	−0.48**	−0.63**
White poverty (%)	0.16	0.07	0.17
Black education (%)	−0.03	−0.27**	−0.12
Black-white income ratio	−30.44*	−24.09	−58.47**
Southern region	6.98**	6.87**	2.84
District size (in thousands)	−0.0066**	0.0012	−0.0057
F	9.98	6.57	11.51
R²	.31	.21	.31
Adjusted R²	.28	.18	.28
N	138	156	162

**p < .05
*p < 10

Table A.13. Expulsion of Black Students: Multivariate Regressions

	Regression Coefficients		
Independent Variable	1971	1972	1973
Black teachers (%)	−0.93*	−1.00*	−0.93*
White poverty (%)	−1.63	−0.12	0.08
Black education (%)	0.06	0.43	0.17
Black-white income ratio	18.89	−65.22	−19.56
Southern region	4.71	−9.15	−2.27
District size (in thousands)	−0.0210	−0.0026	−0.0146
F	6.86	6.08	6.74
R²	.35	.31	.34
Adjusted R²	.30	.26	.29
N	82	89	86

*p < .05

Table A.14. Impact of Other Policy Variables on Blacks: Multivariate Regressions for 1976

Independent Variable	Regression Coefficients		
	Placement in Gifted Classes	Corporal Punishment	Graduation
Black teachers (%)	0.46*	−0.55*	−0.12
White poverty (%)	1.81	0.10	1.01*
Black education (%)	0.93*	0.12	−0.16
Black-white income ratio	46.03	−28.85	13.34
Southern region	−17.98*	−4.65	0.88
District size (in thousands)	0.0446	0.0051	−0.0043
F	7.12	6.72	3.94
R^2	.33	.24	.13
Adjusted R^2	.28	.20	.10
N	95	136	165

*$p < .05$

Appendix B
School Districts Included in the Analysis

ALABAMA
  Huntsville
  Jefferson County
  Mobile County

ALASKA
  Anchorage

ARIZONA
  Mesa Unified
  Phoenix Union
  Tucson

ARKANSAS
  Little Rock
  Pulaski County

CALIFORNIA
  ABC Unified
  Alhambra
  Anaheim Union
  Fresno
  Hacienda–La Puente
  Hayward
  Los Angeles
  Monterey
  Oakland
  Orange
  Palos Verdes
  Pasadena
  Richmond
  Sacramento

San Bernardino
San Diego
San Juan
Stockton

COLORADO
  Adams-Arapahoe County
  Cherry Creek
  Colorado Springs
  Denver
  Pueblo

CONNECTICUT
  Bridgeport

DISTRICT OF COLUMBIA

FLORIDA
  Alachua County
  Bay County
  Brevard County
  Clay County
  Dade County
  Duval County
  Escambia County
  Hillsborough County
  Lake County
  Lee County
  Leon County
  Okaloosa County
  Orange County
  Pasco County

FLORIDA *(continued)*
  Pinellas County
  Seminole County

GEORGIA
  Bibb County
  DeKalb County
  Dougherty County
  Fulton County

ILLINOIS
  Chicago

INDIANA
  Evansville
  Fort Wayne
  Indianapolis
  South Bend

IOWA
  Cedar Rapids
  Des Moines
  Sioux City
  Waterloo

KANSAS
  Kansas City
  Topeka 501
  Wichita 259

KENTUCKY
  Fayette County
  Jefferson County

LOUISIANA
  Bossier Parish
  Caddo Parish
  Calcasieu Parish
  East Baton Rouge
  Jefferson Parish
  Lafayette Parish
  LaFourche Parish
  New Orleans
  Rapides Parish
  St. Landry Parish
  Tangipahoa Parish
  Terrebonne Parish

MARYLAND
  Anne Arundel County
  Baltimore City
  Baltimore County
  Frederick County
  Hartford County
  Montgomery County
  Washington County

MICHIGAN
  Flint
  Lansing

MINNESOTA
  Minneapolis
  St. Paul

MISSISSIPPI
  Jackson

MISSOURI
  Ferguson
  Hazelwood
  Parkway
  St. Joseph
  Springfield

NEBRASKA
  Omaha

NEVADA
  Clark County
  Washoe County

NEW JERSEY
  Camden
  Jersey City
  Newark
  Patterson

NEW MEXICO
  Las Cruces

NEW YORK
  Buffalo
  New York City

NORTH CAROLINA
  Buncome County
  Charlotte-Mecklingberg
  Cumberland County
  Durham County
  Forsyth County
  Greensboro
  Guilford County
  Johnston County

OHIO
  Cincinnati
  Columbus
  Dayton
  Toledo

OKLAHOMA
  Lawton
  Midwest City
  Putnam City
  Tulsa

OREGON
  Portland

PENNSYLVANIA
  Allentown
  Erie
  Philadelphia
  Pittsburgh

SOUTH CAROLINA
  Berkeley County
  Greenville
  Horry County

TENNESSEE
  Davidson County

TEXAS
  Abilene
  Austin
  Dallas
  Ector County
  Edgewood
  El Paso

Fort Worth
Houston
Lubbock
Midland
Northeast
Richardson
San Antonio
Tyler
Waco
Wichita Falls

UTAH
  Salt Lake City

VIRGINIA
  Chesapeake
  Chesterfield County
  Fairfax County
  Hampton
  Henrico
  Newport News
  Norfolk
  Portsmouth
  Prince William County
  Richmond
  Roanoke
  Virginia Beach

WASHINGTON
  Highline
  Kent
  Seattle
  Spokane
  Tacoma
  Vancouver

WEST VIRGINIA
  Cabell County
  Harrison County
  Kanawha County
  Mercer County

WISCONSIN
  Kenosha
  Madison
  Milwaukee

Bibliography

Aaron, Robert, and Glen Powell. 1982. "Feedback Practices as a Function of Teacher and Pupil Race during Reading Group Instruction." *Journal of Negro Education* 51 (Winter): 50–59.

Abney, Glenn F. 1974. "Factors Related to Voter Turnout in Mississippi." *Journal of Politics* 36 (November): 1057–1063.

Adair, Alvis V. 1984 *Desegregation. The Illusion of Black Progress.* New York: University Press of America.

Alexander, Karl L., and Bruce K. Eckland. 1975. "Contextual Effects in the High School Attainment Process." *American Sociological Review* 40 (June): 402–416.

Alexander, Karl L., and Edward McDill. 1976. "Selection and Allocation within Schools." *American Sociological Review* 41 (December): 969–980.

Allport, Gordon W. 1954. *The Nature of Prejudice.* Reading, Mass.: Addison-Wesley.

Alston, Denise A. 1988. "Recruiting Minority Classroom Teachers: State Policies and Practices." In *Capital Ideas,* 1–8. Washington, D.C.: National Governors' Association, March 15.

Alwin, Duane F., and Luther B. Otto. 1977. "High School Context Effects on Aspirations." *Sociology of Education* 50 (October): 259–273.

Anderson, James E. 1984. *Public Policy-Making.* 3rd ed. New York: Praeger.

Anderson, James E., David W. Brady, Charles Bullock III, and Joseph Stewart, Jr. 1984. *Public Policy and Politics in America.* Monterey, Calif.: Brooks/Cole.

Applebee, Arthur N., Judith A. Langer, and Ina V. S. Mullis. 1986. *The Writing Report Card: Writing Achievement in American Schools.* Princeton, N.J.: Educational Testing Service.

Aptheker, Herbert, ed. 1951. *A Documentary History of the Negro People in the United States.* New York: Citadel.

Armor, David J. 1978. *White Flight, Demographic Transition, and the Future of School Desegregation.* Santa Monica: Rand Corporation (R-5931).

Armor, David J. 1980. "White Flight and the Future of School Desegregation." In Walter G. Stephan and Joe R. Feagin, eds., *School Desegregation: Past, Present, and Future,* 187–226. New York: Plenum Press.

Arnez, Nancy L. 1978. "Implementation of Desegregation as a Discriminatory Process." *Journal of Negro Education* 47 (Winter): 28–45.

Austin, Mary C., and Coleman Morrison. 1963. *The First R: The Harvard Report on Reading in Elementary School.* New York: Macmillian.

Baker, James N., with Daniel Shapiro, Pat Wingert, and Nadine Joseph. 1987. "Paddling: Still a Sore Point." *Newsweek* (June 22): 61.

Banfield, Edward C., and James Q. Wilson. 1963. *City Politics.* New York: Vintage.

Banks, James A. 1982. "Educating Minority Youths: An Inventory of Current Theory." *Education and Urban Society* 15 (November): 88–103.

Barbagli, Marzio, and Marcello Dei. 1977. "Socialization into Apathy and Public Subordination." In Jerome Karabel and A. H. Halsey, eds., *Power and Ideology in Education,* 423–431. New York: Oxford University Press.

Barr, Rebecca, and Robert Dreeben. 1977. "Instruction in Classrooms." In L. S. Schulman, ed., *Review of Research in Education,* Vol. 5, 89–162, Itaska, Ill.: Peacock.

Barth, Alan. 1974. *Prophets with Honor: Great Dissents and Great Dissenters in the Supreme Court.* New York: Knopf.

Becker, Gary S. 1975. *Human Capital.* 2nd ed. New York: Columbia University Press.

Bell, Derrick. 1980. "A Model Desegregation Plan." In Derrick Bell, ed., *Shades of Brown: New Perspectives on School Desegregation,* 124–139. New York: Teachers College, Columbia University.

Bennett, Christine, and J. John Harris. 1982. "Suspensions and Expulsions of Male and Black Students." *Urban Education* 16 (January): 399–423.

Bickel, William E. 1982. "Classifying Mentally Retarded Students: A Review of Placement Practices in Special Education." In Kirby A. Heller, Wayne H. Holtzman, and Samuel Messick, eds., *Placing Children in Special Education,* 182–229. Washington, D.C.: National Academy Press.

Birmingham, Stephen. 1977. *Certain People.* Boston: Little, Brown.

Birnie, W. W. 1927. "Education of the Negro in Charleston, South Carolina, Prior to the Civil War." *Journal of Negro History* 12 (January): 13–21.

Blau, Peter M., and Otis Dudley Duncan. 1967. *American Occupational Structure.* New York: John Wiley.

Bloome, David, and Cathy Golden. 1982. "Literacy, Learning, Classroom Processes, and Race." *Journal of Black Studies* 13 (December): 227–240.

Bond, Horace Mann. 1934. *The Education of the Negro in the American Social Order.* New York: Prentice-Hall.

Bosco, James, and Stanley Robin. 1974. "White Flight from Court-Ordered Busing." *Urban Education* 9 (April): 87–98.

Bowles, Samuel, and Herbert Gintis. 1973. "IQ in the U.S. Class Structure." *Social Policy* 3 (January-February): 65–96.

Brady, Nelvia M. 1980. *The Impact of Compensatory Education Programs on Equality of Educational Opportunities in Desegregated Elementary Schools.* Ph.D. dissertation, Michigan State University.

Brantlinger, Ellen A., and Samuel L. Guskin. 1985. "Implications of Social and Cultural Differences for Special Education with Specific Recommendations." *Focus on Exceptional Children* 18 (September): 1–12.

Bridge, Gary R., Charles M. Judd, and Peter R. Mock. 1979. *Determinants of Educational Outcomes: The Impact of Families, Peers, Teachers, and Schools.* Cambridge, Mass.: Ballinger.

Brim, Orville G., and Stanton Wheeler. 1966. *Socialization after Childhood.* New York: John Wiley.

Brookover, Wilbur B., and Edsel L. Erickson. 1975. *The Sociology of Education.* Homewood, Ill.: Dorsey Press.

Brooks, Gary H. 1982. "Black Political Mobilization and White Legislative Behavior." In Lawrence W. Moreland, Tod A. Baker, and Robert T. Steed, eds., *Contemporary Southern Political Attitudes and Behavior,* 221–238. New York: Praeger.

Brophy, Jere E. 1983. "Classroom Organization and Management." *Elementary School Journal* 83 (March): 265–285.

Brophy, Jere E., and Thomas L. Good. 1970. "Teachers' Communication of Differential Expectations for Children's Classroom Performance." *Journal of Educational Psychology* 61 (October): 365–374.

Brophy, Jere E., and Thomas L. Good. 1970. *Teacher Student Relationships: Causes and Consequences.* New York: Holt, Reinhart, and Winston.

Browning, Rufus P., Dale R. Marshall, and David H. Tabb. 1984. *Protest Is Not Enough: The Struggle of Blacks and Hispanics for Equality in Urban Politics.* Berkeley: University of California press.

Bullock, Charles S., III. 1976. "Compliance with School Desegregation Laws: Financial Inducements and Policy Performance." Paper presented at the annual meeting of the American Political Science Association, Chicago, September 2–5.

Bullock, Charles S., III. 1980. "The Office for Civil Rights and Implementation of Desegregation Programs in the Public Schools." *Policy Studies Journal* 8 (Special Issue No. 2): 597–615.

Bullock, Charles S., III, and Christopher Dennis. 1982. "A Diachronic Analysis of Black Registration and Office Holding in Two Southern States." Paper presented at the annual meeting of the Southern Political Science Association, Atlanta.

Bullock, Charles S., III, and Charles M. Lamb. 1984. *Implementation of Civil Rights Policy.* Monterey, Calif.: Brooks/Cole.

Bullock, Charles S., III, and Susan A. MacManus. 1981. "Policy Responsiveness of the Black Electorate." *American Politics Quarterly* 9 (July): 357–368.

Bullock, Charles S., III, and Joseph Stewart, Jr. 1978. "Complaint Processing as a Strategy for Combating Second Generation Discrimination." Paper presented at the annual meeting of the Southern Political Science Association, Atlanta.

Bullock, Charles S., III, and Joseph Stewart, Jr. 1979. "Incidence and Correlates of Second Generation Discrimination." In Marian L. Palley and Michael B. Preston, eds., *Race, Sex, and Policy Problems,* 115–129. Lexington, Mass.: Lexington Books.

Bullock, Henry Allen. 1967. *A History of Negro Education in the South.* Cambridge, Mass.: Harvard University Press.

Burton, Nancy, and Lyle Jones. 1982. "Recent Trends in Achievement Levels of Black and White Youth." *Educational Researcher* 11 (April).

Campbell, David, and Joe Feagin. 1975. "Black Politics in the South: A Descriptive Analysis." *Journal of Politics* 37 (February): 129–159.

Carlberg, Conrad, and Kenneth Kavale. 1980. "The Efficacy of Special versus Regular Class Placement for Exceptional Children: A Meta-Analysis." *Journal of Special Education* 14 (Fall): 295–309.

Carter, David G. 1982. "Second-Generation School Integration Problems for Blacks." *Journal of Black Studies* 13 (December): 175–188.

Cayer, N. Joseph, and Lee Sigelman. 1980. "Minorities and Women in State and Local Government: 1973–1975." *Public Administration Review* 40 (September–October): 443–450.

Cervantes, Robert A. 1984. "Ethnocentric Pedagogy and Minority Student Growth." *Education and Urban Society* 16 (May): 274–293.

Champagne, Richard. 1987. "Putting Color Back into the Constitution." Unpublished manuscript, Department of Political Science, University of Wisconsin–Madison.

Chesler, Mark A., and William M. Cave. 1981. *Sociology of Education.* New York: Macmillian.

Children's Defense Fund. 1974. *Children Out of School in America.* Washington, D.C.: Children's Defense Fund of the Washington Research Project.

Children's Defense Fund. 1975. *School Suspensions: Are They Helping Children?* Washington, D.C.: Children's Defense Fund of the Washington Research Project.

Children's Defense Fund. 1977. *The Elementary and Secondary School Civil Rights Survey: 'Bureaucratic Balderdash' or the Cornerstone of Civil Rights Compliance in Public Schools?* Washington, D.C.: Children's Defense Fund of the Washington Research Project.

Chinn, Philip C., and Selma Hughes. 1987. "Representation of Minority Students in Special Education Classes." *Remedial and Special Education* 8 (July-August): 41–46.

Cicourel, Aaron V., and John I. Kitsuse. 1963. *The Educational Decision-Makers.* Indianapolis, Ind.: Bobbs-Merrill.

Cistone, Peter J. 1975. "The Recruitment and Socialization of School Board Members." In Peter J. Cistone, ed., *Understanding School Boards,* 47–62. Lexington, Mass.: D. C. Heath.

Clifton, Rodney A., Raymond P. Perry, Karen Parsonson, and Stella Hrynuik. 1986. "Effects of Ethnicity and Sex on Teachers' Expectations of Junior High School Students," *Sociology of Education* 59 (January): 58–67.

Cnudde, Charles F., and Donald J. McCrone. 1969. "Party Competition and Welfare Policies in the American States." *American Political Science Review* 63 (September): 858–866.

Cohen, Yinon, and Andrea Tyree. 1986. "Escape from Poverty: Determinants of Intergenerational Mobility of Sons and Daughters of the Poor." *Social Science Quarterly* 67 (December): 803–813.

Cole, Beverly P. 1986. "The Black Educator: An Endangered Species." *Journal of Negro Education* 55 (Summer): 326–334.

Cole, Leonard A. 1974. "Electing Blacks to Municipal Office." *Urban Affairs Quarterly* 10 (September): 17–19.

Cole, Leonard A. 1976. *Blacks in Power.* Princeton: Princeton University Press.

Cole, Richard L. 1971. "The Urban Policy Process: A Note on Structural and Regional Influences." *Social Science Quarterly* 52 (December): 646–655.

Coleman, James S. 1976. "Liberty and Equality in School Desegregation." *Social Policy* 6 (January-February): 9–13.

Coleman, James S. 1981. "The Role of Incentives in School Desegregation." In Adam Yarmolinsky, Lance Liebman, and Corinne S. Schelling, eds., *Race and Schooling in the City,* 182–193. Cambridge, Mass.: Harvard University Press.

Coleman, James S., Ernest Q. Campbell, Carol J. Hobson, James McPartland, Alexander B. Mood, Frederic D. Weinfeld, and Robert L. York. 1966. *Equality of Educational Opportunity.* Washington, D.C.: U.S. Government Printing Office.

Coleman, James S., Sara D. Kelly, and John A. Moore. 1975a. "Recent Trends in School Integration." Paper presented at the annual meeting of the American Educational Research Association, Washington, D.C.

Coleman, James S., Sara D. Kelly, and John A. Moore. 1975b. *Trends in School Segregation, 1968–73*. Working Paper 722-03-01. Washington, D.C.: Urban Institute.

Conant, James B. 1967. *The Comprehensive High School*. New York: McGraw-Hill.

Cooper, Constance C. 1985. "Black Teacher Population Change, 1980–1984 in Southern States." Baltimore, Md.: Coppin State College, mimeo.

Corcoran, Mary, and Greg J. Duncan. 1979. "Work History, Labor Force Attachment, and Earnings Differences between the Races and Sexes." *Journal of Human Resources* 14 (Winter): 3–14.

Corman, Louise, and Jay Gottlieb. 1978. "Mainstreaming Mentally Retarded Children: A Review of Research." In Norman R. Ellis, ed., *International Review of Research in Mental Retardation*, 251–276. New York: Academic Press.

Cruse, Harold W. 1987. *Plural But Equal: A Critical Study of Blacks and Minorities and America's Plural Society*. New York: William Morrow.

Dahl, Robert A. 1961. *Who Governs?* New Haven: Yale University Press.

Damico, Sandra Bowman, and Christopher Sparks. 1986. "Cross-Group Contact Opportunities: Impact on Interpersonal Relationships in Desegregated Middle Schools." *Sociology of Education* 59 (April): 113–123.

Davidson, Chandler, and George Korbel. 1981 "At-Large Elections and Minority Group Representation." *Journal of Politics* 43 (November): 982–1005.

Davies, R. Peter. 1975. *Mixed Ability Grouping: Possibilities and Experiences in the Secondary School*. London: Temple Smith.

Davis, William R. 1934. *The Development and Present Status of Negro Education in East Texas*. New York: Teachers College, Columbia University.

Dawkins, Marvin P. 1983. "Black Students' Occupational Expectations: A National Study of the Impact of School Desegregation." *Urban Education* 18 (April): 98–113.

Dawson, Richard E., and James A. Robinson. 1963. "Inter-Party Competition, Economic Variables and Welfare Policies in the American States." *Journal of Politics* 25 (May): 265–289.

DeMeis, Debra K., and Ralph R. Turner. 1978. "Effects of Students' Race, Physical Attractiveness and Dialect on Teachers' Evaluations." *Contemporary Educational Psychology* 3 (January): 77–86.

Dennis, Jack. 1968. "Major Problems in Political Socialization." *Midwest Political Science Review* 12 (February): 85–114.

Dometrius, Nelson C., and Lee Sigelman. 1988. "Teacher Testing and Racial-Ethnic Representativeness in Public Education." *Social Science Quarterly* 69 (March): 70–82.

Downs, Anthony. 1967. *Inside Bureaucracy*. Boston: Little, Brown.

Downs, Anthony. 1970. *Racism in America and How to Combat it*. Washington, D.C.: U.S. Commission on Civil Rights.

Du Bois, W. E .B., ed. 1901. *The Negro Common School*. Atlanta: Atlanta University Press.

Duncan, Greg J. 1984. *Years of Poverty, Years of Plenty*. Ann Arbor, Mich.: Institute for Social Research, University of Michigan.

Dunn, Lloyd M. 1968. "Special Education for the Mildly Retarded—Is Much of It Justifiable?" *Exceptional Children* 35 (September): 5–22.

Dusek, Jerome B., and Gail Joseph. 1983. "The Bases of Teacher Expectancies: A Meta-Analysis." *Journal of Educational Psychology* 75 (June): 327–346.

Dye, Thomas R. 1966. *Politics, Economics and the Public.* Chicago: Rand McNally.

Dye, Thomas R. 1968. "Urban School Desegregation: A Comparative Analysis." *Urban Affairs Quarterly* 4 (December): 141–166.

Dye, Thomas R., ed. 1969. *American Public Policy: Documents and Essays.* Columbus, Ohio: Merrill.

Dye, Thomas R., and James Renick. 1981. "Political Power and City Jobs: Determinants of Minority Employment." *Social Science Quarterly* 62 (September): 475–486.

Eder, Donna. 1981. "Ability Grouping as a Self-Fulfilling Prophecy." *Sociology of Education* 54 (July): 151–162.

Eisinger, Peter K. 1982a. "Black Employment in Municipal Jobs: The Impact of Black Political Power." *American Political Science Review* 76 (June): 380–392.

Eisinger, Peter K. 1982b. "The Economic Conditions of Black Employment in Municipal Bureaucracies." *American Journal of Political Science* 26 (November): 754–771.

Elazar, Daniel J. 1984. *American Federalism: A View from the States.* 3rd ed. New York: Harper and Row.

England, Robert E., and Kenneth J. Meier. 1985. "From Desegregation to Integration: Second Generation Discrimination as an Institutional Impediment." *American Politics Quarterly* 13 (April): 227–247.

England, Robert E., and David R. Morgan. 1986. *Desegregating Big City Schools: Strategies, Outcomes, and Impacts.* New York: Associated Faculty Press.

England, Robert E., Kenneth J. Meier, and Luis R. Fraga. 1986. "Second Generation School Discrimination: A Longitudinal Analysis." Paper presented at the annual meeting of the Southwest Political Science Association, March 19–22, San Antonio.

Engstrom, Richard L., and Michael D. McDonald. 1981. "The Election of Blacks to City Councils." *American Political Science Review* 75 (June): 344–354.

Engstrom, Richard L., and Michael D. McDonald. 1982. "The Underrepresentation of Blacks on City Councils." *Journal of Politics* 44 (November): 1088–1105.

Entwisle, Doris R., and Leslie A. Hayduck. 1981. "Academic Expectations and the School Attainment of Young Children." *Sociology of Education* 54 (January): 34–50.

Epps, Edgar G. 1981. "Minority Children: Desegregation, Self-Evaluation, and Achievement Orientation." In Willis D. Hawley, ed., *Effective School Desegregation: Equity, Quality and Feasibility,* 85–106. Beverly Hills, Calif.: Sage.

Epstein, Benjamin. 1971. "Displacement and Present Status of Black School Principals in Desegregated School Districts." Testimony before the U.S. Senate Select Committee on Equal Educational Opportunity, June 14, 4906–4907. Washington, D.C.: U.S. Government Printing Office.

Epstein, Joyce L. 1985. "After the Bus Arrives: Resegregation in Desegregated Schools." *Journal of Social Issues* 41 (Fall): 23–43.

Epstein, Joyce L. 1986. *After the Bus Arrives: Resegregation in Desegregated Schools.* Baltimore: Johns Hopkins University Press.

Eulau, Heinz, and Paul D. Karps. 1977. "The Puzzle of Representation: Specifying Components of Responsiveness." *Legislative Studies Quarterly* 2 (August): 233–254.

Eulau, Heinz, John C. Wahlke, William Buchanan, and Leroy C. Ferguson. 1959. "The Role of the Representative: Some Empirical Observations on the Theory of Edmund Burke." *American Political Science Review* 53 (September): 742–756.

Everhart, Robert B. 1983. *Reading, Writing, and Resistance.* London: Routledge and Kegan Paul.

Evertson, Carolyn M. 1986. "Do Teachers Make a Difference? Issues for the Eighties." *Education and Urban Society* 18 (February): 195–210.

Eyler, Janet, Valerie J. Cook, and Leslie E. Ward. 1983. "Resegregation: Segregation within Desegregated Schools." In Christine H. Rossell and Willis D. Hawley, eds. *The Consequences of School Desegregation,* 126–162. Philadelphia: Temple University Press.

Eyler, Janet, Valerie J. Cook, Rachel Thompkins, William Trent, and Leslie E. Ward. 1981. "Resegregation: Segregation within Desegregated Schools." In Christine Rossell et al., eds., *Assessment of Current Knowledge About the Effectiveness of School Desegregation Strategies,* 210–329. Nashville, Tenn.: Institute of Public Policy Studies, Vanderbilt University.

Farley, Reynolds. 1975. "Racial Integration in the Public Schools, 1967 to 1972: Assessing the Effects of Governmental Politics." *Sociological Forces* 8 (January): 3–26.

Farley, Reynolds. 1984. *Blacks and Whites: Narrowing the Gap.* Cambridge, Mass.: Harvard University Press.

Farley, Reynolds, and Walter R. Allen. 1987. *The Color Line and the Quality of Life in America.* New York: Russel Sage Foundation.

Farley, Reynolds, Toni Richards, and Clarence Wurdock. 1980. "School Desegregation and White Flight: An Investigation of Competing Models and Their Discrepant Findings." *Sociology of Education* 53 (July): 123–139.

Farrell, Walter C., James L. Olson, William W. Malloy, and Wesley L. Boykin. 1984. "Discrimination in Educational Placement and Referral." *Integrated Education* 20 (July): 120–123.

Feagin, Joe R. 1980. "School Desegregation: A Political-Economic Perspective." In Walter G. Stephan and Joe R. Feagin, eds., *School Desegregation: Past, Present and Future,* 25–50. New York: Plenum Press.

Feagin, Joe R., and Clairece Booher Feagin. 1986. *Discrimination American Style.* 2nd ed. Malabar, Fla.: Robert E. Krieger Publishing Co.

Featherman, David L., and Robert M. Hauser. 1976. "Changes in the Socioeconomic Stratification of the Races, 1962–1973." *American Journal of Sociology* 82 (November): 621–651.

Felice, Lawrence G., and Ronald L. Richardson. 1977. "The Effects of Busing and School Desegregation on Majority and Minority Student Dropout Rates." *Journal of Educational Research* 70 (May-June): 242–246.

Felmlee, Diane, and Donna Eder. 1983. "Contextual Effects in the Classroom: The

Impact of Ability Groups on Student Attention.'' *Sociology of Education* 56 (April): 77–87.

Fernández, Ricardo R., and Judith T. Guskin. 1981. "Hispanic Students and School Desegregation." In Willis D. Hawley, ed., *Effective School Desegregation: Equity, Quality, and Feasibility,* 107–140. Beverly Hills, Calif.: Sage.

Findley, Warren, and Miriam Bryan. 1975. *The Pros and Cons of Ability Grouping.* Bloomington, Ind.: Phi Delta Kappa Educational Foundation.

Finley, Merrilee K. 1984. "Teachers and Tracking in a Comprehensive High School." *Sociology of Education* 57 (October): 233–243.

Finn, Jeremy D. 1982. "Patterns in Special Education Placement as Revealed by the OCR Surveys." In Kirby A. Heller, Wayne H. Holtzman, and Samuel Messick, eds., *Placing Children in Special Education,* 322–381. Washington, D.C.: National Academy Press.

Fisher, Charles W. 1970. *Minorities Civil Rights and Protest.* Belmont, Calf.: Dickenson.

Fitzgerald, Michael R., and David R. Morgan. 1977. "Changing Patterns of Urban School Desegregation." *American Politics Quarterly* 5 (October): 437–463.

Flaxman, Erwin, ed. 1976. *Educating the Disadvantaged.* New York: AMS Press.

Foner, Philip S., ed. 1955. *The Life and Writings of Frederick Douglass,* Vol. 4. New York: International Publishers.

Forbes, Roy H. 1985. "Academic Achievement of Historically Lower-Achieving Students during the Seventies." *Phi Delta Kappan* 66 (April): 542–543.

Fraga, Luis R., Kenneth J. Meier, and Robert E. England. 1986. "Hispanic Americans and Educational Policy: Limits to Equal Access." *Journal of Politics* 48 (November): 850–876.

Franseth, Jane. 1966. "Does Grouping Make a Difference in Pupil Learning?" In Anne Morgenstern, ed., *Grouping in Elementary School,* 14–21. New York: Pitman Publishing.

Free, Lloyd A., and Hadley Cantril. 1967. *The Political Beliefs of Americans.* New Brunswick, N.J.: Rutgers University Press.

Freeman, Richard B. 1977. "Political Power, Desegregation, and Employment of Black Schoolteachers." *Journal of Political Economy* 85 (April): 299–322.

Freire, Paulo. 1970. *Pedagogy of the Oppressed.* New York: Herder and Herder.

Friedrich, Carl J. 1950. *Constitutional Government and Democracy.* Boston: Little, Brown.

Friesema, H. Paul, and Ronald D. Hedlund. 1974. "The Reality of Representational Roles." In Norman R. Luttbeg, *Public Opinion and Public Policy,* 413–417. Homewood, Ill.: Dorsey Press.

Gallagher, James J. 1972. "The Special Education Contract for Mildly Handicapped Children." *Exceptional Children* 38 (March): 527–535.

Gamson, William. 1975. *The Strategy of Social Protest.* Homewood, Ill.: Dorsey Press.

Garrison, Mortimer, and Donald D. Hammill. 1971. "Who Are the Retarded?" *Exceptional Children* 38 (September): 13–20.

Gartner, Alan, and Dorothy Kerzner Lipsky. 1987. "Beyond Special Education: Toward a Quality System for All Students.'' *Harvard Educational Review* 57 (November): 367–395.

Gates, Robbins L. 1964. *The Making of Massive Resistance: Virginia's Politics of Public School Desegregation, 1954–1956.* Chapel Hill: University of North Carolina Press.

Gay, G. 1974. ''Differential Dyadic Interactions of Black and White Teachers with Black and White Pupils in Recently Desegregated Social Studies Classrooms.'' Office of Education Project No. 2F113.

General Accounting Office. 1984. *Education Block Grant Alters State Role and Provides Greater Local Discretion.* Washington, D.C.

Gerard, Harold B., Terrence D. Jackson, and Edward S. Conollcy. 1975. ''Social Contact in the Desegregated Classroom.'' In Harold B. Gerard and Norman V. Miller, eds., *School Desegregation,* 211–242. New York: Plenum Press.

Gerber, David A. 1976. *Black Ohio and the Color Line, 1860–1915.* Urbana: University of Illinois Press.

Giles, Micheal W. 1975. ''Black Concentration and School District Size as Predictors of School Segregation: The Impact of Federal Enforcement.'' *Sociology of Education* 48 (Fall): 11–19.

Giles, Micheal W. 1978. ''White Enrollment Stability and School Desegregation: A Two-Level Analysis.'' *American Sociological Review* 43 (December): 848–864.

Giles, Micheal W., and Arthur S. Evans. 1985. ''External Threat, Perceived Threat, and Group Identity.'' *Social Science Quarterly* 66 (March): 50–66.

Giles, Micheal W., and Arthur S. Evans. 1986. ''The Power Approach to Intergroup Hostility.'' *Journal of Conflict Resolution* 30 (September): 469–486.

Giles, Micheal W., and Douglas S. Gatlin. 1980. ''Mass Level Compliance with Public Policy: The Case of School Desegregation.'' *Journal of Politics* 37 (August): 722–746.

Goldberg, Miriam, and A. Harry Passow. 1966. ''The Effects of Ability Grouping.'' In Anne Morgenstern, ed., *Grouping in Elementary School,* 22–39. New York: Pitman Publishing.

Goldberg, Miriam L., A. Harry Passow, and Joseph Justman. 1966. *The Effects of Ability Grouping.* New York: Teachers College, Columbia University.

Good, Thomas L. 1970. ''Which Pupils Do Teachers Call On?'' *The Elementary School Journal* 70 (January): 190–198.

Good, Thomas L., and Harris M. Cooper. 1983. *Pygmalion Grows Up.* New York: Longman.

Grant, Linda. 1984. ''Black Females' 'Place' in Desegregated Classrooms.'' *Sociology of Education* 57 (April): 96–111.

Groff, Patrick J. 1962. ''A Survey of Basic Reading Group Practices.'' *Reading Teacher* 15 (January): 232–235.

Hall, Grace, and Alan Saltzstein. 1977. ''Equal Employment Opportunity for Minorities in Municipal Government.'' *Social Science Quarterly* 57 (March): 864–872.

Harmel, Robert, Keith Hamm, and Robert Thompson. 1983. ''Black Voting Cohesion and Distinctiveness in Southern Legislatures.'' *Social Science Quarterly* 64 (March): 183–192.

Harrison, Bennett. 1972. *Education, Training, and the Urban Ghetto.* Baltimore: Johns Hopkins University Press.

Hauser, Robert M., William H. Sewell, and Duane F. Alwin. 1976. "High School Effects on Achievement." In William H. Sewell, Robert M. Hauser, and David L. Featherman, eds., *Schooling and Achievement in American Society,* 309–342. New York: Academic Press.

Hawkins, Michael L. 1966. "Mobility of Students in Reading Groups." *Reading Teacher* 20 (November): 136–140.

Hawley, Willis D. 1981. "Equality and Quality in Education: Characteristics of Effective Desegregated Schools." In Willis D. Hawley, ed., *Effective School Desegregation: Equity, Quality, and Feasibility,* 297–307. Beverly Hills, Calif.: Sage.

Hawley, Willis D., et al. 1983. *Strategies for Effective Desegregation.* Lexington, Mass.: Lexington Books.

Hawley, Willis, and Susan Rosenholtz. 1984. "Good Schools: What Research Says about Improving Student Achievement." *Peabody Journal of Education* 61 (Summer): 1–178.

Hedlund, Ronald D., and H. Paul Friesema. 1972. "Representatives' Perceptions of Constituency Opinion." *Journal of Politics* 34 (August): 730–752.

Helig, Peggy, and Robert J. Mundt. 1983. "The Effect of Adopting Districts on Representational Equity." *Social Science Quarterly* 64 (June): 393–397.

Heller, Kirby A. 1982. "Effects of Special Education Placement on Mentally Retarded Children." In Kirby A. Heller, Wayne H. Holtzman, and Samuel Messick, eds., *Placing Children in Special Education,* 262–299. Washington, D.C.: National Academy Press.

Heller, Kirby A., Wayne H. Holtzman, and Samuel Messick, eds. 1982. *Placing Children in Special Education.* Washington, D.C.: National Academy Press.

Hellriegel, Don, and Larry Short. 1972. "Equal Employment Opportunity in the Federal Government: A Comparative Analysis." *Public Administration Review* 32 (November-December): 852–858.

Henderson, Lenneal J., and Michael B. Preston. 1984. "Blacks, Public Employment, and Public Interest Theory." In Mitchell F. Rice and Woodrow Jones, Jr., eds. *Contemporary Public Policy Perspectives and Black Americans,* 33–48. Westport, Conn.: Greenwood Press.

Heohn, Arthur J. 1954. "A Study of Social Status Differentiation in the Classroom Behavior of Nineteen Third Grade Teachers." *Journal of Social Psychology* 39 (May): 269–292.

Heyns, Barbara. 1974. "Social Selection and Stratification within Schools." *American Journal of Sociology* 79 (May): 1434–1451.

Hobbs, Nicholas. 1975. *The Futures of Children: Categories, Labels, and Their Consequences.* San Francisco: Jossey-Bass.

Hochschild, Jennifer L. 1984. *The New American Dilemma: Liberal Democracy and School Desegregation.* New Haven: Yale University Press.

Hofferbert, Richard I. 1974. *The Study of Public Policy.* Indianapolis: Bobbs-Merrill.

Holliday, Bertha Garrett. 1985. "Differential Effects of Children's Self-Perceptions and Teachers' Perceptions on Black Children's Academic Achievement." *Journal of Negro Education* 54 (Winter): 71–81.

Howard, Lawrence C. 1975. "Black Praxis of Governance: Toward an Alternative Paradigm for Public Administration." *Journal of Afro-American Issues* 3 (Spring): 143–159.

Hughes, Larry W., William M. Gordon, and Larry W. Hillman. 1980. *Desegregating America's Schools*. New York: Longman.

Hutchins, Matthew, and Lee Sigelman. 1981. "Black Employment in State and Local Government." *Social Science Quarterly* 62 (March): 79–87.

Jackman, Mary R. 1978. "General and Applied Tolerance." *American Journal of Political Science* 22 (May): 302–324.

Jackman, Mary R. 1981. "Education and Policy Commitment to Racial Integration." *American Journal of Political Science* 25 (May): 256–271.

Jackson, Gregg, and Cecilia Cosca. 1974. "The Inequality of Educational Opportunity in the Southwest." *American Educational Research Journal* 11 (October): 3–23.

Janowitz, Morris. 1969. *Institutional Building in Urban Education*. New York: Russell Sage Foundation.

Jencks, Christopher, et al. 1972. *Inequality: A Reassessment of the Effect of Family and Schooling in America*. New York: Harper & Row.

Johnson, Charles S. 1938. *The Negro College Graduate*. Chapel Hill: University of North Carolina Press.

Jones, Clinton B. 1976. "The Impact of Local Election Systems and Black Representation." *Urban Affairs Quarterly* 11 (March): 345–356.

Jones, Reginald L., ed. 1976. *Mainstreaming and the Minority Child*. Reston, Va.: Council for Exceptional Children.

Jones, Reginald L., and Frank Wilderson. 1976. "Mainstreaming and the Minority Child: An Overview of Issues and a Perspective." In Reginald L. Jones, ed., *Mainstreaming and the Minority Child*, 1–14. Reston, Va.: Council for Exceptional Children.

Kaeser, Susan C. 1979. "Suspensions in School Discipline." *Education and Urban Sociology* 11 (August): 465–486.

Karnig, Albert K. 1976. "Black Representation on City Councils." *Urban Affairs Quarterly* 12 (December): 223–242.

Karnig, Albert K. 1979. "Black Resources and City Council Representation." *Journal of Politics* 41 (February): 134–149.

Karnig, Albert K., and Susan Welch. 1979. "Sex and Ethnic Differences in Municipal Representation." *Social Science Quarterly* 60 (December): 465–481.

Karnig, Albert K., and Susan Welch. 1980. *Black Representation and Urban Policy*. Chicago: University of Chicago Press.

Karnig, Albert K., and Susan Welch. 1982. "Electoral Structure and Black Representation on City Councils." *Social Science Quarterly* 63 (March): 99–114.

Katzman, Martin T. 1978. *The Quality of Municipal Services: Central City Decline and Middle-Class Flight*. Cambridge, Mass.: Harvard University Press.

Katzman, Martin T. 1983. "The Flight of Blacks from Central City Public Schools." *Urban Education* 18 (October): 259–283.

Keech, William R. 1968. *The Impact of Negro Voting.* Chicago: Rand McNally.

Keller, Ernest. 1978. "The Impact of Black Mayors on Urban Policy." *The Annals* 439: 40–52.

Kessel, John H. 1968. "The Supreme Court and the American People." In Sheldon Goldman and Thomas P. Jahnige, eds., *The Federal Judicial System: Readings in Process and Behavior,* 77–91. New York: Holt, Rinehart, and Winston.

Key, V. O. 1956. *American State Politics.* New York: Knopf.

Kingsley, J. Donald. 1944. *Representative Bureaucracy.* Yellow Springs, Ohio: Antioch Press.

Kirp, David L. 1973. "Schools as Sorters: The Constitutional and Policy Implications of Student Classification." *University of Pennsylvania Law Review* 121 (April): 705–797.

Klingberg, Frank J. 1941. *The Appraisal of the Negro in Colonial South Carolina: A Study in Americanization.* Washington, D.C.: Associated Publishers.

Kluger, Richard. 1975. *Simple Justice.* New York: Knopf.

Knowles, Louis L., and Kenneth Prewitt. 1969. *Institutional Racism in America.* Englewood Cliffs, N.J.: Prentice-Hall.

Krislov, Samuel. 1965. *The Supreme Court in the Political Process.* New York: Macmillian.

Kuklinski, James H. 1979. "Representative-Constituency Linkages: A Review Article." *Legislative Studies Quarterly* 4 (February): 121–140.

Kulik, Chen-Lin, and James A. Kulik. 1982. "Effects of Ability Grouping on Secondary School Students." *American Educational Research Journal* 19 (Fall): 415–428.

Lanier, J., and J. Wittmer. 1977. "Teacher Prejudice in Referral of Students to EMR Programs." *The School Counselor* 24: 165–170.

Lapointe, Archie E. 1984. "The Good News about American Education." *Phi Delta Kappan* 65 (June): 663–667.

Lasswell, Harold D. 1936. *Politics: Who Gets What, When, How?* New York: McGraw-Hill.

Leacock, Eleanor B. 1969. *Teaching and Learning in City Schools.* New York: Basic Books.

Levin, Betsy, and Phillip Moise. 1975. "Litigation in the Seventies and the Use of Social Science Evidence: An Annotated Guide." *Law and Contemporary Problems* 39 (Winter): 50–133.

Levin, Henry M. 1975. "Education, Life Chances, and the Courts: The Role of Social Science Evidence." *Law and Contemporary Problems* 39 (Spring): 217–239.

Levine, Charles H. 1974. *Racial Conflict and the American Mayor.* Lexington, Mass.: Lexington Books.

Levitan, David M. 1946. "The Responsibility of Administrative Officials in a Democratic Society." *Political Science Quarterly* 61 (December): 562–598.

Levy, Leonard W. 1957. *The Law of the Commonwealth and Chief Justice Shaw.* Cambridge, Mass.: Harvard University Press.

Lewis, Anthony. 1965. *Portrait of a Decade.* New York: Bantam.

Lewis-Beck, Michael, and Tom W. Rice. 1985. "Government Growth in the United States." *Journal of Politics* 47 (February): 2–30.

Lieberson, Stanley. 1980. *A Piece of the Pie: Blacks and White Immigrants since 1980.* Berkeley, Calif.: University of California Press.

Lightfoot, Sara L. 1980. "Families as Educators: The Forgotten People of *Brown.*" In Derrick Bell, ed., *Shades of Brown: New Perspectives on School Desegregation,* 2–19. New York: Teachers College, Columbia University.

Lineberry, Robert L. 1978. "Reform, Representation, and Policy." *Social Science Quarterly* 59 (June): 173–177.

Lineberry, Robert L., and Edmund P. Fowler. 1967. "Reformism and Public Policies in American Cities." *American Political Science Review* 61 (September): 701–716.

Lipsky, Michael. 1980. *Street Level Bureaucracy.* New York: Russell Sage Foundation.

Long, Norton E. 1952. "Bureaucracy and Constitutionalism." *American Political Science Review* 46 (September): 808–818.

Longshore, Douglas. 1982. "Race Composition and White Hostility: A Research Note on the Problem of Control in Desegregated Schools." *Social Forces* 61 (September): 73–78.

Lowery, David, and William D. Berry. 1983. "The Growth of Government in the United States." *American Journal of Political Science* 27 (November): 665–694.

Mackler, Bernard. 1969. "Grouping in the Ghetto." *Education and Urban Society* 2 (November): 80–96.

McConahay, John B. 1981. "Reducing Racial Prejudice in Desegregated Schools." In Willis D. Hawley, ed., *Effective School Desegregation: Equity, Quality, and Feasibility,* 35–53. Beverly Hills, Calif.: Sage.

MacManus, Susan A. 1978. "City Council Election Procedures and Minority Representation: Are They Related?" *Social Science Quarterly* 59 (June): 153–161.

McPartland, James M., and Jomills H. Braddock. 1981. "Going to College and Getting a Good Job: The Impact of Desegregation." In Willis D. Hawley, ed., *Effective School Desegregation: Equity, Quality, and Feasibility,* 141–156. Beverly Hills, Cailf.: Sage.

Magnetti, Suzanne S. 1982. "Some Potential Incentives of Special Education Funding Practices." In Kirby A. Heller, Wayne Holtzman, and Samuel Messick, eds., *Placing Children in Special Education,* 300–321. Washington, D.C.: National Academy Press.

Mangold, L. C. 1974. "Teacher Pupil Dyadic Interactions in Desegregated Elementary School Classrooms." D.Ed. dissertation, University of Texas at Austin.

Mann, Dale. 1974. "The Politics of Representation in Educational Administration." *Education in Urban Society* 6 (May): 297–317.

Marshall, Harvey. 1979. "White Movement to the Suburbs: A Comparison of Explanations." *American Sociological Review* 44 (December): 975–994.

Marwit, Karen S., Samuel J. Marwit, and Elaine Walker. 1978. "Effects of Student Race and Physical Attractiveness on Teachers' Judgments of Transgressions." *Journal of Educational Psychology* 70 (December): 911–915.

Mathis, Dolores W. 1975. *Differences in Teacher Interaction with Afro-American and Anglo-American Students in the Same Classroom.* Ph.D. dissertation, University of Michigan.

Mazmanian, Daniel A., and Paul A. Sabatier. 1983. *Implementation and Public Policy.* Glenview, Ill.: Scott-Foresman.

Meier, Kenneth J. 1984. "Teachers, Students and Discrimination: The Policy Impact of Black Representation." *Journal of Politics* 46 (February): 252–263.

Meier, Kenneth J. 1985. *Regulation: Politics, Bureaucracy and Economics.* New York: St. Martin's Press.

Meier, Kenneth J., and Robert E. England. 1984. "Black Representation and Educational Policy: Are They Related?" *American Political Science Review* 78 (June): 392–403.

Meier, Kenneth J., and Lloyd G. Nigro. 1976. "Representative Bureaucracy and Policy Preferences." *Public Administration Review* 36 (July-August): 458–470.

Mercer, Jane R. 1972. "Discussion of Alternative Value Frames for Classification of Exceptional Children." Working paper prepared for Project on Classification of Exceptional Children, Vanderbilt University, Nashville, Tenn.

Mercer, Jane R. 1973. *Labeling the Mentally Retarded: Clinical and Social System Perspectives on Mental Retardation.* Berkeley: University of California Press.

Messick, Samuel. 1984. "Assessment in Context: Appraising Student Performance in Relation to Instructional Quality." *Educational Researcher* 13 (March): 3–8.

Metz, Mary Haywood. 1978. *Classrooms and Corridors: The Crisis of Authority in Desegregated Secondary Schools.* Berkeley: University of California Press.

Miles, Rufus E. 1978. "The Origin and Meaning of Miles' Law." *Public Administration Review* 38 (September-October): 399–403.

Miller, Warren E., and Donald E. Stokes. 1963. "Constituency Influence in Congress." *American Political Science Review* 57 (March): 45–56.

Milton, Sande. 1983. "Participation in Local School Board Elections." *Social Science Quarterly* 64 (September): 647–654.

Minar, David W. 1966. "The Community Basis of Conflict in School System Politics." *American Sociological Review* 31 (December): 822–835.

Mladenka, Kenneth R. 1981. "Citizen Demands for Urban Services." *American Journal of Political Science* 25 (November): 693–714.

Monroe, Alan D. 1975. *Public Opinion in America.* New York: Dodd Mead.

Moore, Archie B. 1977. "The Disturbing Revelation of the Predicament of Black Principals in Southern School Districts." *Urban Education* 12 (July): 213–216.

Moore, Helen A., and David R. Johnson. 1983. "A Reexamination of Elementary School Teachers' Expectations: Evidence of Sex and Ethnic Segmentation." *Social Science Quarterly* 64 (September): 460–475.

Morgan, David R., and Robert E. England. 1982. "Large District School Desegregation: A Preliminary Assessment of Techniques." *Social Science Quarterly* 63 (December): 688–700.

Morgan, David R., and Robert E. England. 1984. "School Desegregation and White Enrollment Decline." *Integrateducation* 21 (July): 199–201.

Morgenstern, Anne. 1966. "Historical Survey of Grouping Practices in the Elementary School." In Anne Morgenstern, ed., *Grouping in the Elementary School,* 3–13. New York: Pittman.

Mosher, Frederick C. 1968. *Democracy and the Public Service.* New York: Oxford University Press.

Mundt, Robert J., and Peggy Helig. 1982. "District Representation: Demand and Effects in the Urban South." *Journal of Politics* 44 (November): 1035–1049.

Muse, Benjamin. 1961. *Virginia's Massive Resistance.* Bloomington: Indiana University Press.

Muse, Benjamin. 1964. *Ten Years of Prelude: The Story of Integration since the Supreme Court's 1954 Decision.* New York: Viking.

Myers, David, Ann M. Milne, Keith Baker, and Alan Ginsburg. 1987. "Student Discipline and High School Performance." *Sociology of Education* 60 (January): 18–33.

National Academy of Education. 1987. *The Nation's Report Card.* Cambridge, Mass.

National Education Association. 1968. *Ability Grouping.* Research Summary 1968-S3. Washington, D.C.

National Institute of Education. 1977. *Resegregation: A Second Generation School Desegregation Issue.* Washington, D.C.: U.S. Government Printing Office.

National Institute of Education. 1979. *In School Alternatives to Suspension.* Washington, D.C.: U.S. Government Printing Office.

Nelson, William. 1972. *Black Politics in Gary.* Washington, D.C.: Joint Center for Political Studies.

Nelson, William, and Phillip Meranto. 1976. *Electing Black Mayors.* Columbus: Ohio State University Press.

Nordlinger, Eric A. 1981. *On the Autonomy of the Democratic State.* Cambridge, Mass.: Harvard University Press.

Oakes, Jeannie. 1985. *Keeping Track: How Schools Structure Inequality.* New Haven: Yale University Press.

Oakes, Jeannie. 1988. "Tracking: Can Schools Take a Different Route?" *National Education Association* (January): 41–47.

Office for Civil Rights. 1975. "Student Discipline." HEW Fact Sheet. May. Washington, D.C.

Ogbu, John U. 1978. *Minority Education and Caste: The American System in Cross-Cultural Perspective.* New York: Academic Press.

Orfield, Gary. 1969. *The Reconstruction of Southern Education: The Schools and the 1964 Civil Rights Act.* New York: John Wiley Interscience.

Ortiz, Vilma. 1986. "Reading Activities and Reading Proficiency among Hispanic, Black, and White Students." *American Journal of Education* 95 (November): 58–76.

Panetta, Leon E., and Peter Gall. 1971. *Bring Us Together: The Nixon Team and the Civil Rights Retreat.* Philadelphia: Lippincott.

Parent, Wayne, and Paul Stekler. 1985. "The Political Implications of Economic Stratification in the Black Community." *Western Political Quarterly* 38 (December): 521–538.

Peltason, Jack W. 1971. *Fifty-Eight Lonely Men: Southern Federal Judges and School Desegregation.* Urbana: University of Illinois Press.

Perlman, Joel. 1987. "A Piece of the Educational Pie." *Sociology of Education* 60 (January): 54–61.

Persell, Caroline Hodges. 1977. *Education and Inequality.* New York: The Free Press.

Peterson, Jimmy Lee. 1976. *The Changes in the Educational System Resulting from the Growth of Black Political Participation and the Involvement of the Federal Government.* Ph.D. dissertation, University of Michigan.

Peterson, Paul E. 1985. *The Politics of School Reform, 1870–1940.* Chicago: University of Chicago Press.

Pettigrew, Thomas F. 1971. *Racially Separate or Together?* New York: McGraw-Hill.

Pettigrew, Thomas F. 1976. "Black Mayoral Campaigns." In Herrington J. Bryce, ed., *Urban Governance and Minorities,* 14–29. New York: Praeger.

Pettigrew, Thomas F., and Robert L. Green. 1976. "School Desegregation in Large Cities: A Critique of the Coleman 'White Flight' Thesis." *Harvard Education Review* 46 (February): 1–53.

Pitkin, Hanna F. 1967. *The Concept of Representation.* Berkeley: University of California Press.

Piven, Frances Fox, and Richard Cloward. 1971. *Regulating the Poor.* New York: Pantheon Books.

Poinsett, Alex. 1970. *Black Power Gary Style.* Chicago: Johnson.

Polloway, Edward A. 1984. "The Integration of Mildly Retarded Students in the Schools: A Historical Review." *Remedial and Special Education* 5 (July-August): 18–28.

Pratt, Theodore B., ed. 1983. *National Assessment of Educational Progress 1969–1983: A Bibliography of Documents in the Eric Database.* Denver: National Assessment of Educational Progress.

Pressman, Jeffrey L., and Aaron B. Wildavsky. 1973. *Implementation.* Berkeley: University of California Press.

Preston, Michael B. 1977. "Minority Employment and Collective Bargaining in the Public Sector." *Public Administration Review* 37 (September-October): 511–514.

Prewitt, Kenneth. 1970. "Political Ambitions, Volunteerism, and Electoral Accountability." *American Political Science Review* 64 (March): 5–17.

Ramirez, Manuel, and Alfredo Castaneda. 1974. *Cultural Democracy, Bicognitive Development, and Education.* New York: Academic Press.

Ravitch, Diane. 1978. "The White Flight Controversy." *The Public Interest* 51 (Spring): 135–149.

Ravitch, Diane. 1983. *The Troubled Crusade: American Education 1945–1980.* New York: Basic Books.

Read, Frank T. 1977. "Judicial Evolution of the Law of School Integration since Brown v. Board of Education." In Betsy Levin and Willis Hawley, eds., *The Courts, Social Science, and School Desegregation,* 147–179. New Brunswick, N.J.: Transaction Books.

Redford, Emmette S. 1969. *Democracy in the Administrative State.* New York: Oxford University Press.

Redl, Fritz. 1975. "Disruptive Behavior in the Classroom." *School Review* 83 (August): 569–594.

Reissman, Frank, and Colin Greer. 1976. "Editorial: Desegregation 1976." *Social Policy* 6 (January-February): 2–3.

Richardson, Ronald L., and S. Craig Gerlach. 1980. "Black Dropouts: A Study of Significant Factors Contributing to a Black Student's Decision." *Urban Education* 14 (January): 489–494.

Ripley, Randall B., and Grace A. Franklin. 1986. *Policy Implementation and Bureaucracy.* 2nd ed. Chicago: Dorsey Press.

Ripley, Randall B., and Grace A. Franklin. 1985. *Congress, the Bureaucracy, and Public Policy.* 3rd ed. Homewood, Ill.: Dorsey Press.

Rist, Ray C. 1970. "Student Social Class and Teacher Expectations: The Self-Fulfilling Prophecy in Ghetto Education." *Harvard Educational Review* 40 (August): 411–450.

Rist, Ray C. 1973. *The Urban School: A Factory for Failure.* Cambridge, Mass.: MIT Press.

Rist, Ray C. 1978. *The Invisible Children: School Integration in American Society.* Cambridge, Mass.: Harvard University Press.

Ritterband, Paul. 1976. "Ethnicity and School Disorder." *Education and Urban Society* 8 (August): 383–400.

Robinson, Theodore P., and Thomas R. Dye. 1978. "Reformism and Black Representation on City Councils." *Social Science Quarterly* 59 (June): 133–41.

Robinson, Theodore P., and Robert E. England. 1981. "Black Representation on Central City School Boards Revisited." *Social Science Quarterly* 62 (September): 495–502.

Robinson, Theodore P., Robert E. England, and Kenneth J. Meier. 1985. "Black Resources and Black School Board Representation: Does Political Structure Matter?" *Social Science Quarterly* 66 (December): 976–982.

Rodgers, Harrell R., and Charles S. Bullock III. 1972. *Law and Social Change.* New York: McGraw-Hill.

Rodgers, Harrell R., and Charles S. Bullock III. 1976a. *Coercion to Compliance.* Lexington, Mass.: D. C. Heath.

Rodgers, Harrell R., and Charles S. Bullock III. 1976b. "School Desegregation: A Multivariate Test of the Role of Law in Effectuating Social Change." *American Politics Quarterly* 4 (April): 153–176.

Romzek, Barbara S., and J. Stephan Hendricks. 1982. "Organizational Involvement and Representative Bureaucracy: Can We Have It Both Ways?" *American Political Science Review* 76 (March): 75–82.

Rosenbaum, James E. 1976. *Making Inequality: The Hidden Curriculum of High School Tracking.* New York: John Wiley.

Rosenbaum, James R. 1980. "Track Misperceptions and Frustrated College Plans." *Sociology of Education* 53 (April): 74–88.

Rosenthal, Robert, and Lenore Jacobson. 1968. *Pygmalion in the Classroom: Teacher Expectation and Pupils' Intellectual Development.* New York: Holt, Reinhart and Winston.

Rourke, Francis E. 1984. *Bureaucracy, Politics and Public Policy.* 3rd ed. Boston: Little, Brown.

Rowan, Brian, and Andrew W. Miracle. 1983. "Systems of Ability Grouping and the Stratification of Achievement in Elementary Schools." *Sociology of Education* 56 (July): 133–144.

Rubovits, Pamela C., and Martin L. Maehr. 1973. "Pygmalion Black and White." *Journal of Personality and Social Psychology* 25 (February): 210–218.

Ryan, William. 1976. *Blaming the Victim.* New York: Random House.

St. John, Nancy. 1971. "Thirty-Six Teachers, Their Characteristics, and Outcomes for Black and White Pupils." *American Educational Research Journal* 8 (November): 635–648.

St. John, Nancy. 1975. *School Desegregation Outcomes for Children.* New York: John Wiley.

Saltzstein, Grace Hall. 1979. "Representative Bureaucracy and Bureaucratic Responsibility." *Administration and Society* 10 (February): 465–475.

Saltzstein, Grace Hall. 1983. "Personnel Directors and Female Employment Representation." *Social Science Quarterly* 64 (December): 734–746.

San Miguel, Guadalupe. 1982. "Mexican American Organizations and the Changing Politics of School Desegregation in Texas, 1945–1980." *Social Science Quarterly* 63 (December): 701–715.

Schafer, Walker E., and Carol Olexa. 1971. *Tracking and Opportunity: The Locking Out Process and Beyond.* Scranton, Pa.: Chandler.

Schechter, Ellen. 1987. *The New Jersey Provisional Teacher Program: A Third Year Report.* Trenton, N.J.: State Department of Education.

Scholfield, Janet W. 1981. "Desegregation School Practices and Student Race Relations Outcomes." In Willis D. Hawley, ed., *Assessment of Current Knowledge About the Effectiveness of School Desegregation Strategies,* 88–171. Nashville, Tenn.: Institute for Public Policy Studies, Vanderbilt University.

Schultz, Theodore W. 1961. "Investment in Human Capital." *American Economic Review* 51 (March): 1–17.

Scott, Hugh J. 1980. *The Black School Superintendent.* Washington, D.C.: Howard University Press.

Scritchfield, Shirley A., and J. Steven Picou. 1982. "The Structural Significance of Other Influence for Status Attainment Processes: Black-White Variations." *Sociology of Education* 55 (March): 22–30.

Semmel, Melvyn I., Jay Gottlieb, and Nancy M. Robinson. 1979. "Mainstreaming: Perspectives on Educating Handicapped Children in the Public School." In David C. Berliner, ed., *Review of Research in Education, Volume 7,* 223–281. Washington, D.C.: American Educational Research Association.

Sharkansky, Ira, and Richard I. Hofferbert. 1969. "Dimensions of State Politics, Economics, and Public Policy." *American Political Science Review* 63 (September): 867–880.

Shepard, Lorrie A. 1987. "The New Push for Excellence: Widening the Schism between Regular and Special Education." *Exceptional Children* 53 (January): 327–329.

Shonkoff, Jack P. 1982. "Biological and Social Factors Contributing to Mild Mental Retardation." In Kirby A. Heller, Wayne H. Holtzman, and Samuel Messick, eds., *Placing Children in Special Education,* 133–181. Washington D.C.: National Academy Press.

Sigelman, Lee, and Albert K. Karnig. 1976. "Black Representation in American States—Comparison of Bureaucracies and Legislatures." *American Politics Quarterly* 4 (April): 237–246.

Sigelman, Lee, and Albert K. Karnig. 1977. "Black Education and Bureaucratic Employment." *Social Science Quarterly* 57 (March): 858–863.

Silver, Catherine Bodard. 1973. *Black Teachers in Urban Schools.* New York: Praeger.

Simmons, Cassandra A., and Nelvia M. Brady. 1981. "The Impact of Ability Group Placement Decisions on the Equality of Educational Opportunity in Desegregated Elementary Schools." *Urban Review* 13 (Summer): 129–133.

Simon, Herbert A. 1969. *The Sciences of the Artificial.* Cambridge, Mass.: MIT Press.

Singer, Judith D., and John A. Butler. 1987. "The Education for All Handicapped Children Act: Schools as Agents for Social Reform." *Harvard Education Review* 57 (May): 125–152.

Singer, Judith D., John A. Butler, Judith S. Palfrey, and Deborah K. Walker. 1986. "Characteristics of Special Education Placement: Findings from Probability Samples in Five Metropolitan School Districts." *Journal of Special Education* 20 (Fall): 319–337.

Slavin, Robert E. 1980. "Cooperative Learning in Teams: State of the Art." *Educational Psychologist* 15 (Summer): 93–111.

Slavin, Robert E. 1981. "Cooperative Learning and Desegregation." In Willis D. Hawley, ed., *Effective School Desegregation: Equity, Quality, and Feasibility,* 255–244. Beverly Hills: Sage.

Slavin, Robert E. 1982. *Cooperative Learning.* New York: Longman.

Slavin, Robert E., and Eileen Dickle. 1981. "Effects of Cooperative Learning Teams on Student Achievement and Race Relations." *Sociology of Education* 54 (July): 174–198.

Sleeter, Christine E., and Carl A. Grant. 1985. "Race, Class, and Gender in an Urban School." *Urban Education* 20 (April): 37–60.

Sloan, Lee. 1969. "Good Government and the Politics of Race." *Social Problems* 17 (Fall): 161–175.

Smith, Bob. 1965. *They Closed Their Schools: Prince Edward County, Virginia, 1951–1954.* Chapel Hill: University of North Carolina Press.

Smith, Elsie J., and Lee N. June. 1982. "The Role of the Counselor in Desegregated Schools." *Journal of Black Studies* 13 (December): 227–240.

Smith, James P., and Finis R. Welch. 1986. *Closing the Gap: Forty Years of Economic Progress for Blacks.* Santa Monica, Calif.: Rand Corporation.

Smith, John, and Bette M. Smith. 1974. "Desegregation in the South and the Demise of the Black Educator." *Journal of Social and Behavioral Sciences* 20 (Winter): 28–40.

Smith, Marzell, and Charles D. Dziuban. 1977. "The Gap between Desegregation Research and Remedy." *Integrated Education* 15 (November-December): 51–55.

Southern Regional Council. 1973. *The Student Pushout: Victim of Continued Resistance to Desegregation.* Atlanta.

Stedman, Jim. 1983. *The Consolidation of the Emergency School Aid Act—A Brief Analysis of Its Impact.* Washington, D.C.: Congressional Research Service.

Stewart, Joseph, Jr., and Charles S. Bullock III. 1981. "Implementing Equal Education Opportunity Policy." *Administration and Society* 12 (February): 427–446.

Stewart, Joseph, Jr., and James F. Sheffield, Jr. 1987. "Does Interest Group Litigation Matter?" The Case of Black Political Mobilization in Mississippi." *Journal of Politics* 49 (August): 780–800.

Stone, Chuck. 1971. *Black Political Power in America.* New York: Dell.

Stone, Clarence N., Robert K. Whelan, and William J. Murin. 1979. *Urban Policy and Politics in a Bureaucratic Age.* Englewood Cliffs, N.J.: Prentice-Hall.

Subramaniam, V. 1967. "Representative Bureaucracy: A Reassessment." *American Political Science Review* 61 (December): 1010–1019.

Sydnor, Charles S. 1966. *Slavery in Mississippi.* Baton Rouge: Louisiana State University Press.

Taebel, Delbert A. 1977. "Politics of School Board Elections." *Urban Education* 12 (July): 153–166.

Taebel, Delbert. 1978. "Minority Representation on City Councils." *Social Science Quarterly* 59 (June): 142–152.

Taeuber, Karl E., and David R. James. 1982. "Racial Segregation among Public and Private Schools." *Sociology of Education* 55 (April-July): 133–143.

Taeuber, Karl E., and Anna F. Taeuber. 1965. *Negroes in Cities.* Chicago: Aldine.

Thomas, Gail E., and Frank Brown. 1982. "What Does Educational Research Tell Us about School Desegregation Effects?" *Journal of Black Studies* 13 (December): 155–174.

Thompson, Frank J. 1978. "Civil Servants and the Deprived: Socio-Political and Occupational Explanations of Attitudes Toward Minority Hiring." *American Journal of Political Science* 22 (May): 325–347.

Tindall, George Brown. 1952. *South Carolina Negroes, 1877–1900.* Columbia: University of South Carolina Press.

Traxler, Harrison Anthony. 1914. "Slavery in Missouri, 1804–1865." *John Hopkins University Studies in Historical and Political Science* 32 (2): 191–441.

Trent, William T. 1981. "Expert Opinion on School Desegregation Issues." In Willis D. Hawley, ed., *Assessment of Current Knowledge about the Effectiveness of School Desegregation Strategies,* 241–293. Nashville, Tenn.: Institute for Public Policy Studies, Vanderbilt University.

Tucker, Harvey, and Harmon Zeigler. 1980. *Professionals versus the Public.* New York: Longman.

Tufte, Edward R. 1974. *Data Analysis for Politics and Policy.* Englewood Cliffs, N.J.: Prentice-Hall.

Tushnet, Mark V. 1987. *The NAACP's Legal Strategy against Segregated Education, 1925–1950.* Chapel Hill: University of North Carolina Press.

Tyack, David B. 1974. *The One Best System: A History of American Urban Education.* Cambridge, Mass.: Harvard University Press.

U.S. Bureau of the Census. 1985. *1980 Housing and Population Survey, File STF-3.* Washington, D.C.

U.S. Commission on Civil Rights. 1969. *Federal Enforcement of School Desegregation.* Washington, D.C.: U.S. Government Printing Office.

U.S. Commission on Civil Rights. 1975. *School Desegregation in Boston.* Washington, D.C.: U.S. Government Printing Office.

U.S. Commission on Civil Rights. 1976. *Fulfilling the Letter and Spirit of the Law: Desegregation of the Nation's Schools.* Washington D.C.: U.S. Government Printing Office.

U.S. Commission on Civil Rights. 1977. *Statement on Metropolitan School Desegregation.* Washington, D.C.: U.S. Government Printing Office.

U.S. Commission on Civil Rights. 1979. *Desegregation of the Nation's Public Schools: A Status Report.* Washington, D.C.: U.S. Government Printing Office.

Usdan, Michael D. 1984. "New Trends in Urban Demography." *Education and Urban Society* 16 (August): 399–414.

Uslaner, Eric M., and Ronald E. Weber. 1983. "Policy Congruence and American State Elites." *Journal of Politics* 45 (February): 183–196.

Verba, Sidney, and Norman H. Nie. 1972. *Participation in America.* New York: Harper and Row.

Wainscott, Stephen H., and J. David Woodard. 1988. "Second Thoughts on Second-Generation Discrimination." *American Politics Quarterly* 16 (April): 171–192.

Wakefield, Howard E. 1971. "Rural School Boards." In Lee C. Deighton, ed., *Encyclopedia of Education,* Vol. 8, 70–73. New York: Macmillian.

Wald, Kenneth, D., and Carole Sutherland. 1982. "Black Public Officials and the Dynamics of Representation." In Lawrence W. Moreland, Tod A. Baker, and Robert P. Steed, eds., *Contemporary Southern Political Attitudes and Behavior,* 239–253. New York: Praeger.

Wasby, Stephen L. 1970. *The Impact of the United States Supreme Court: Some Perspectives.* Homewood, Ill.: Dorsey Press.

Weber, Max. 1946. *From Max Weber: Essays in Sociology,* trans. H. H. Gerth and C. Wright Mills. New York: Oxford University Press.

Weinberg, Meyer. 1977. *A Chance to Learn: The History of Race and Education in the United States.* London: Cambridge University Press.

Weinberg, Meyer. 1983. *The Search for Quality Integrated Education.* Westport, Conn.: Greenwood Press.

Weisberg, Robert. 1978. "Collective vs. Dyadic Representation in Congress." *American Political Science Review* 72 (June): 535–547.

Welch, Finis. 1987. "A Reconsideration of the Impact of School Desegregation Programs on White Public School Enrollment, 1968–1976." *Sociology of Education* 58 (July): 215–221.

Welch, Susan, and Lorn Foster. 1987. "Class and Conservatism in the Black Community." *American Politics Quarterly* 15 (October): 445–470.

Welch, Susan, and John R. Hibbing. 1984. "Hispanic Representation in the U.S. Congress." *Social Science Quarterly* 65 (June): 328–335.

Welch, Susan, and Albert K. Karnig. 1978. "Representation of Blacks on Big City School Boards." *Social Science Quarterly* 59 (June): 162–172.

Welch, Susan, and Albert K. Karnig. 1979a. "The Impact of Black Elected Officials on Urban Social Expenditures." *Policy Studies Journal* 7 (Summer): 707–714.

Welch, Susan, and Albert K. Karnig. 1979b. "The Impact of Black Elected Officials on Urban Expenditures and Intergovernmental Revenues." In Dale R. Marshall, ed., *Urban Policymaking,* 101–126. Beverly Hills: Sage.

Williams, Junious. 1979. "In-School Alternatives to Suspensions: Why Bother?" In Antoine M. Garibaldi, ed., *In-School Alternatives to Suspension: Conference Report,* 1–22. Washington, D.C.: U.S. Government Printing Office.

Williams, Trevor. 1976. "Teacher Prophecies and the Inheritance of Inequality." *Sociology of Education* 49 (July): 223–236.

Willie, Charles V., and Michael Fultz. 1984. "Do Mandatory School Desegregation Plans Foster White Flight?" In Charles V. Willie, ed., *School Desegregation Plans That Work,* 163–172. Westport, Conn.: Greenwood Press.

Wilson, Barry J., and Donald W. Schmits. 1978. "What's New in Ability Grouping?" *Phi Delta Kappan* 59 (March): 535–536.

Wilson, Franklin D. 1985. ''The Impact of School Desegregation Programs on White Public-School Enrollment, 1968–1976.'' *Sociology of Education* 58 (July): 137–153.

Winn, Mylon. 1984. ''Black Public Administrators and Opposing Expectations.'' In Mitchell F. Rice and Woodrow Jones, Jr., eds., *Contemporary Public Policy Perspectives and Black Americans,* 187–196. Westport, Conn.: Greenwood Press.

Wolfinger, Raymond E., and Steven J. Rosenstone. 1980. *Who Votes?* New Haven: Yale University Press.

Woodson, Carter G. 1919. *The Education of the Negro Prior to 1861.* Washington, D.C.: Associated Publishers.

Ysseldyke, James E., Martha Thurlow, Janet Graden, Caren Wesson, Bob Algozzine, and Stanley Deno. 1983. ''Generalizations from Five Years of Research on Assessment and Decision Making: The University of Minnesota Institute.'' *Exceptional Education Quarterly* 4 (Spring): 75–93.

Yudof, Mark G. 1975. ''Suspensions and Expulsions of Black Students from the Public Schools.'' *Law and Contemporary Problems* 39 (Spring): 374–411.

Yudof, Mark G. 1981. ''Implementing Desegregation Decrees.'' In Willis D. Hawley, ed., *Effective School Desegregation: Equity, Quality, and Feasibility,* 245–262. Beverly Hills: Sage.

Zeigler, L. Harmon, and M. Kent Jennings, with G. Wayne Peak. 1974. *Governing American Schools.* North Scituate, Mass.: Duxbury.

Zettel, Jeffrey J., and Alan Abeson. 1978. ''The Right to a Free Appropriate Public Education.'' In Clifford P. Hooker, ed., *The Courts and Education,* 188–216. Chicago: University of Chicago Press.

Court Cases

Adams v. *Richardson*, 351 F. Supp. 636 (1972).
Alexander v. *Holmes County Board of Education*, 396 U.S. 19 (1969).
Alston v. *School Board of Norfolk*, 112 F. 2d 992 (1940).
Black Coalition v. *Portland School District No. 1*, 484 F. 2d 1040 (1973).
Black Students, etc., ex rel Shoemaker v. *Williams*, 317 F. Supp. 1211 (1970).
Borders v. *Rippy*, 247 F. 2d 268 (1957).
Brown v. *Board of Education*, 347 U.S. 483 (1954).
Brown v. *Board of Education*, 349 U.S. 294 (1955).
Claybrook v. *City of Owensboro*, 16 F. 297 (D. Kentucky 1883).
Cumming v. *County Board of Education*, 175 U.S. 545 (1899).
Dunn v. *Tyler Independent School District*, 327 F. Supp. 528 (1971).
Green v. *New Kent County School Board*, 391 U.S. 390 (1968).
Hawkins v. *Coleman*, 376 F. Supp. 1330 (1974).
Hobson v. *Hansen*, 269 F. Supp. 401 (1967).
In re Wallace, 4 Race Relations Law Reporter 97 (1959).
In the Matter of Board of Education of Cook County, Georgia, HEW Administrative Proceeding (October 18, 1972).
Kelly v. *Metroloplitan County Board of Education* 293 F. Supp. 485 (1968).
Larry P. v. *Riles*, 343 F. Supp. 1306 (1972).
Larry P. v. *Riles*, 495 F. Supp. 926 (1979).
Larry P. v. *Riles*, 793 F. 2d 969 (1984).
Lemon v. *Bossier Parish School Board*, 444 F. 2d 1400 (1971).
McNeal v. *Tate County Board of Education*, 508 F. 2d 1017 (1975).
Missouri ex rel Gaines v. *Canada*, 305 U.S. 337 (1938).
Moses v. *Washington County School Board*, 330 F. Supp. 1340 (1971).
Plessy v. *Ferguson*, 163 U.S. 537 (1896).
Puitt v. *Commissioners*, 94 N.C. 519 (1886).
Roberts v. *City of Boston*, 5 Cush. 198 (1849).
Singleton v. *Jackson Municipal Separate School District*, 419 F. 2d 1211 (1969).
Stell v. *Savannah-Chatham County Board of Education*, 333 F. 2d 55 (1964).
Stevenson v. *Board of Education of Wheeler County, Georgia*, 462 F. 2d 1154 (1970).

United States v. *Gadsden County School District*, 572 F. 2d 1049 (1978).
United States v. *Georgia*, Civil No. 12972, N.D. Ga. (1969).
United States v. *Sunflower County School District*, 430 F. 2d 839 (1970).
United States v. *Tunica County School District*, 421 F. 2d 1236 (1970).
Woods v. *Wright*, 334 F. 2d 369 (1964).

Index